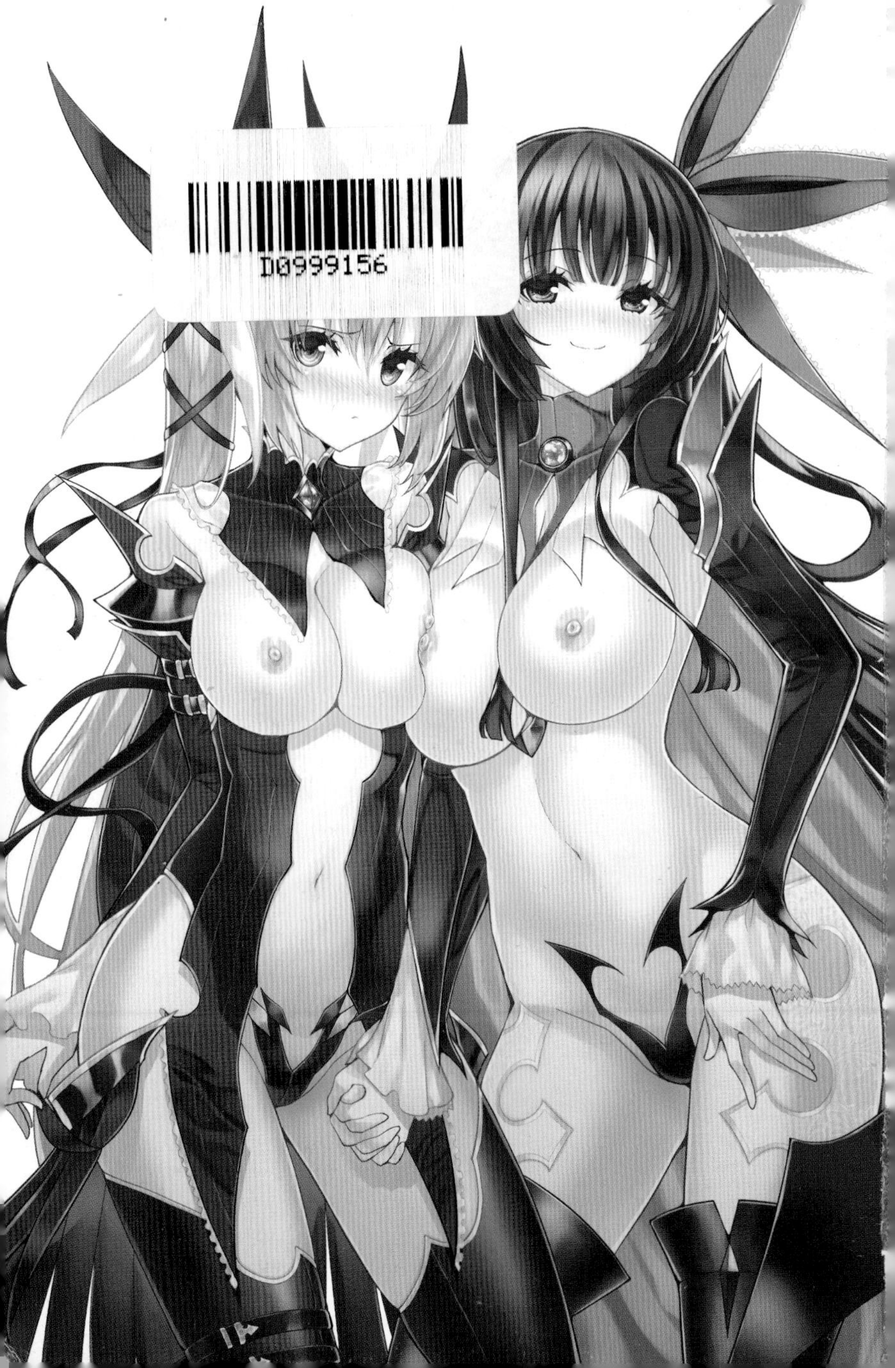

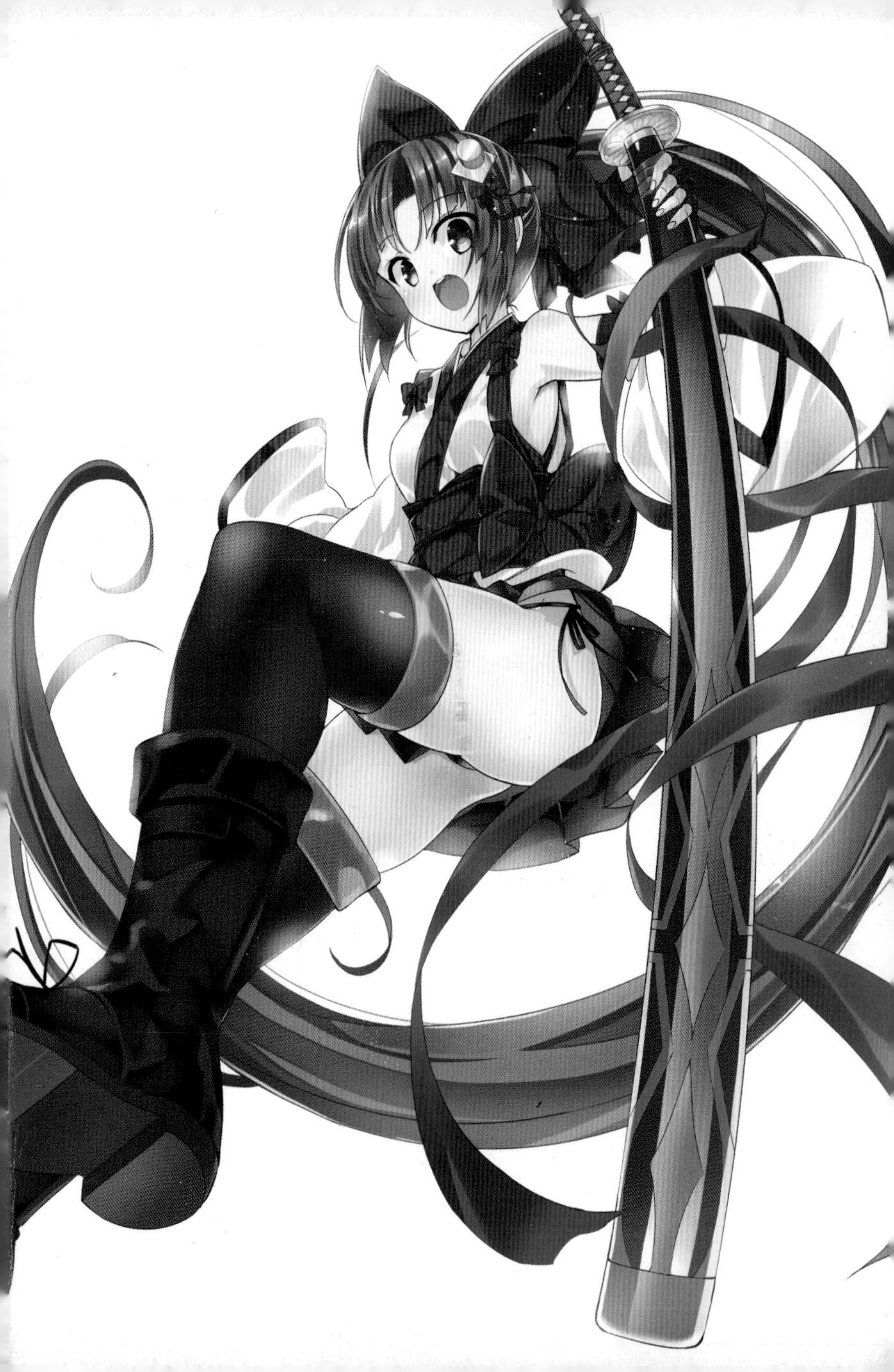

Cast of Characters

Amasaki Mio

First-year A-ranked Magika student who has formed a contract with the diva Phoenix. As the daughter of a famous magical family, her goal is to become Magika student council president.

Hayashizaki Kanae

Second-year Kengika student and Kazuki's "little" sister. Ranked just after Kazuki in the Hayashizaki School, she also goes by the name "Stormcat." She is the Kengika student council president.

Hayashizaki Kazuki

First-year E-ranked Magika student. A master swordsman of the Hayashizaki School, he entered the Magika after receiving the Enigma.

Lemegeton

The diva with whom Kazuki has formed a contract. The demon king ruling over the 72 pillars, she is able to wield all magic used by them. However, in order for her to do so, Kazuki must earn their summoners' affections.

Otonashi Kaguya

Second-year Magika student. She is the strongest summoner in the school and the Magika student council president. Bound to the diva Asmodeus, she is known by the name "Nightmare Bringer."

Hiakari Koyuki

First-year A-ranked Magika student. An elf born with incredible magical strength, she successfully formed a contract with Vepar.

Magika SWORDSMAN AND SUMMONER

The Story So Far...

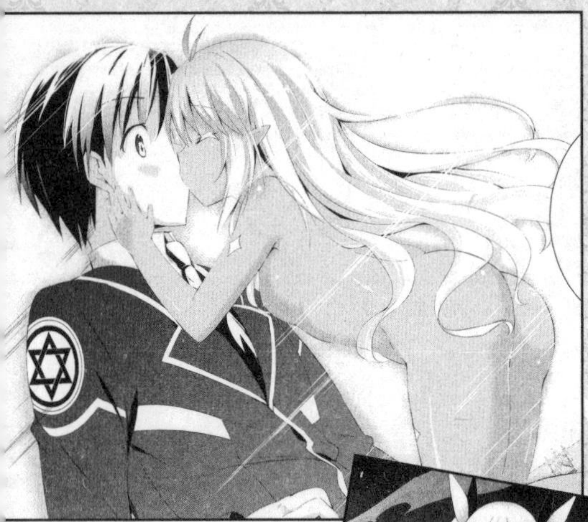

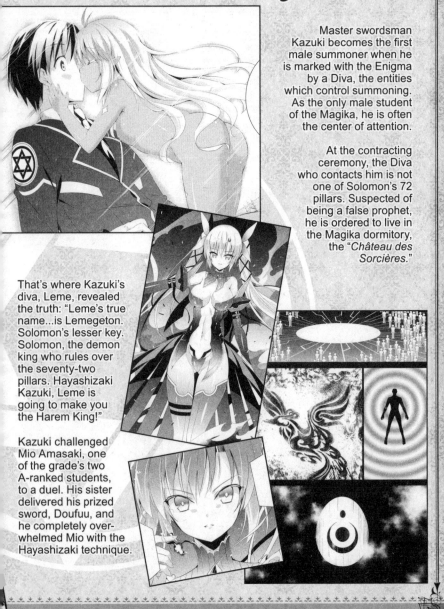

Master swordsman Kazuki becomes the first male summoner when he is marked with the Enigma by a Diva, the entities which control summoning. As the only male student of the Magika, he is often the center of attention.

At the contracting ceremony, the Diva who contacts him is not one of Solomon's 72 pillars. Suspected of being a false prophet, he is ordered to live in the Magika dormitory, the "*Château des Sorcières.*"

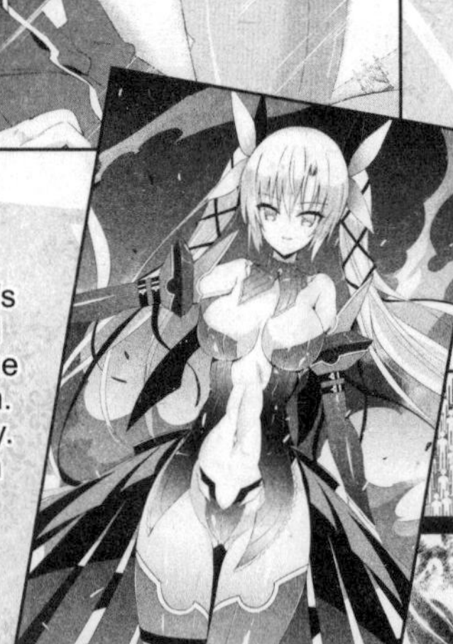

That's where Kazuki's diva, Leme, revealed the truth: "Leme's true name...is Lemegeton. Solomon's lesser key. Solomon, the demon king who rules over the seventy-two pillars. Hayashizaki Kazuki, Leme is going to make you the Harem King!"

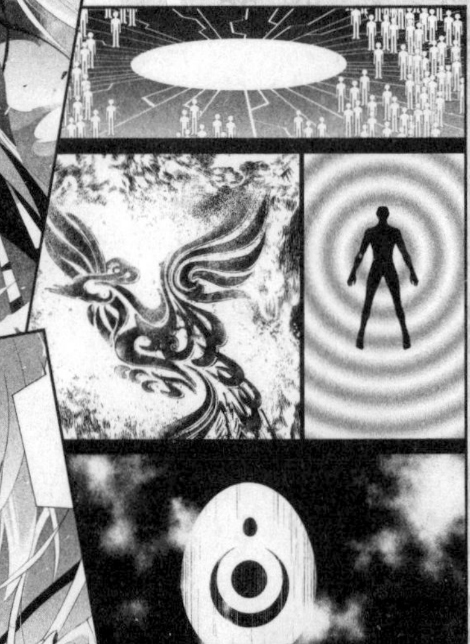

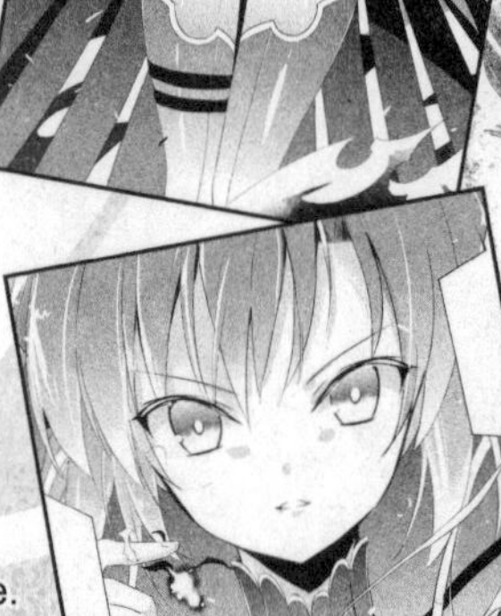

Kazuki challenged Mio Amasaki, one of the grade's two A-ranked students, to a duel. His sister delivered his prized sword, Doufuu, and he completely overwhelmed Mio with the Hayashizaki technique.

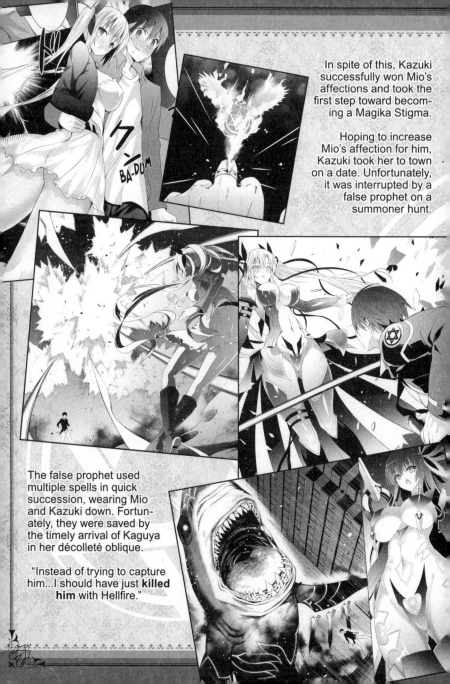

In spite of this, Kazuki successfully won Mio's affections and took the first step toward becoming a Magika Stigma.

Hoping to increase Mio's affection for him, Kazuki took her to town on a date. Unfortunately, it was interrupted by a false prophet on a summoner hunt.

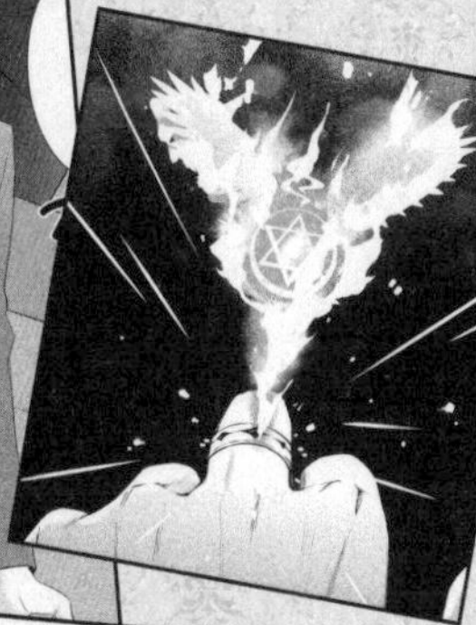

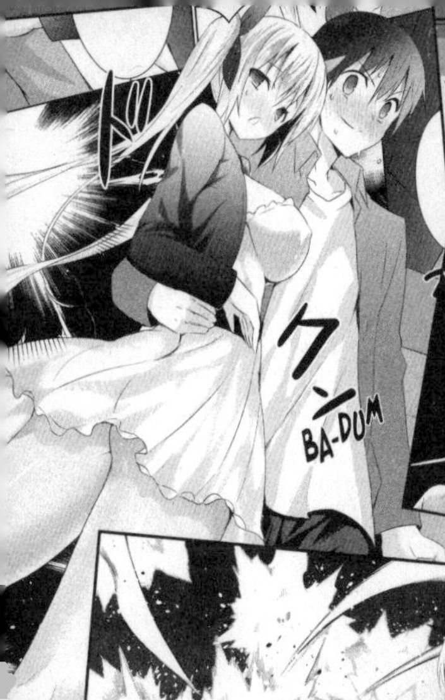
BA-DUM

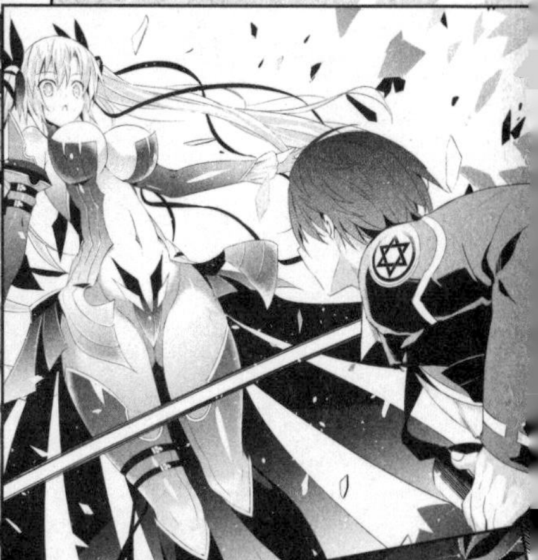

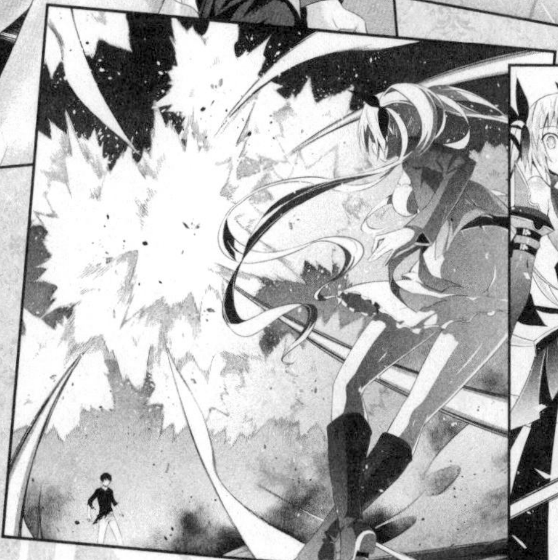

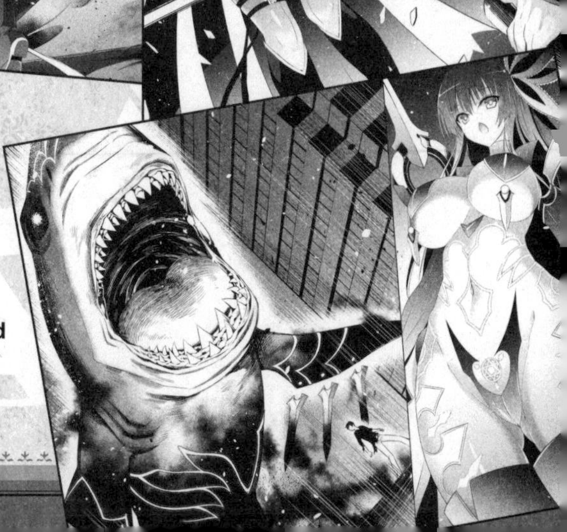

The false prophet used multiple spells in quick succession, wearing Mio and Kazuki down. Fortunately, they were saved by the timely arrival of Kaguya in her décolleté oblique.

"Instead of trying to capture him...I should have just **killed him** with Hellfire."

魔技科の剣士と召喚魔王

3

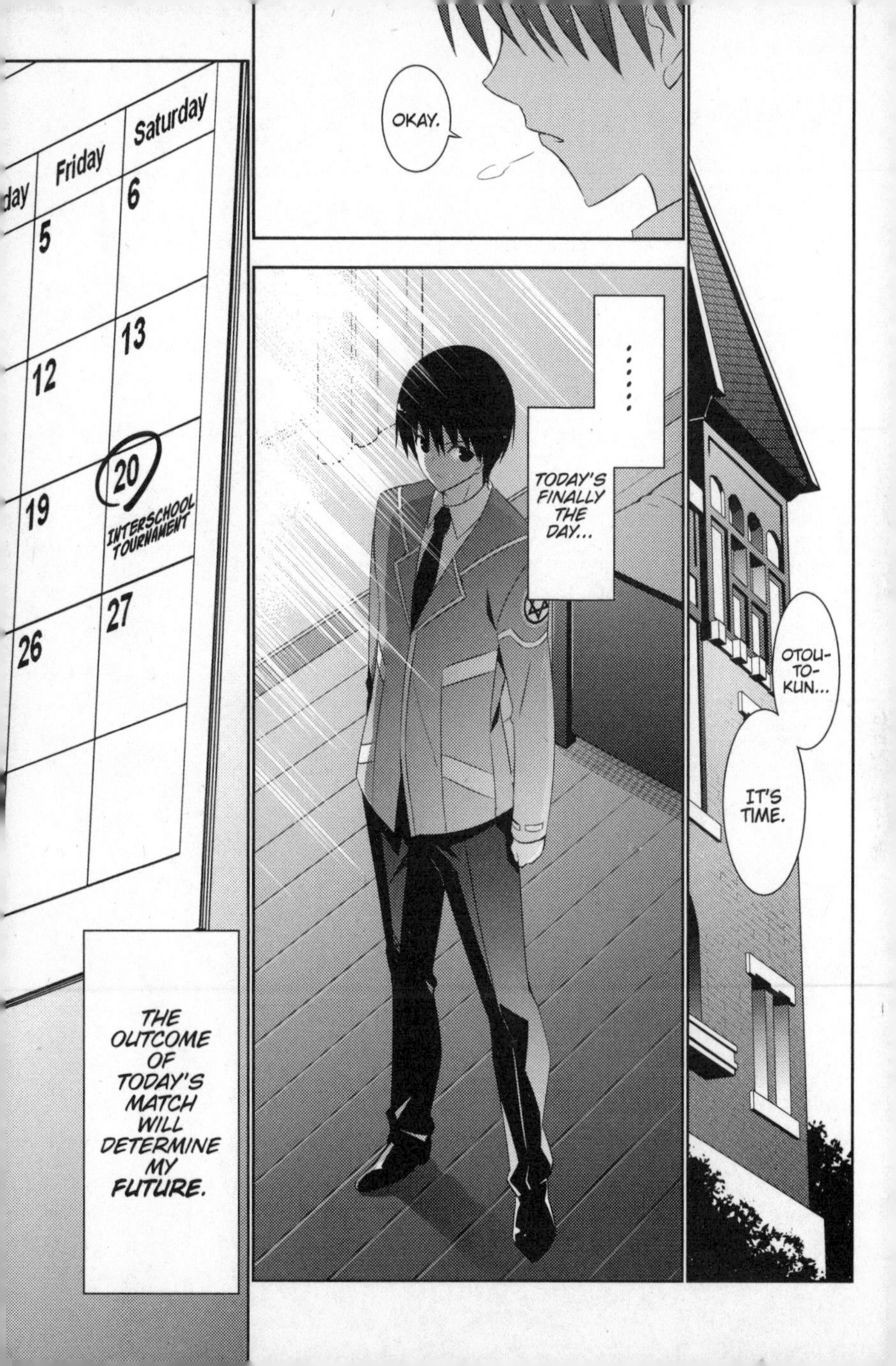

OTOU-TO-KUN...
IT'S TIME.
OKAY.
......
TODAY'S FINALLY THE DAY...
day
Friday
Saturday
5
6
12
13
19
20
INTERSCHOOL TOURNAMENT
26
27
THE OUTCOME OF TODAY'S MATCH WILL DETERMINE MY FUTURE.

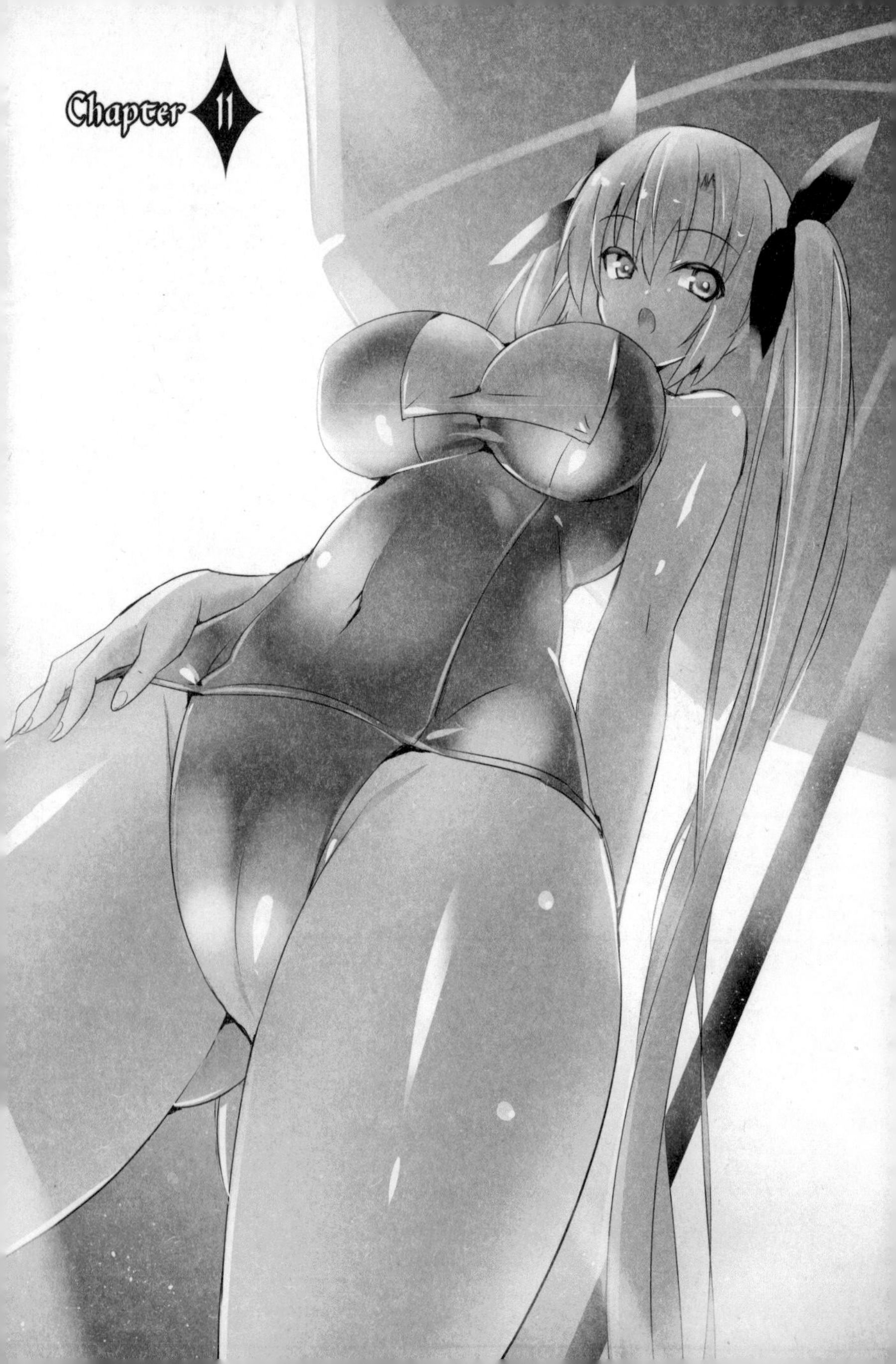
Chapter 11

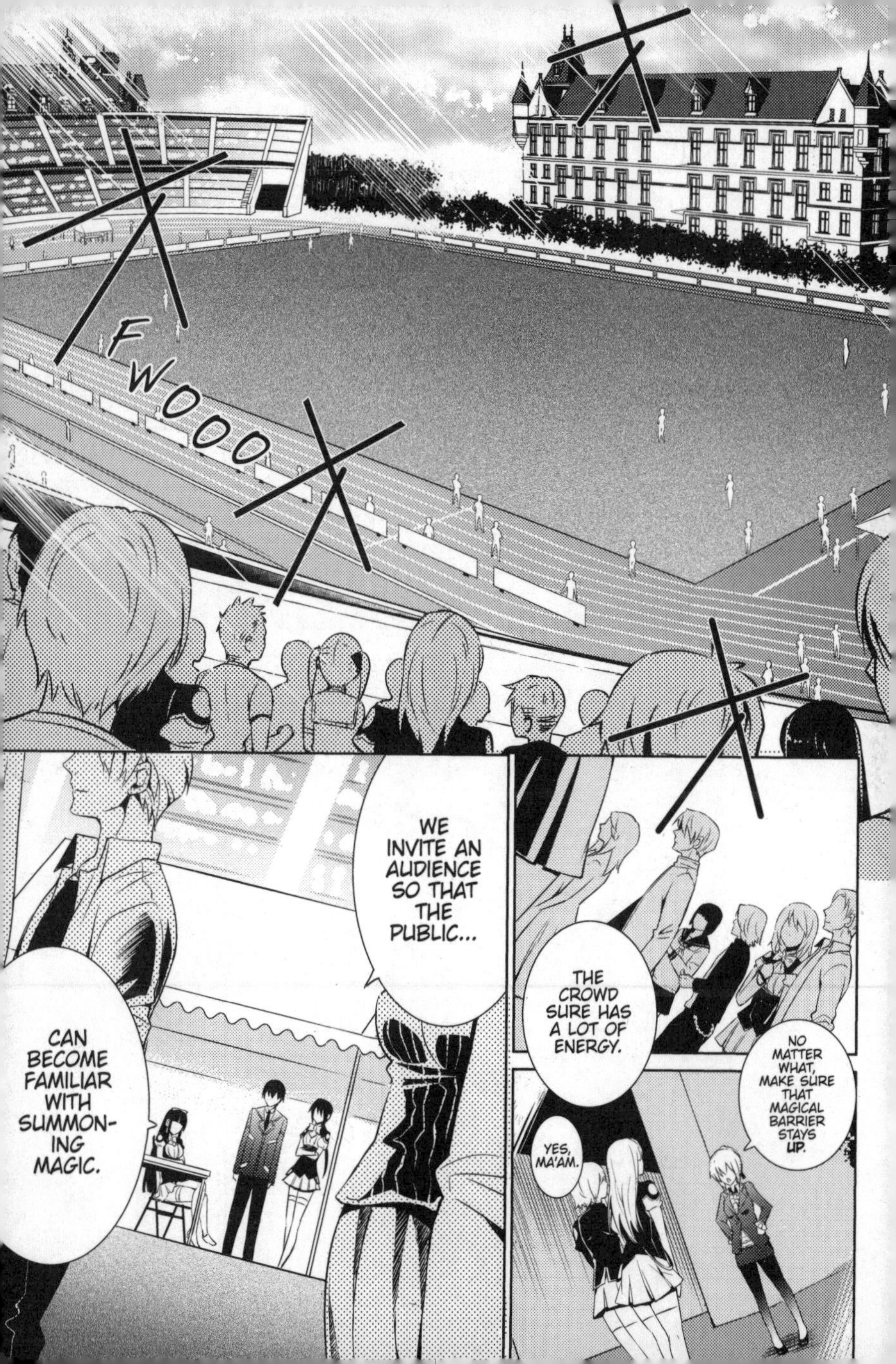
FWOOOO
THE CROWD SURE HAS A LOT OF ENERGY.
NO MATTER WHAT, MAKE SURE THAT MAGICAL BARRIER STAYS **UP**.
YES, MA'AM.
WE INVITE AN AUDIENCE SO THAT THE PUBLIC...
CAN BECOME FAMILIAR WITH SUMMONING MAGIC.

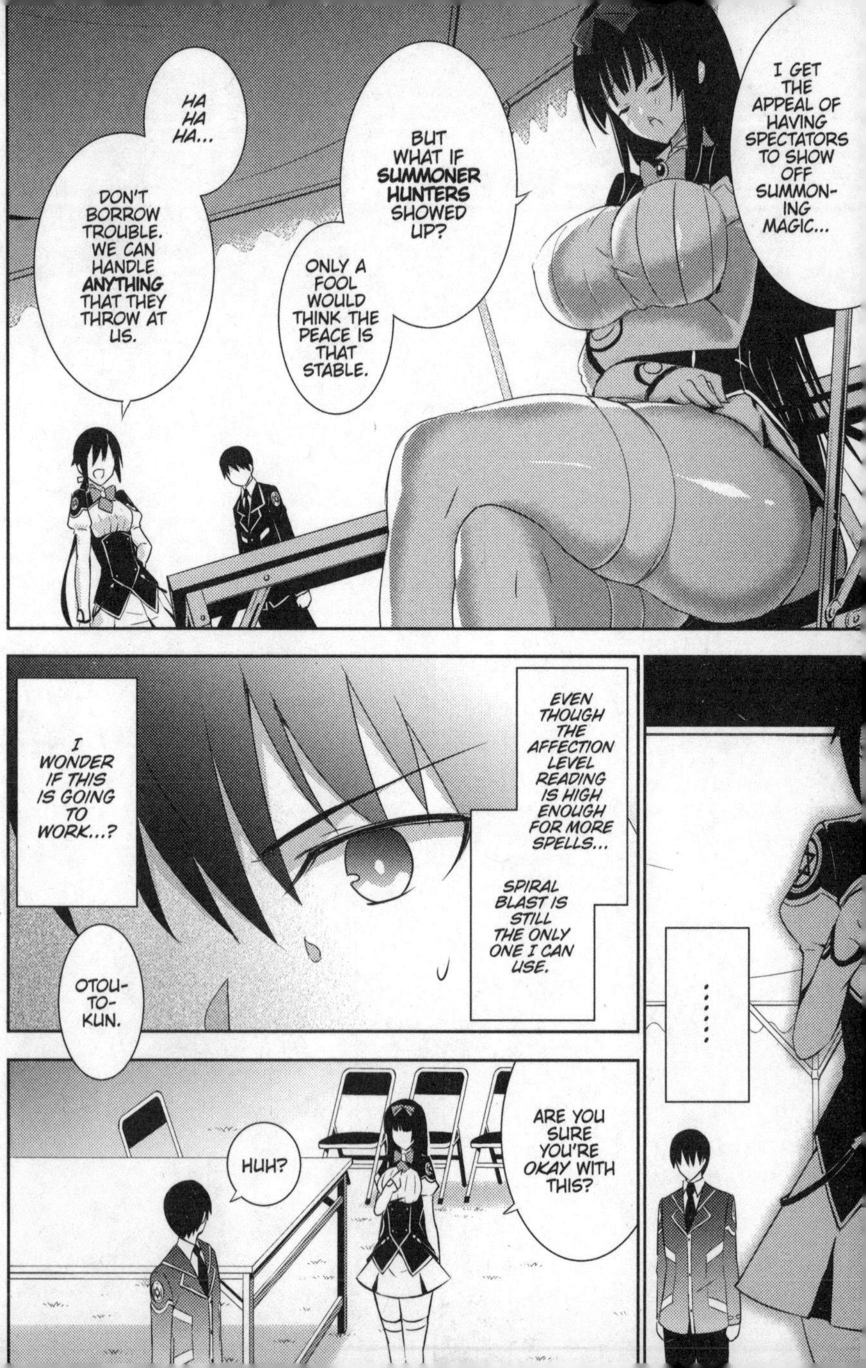
I GET THE APPEAL OF HAVING SPECTATORS TO SHOW OFF SUMMONING MAGIC...
BUT WHAT IF **SUMMONER HUNTERS** SHOWED UP?
ONLY A FOOL WOULD THINK THE PEACE IS THAT STABLE.
HA HA HA...
DON'T BORROW TROUBLE. WE CAN HANDLE **ANYTHING** THAT THEY THROW AT US.
......
EVEN THOUGH THE AFFECTION LEVEL READING IS HIGH ENOUGH FOR MORE SPELLS...
SPIRAL BLAST IS STILL THE ONLY ONE I CAN USE.
I WONDER IF THIS IS GOING TO WORK...?
OTOUTO-KUN.
ARE YOU SURE YOU'RE *OKAY* WITH THIS?
HUH?

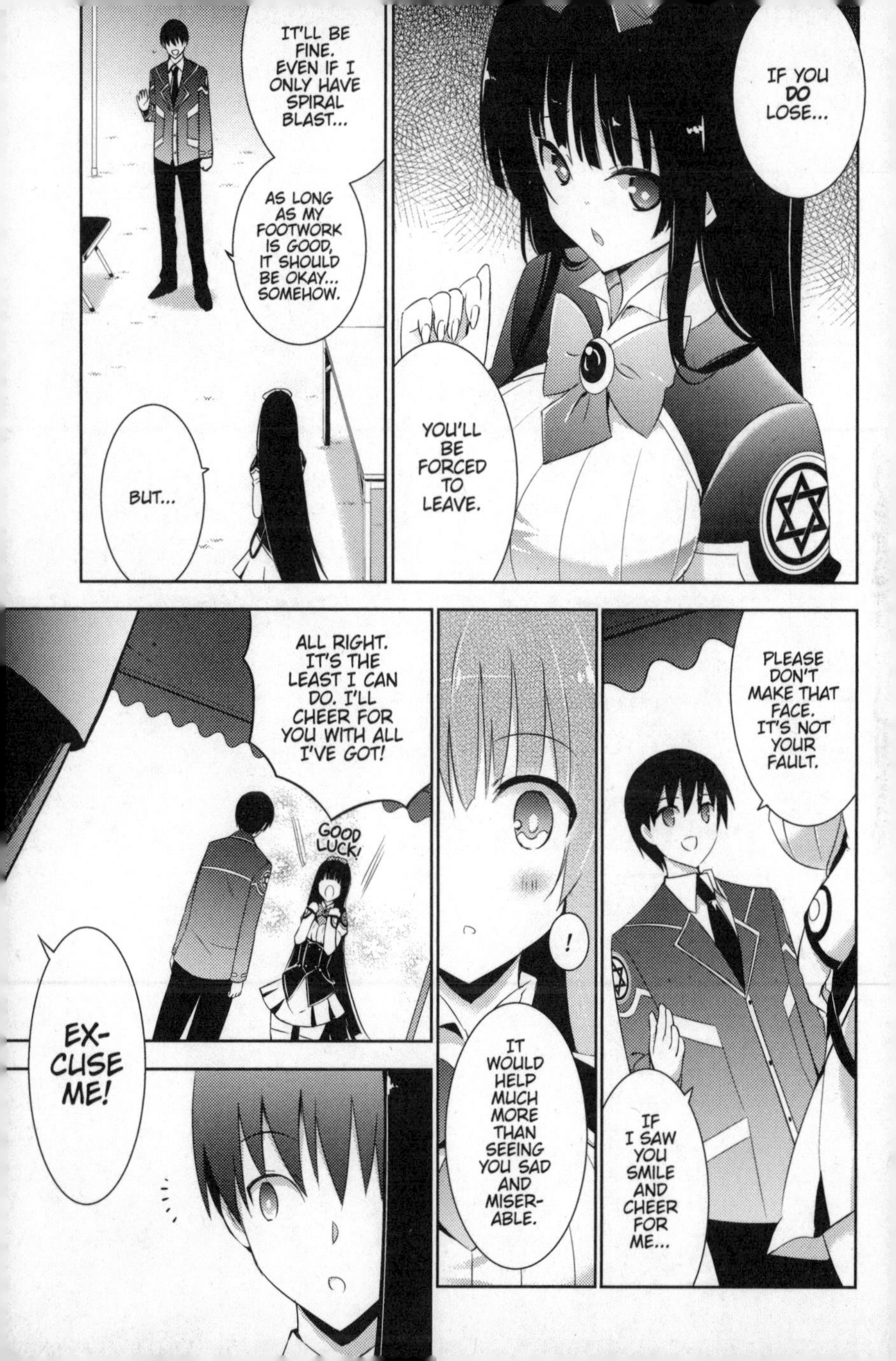
IF YOU DO LOSE...
YOU'LL BE FORCED TO LEAVE.
IT'LL BE FINE. EVEN IF I ONLY HAVE SPIRAL BLAST...
AS LONG AS MY FOOTWORK IS GOOD, IT SHOULD BE OKAY... SOMEHOW.
BUT...
PLEASE DON'T MAKE THAT FACE. IT'S NOT YOUR FAULT.
IF I SAW YOU SMILE AND CHEER FOR ME...
!
IT WOULD HELP MUCH MORE THAN SEEING YOU SAD AND MISER-ABLE.
ALL RIGHT. IT'S THE LEAST I CAN DO. I'LL CHEER FOR YOU WITH ALL I'VE GOT!
GOOD LUCK!
EX-CUSE ME!

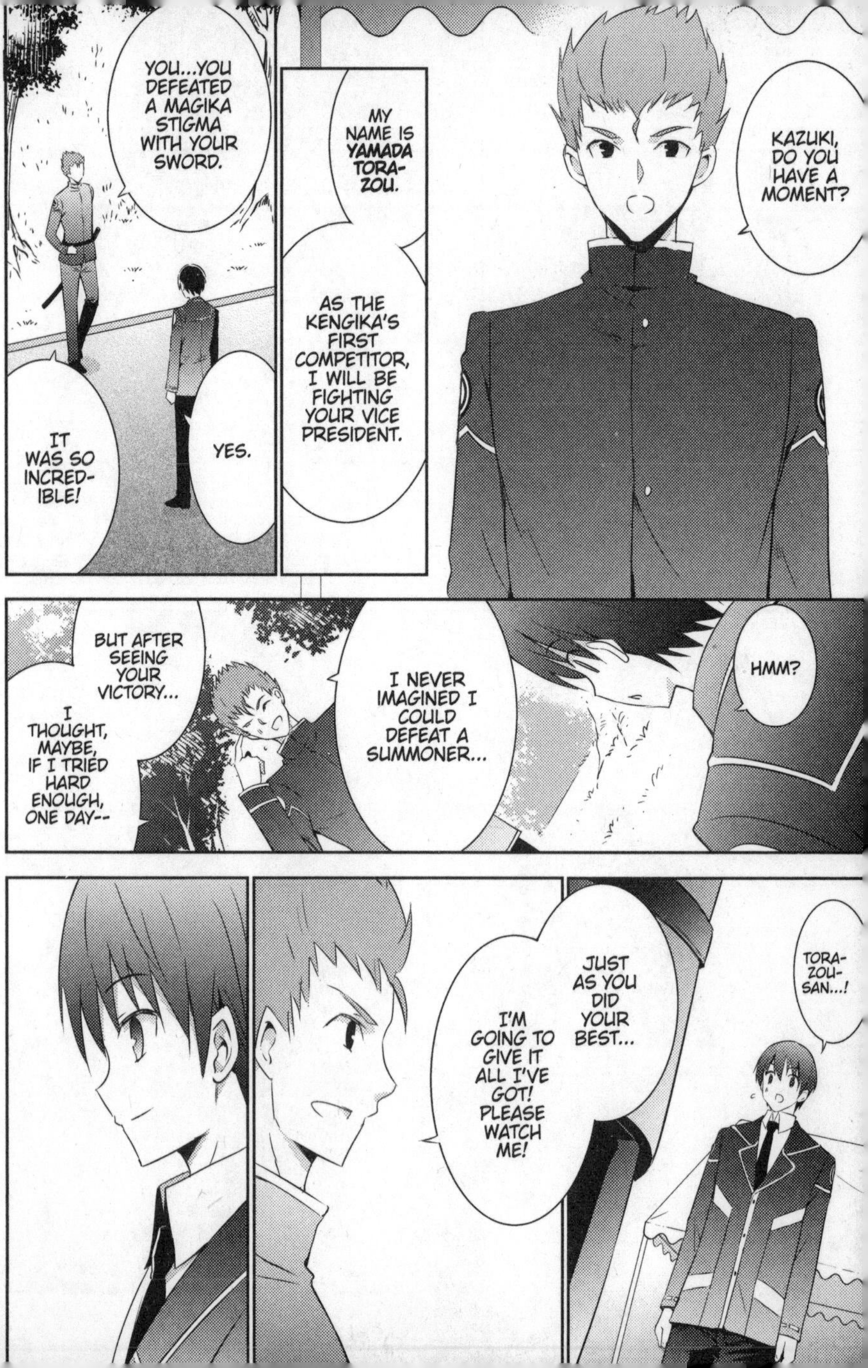
KAZUKI, DO YOU HAVE A MOMENT?
MY NAME IS YAMADA TORAZOU.
AS THE KENGIKA'S FIRST COMPETITOR, I WILL BE FIGHTING YOUR VICE PRESIDENT.
YOU...YOU DEFEATED A MAGIKA STIGMA WITH YOUR SWORD.
YES.
IT WAS SO INCREDIBLE!
HMM?
I NEVER IMAGINED I COULD DEFEAT A SUMMONER...
BUT AFTER SEEING YOUR VICTORY...
I THOUGHT, MAYBE, IF I TRIED HARD ENOUGH, ONE DAY--
TORAZOU-SAN...!
JUST AS YOU DID YOUR BEST...
I'M GOING TO GIVE IT ALL I'VE GOT! PLEASE WATCH ME!

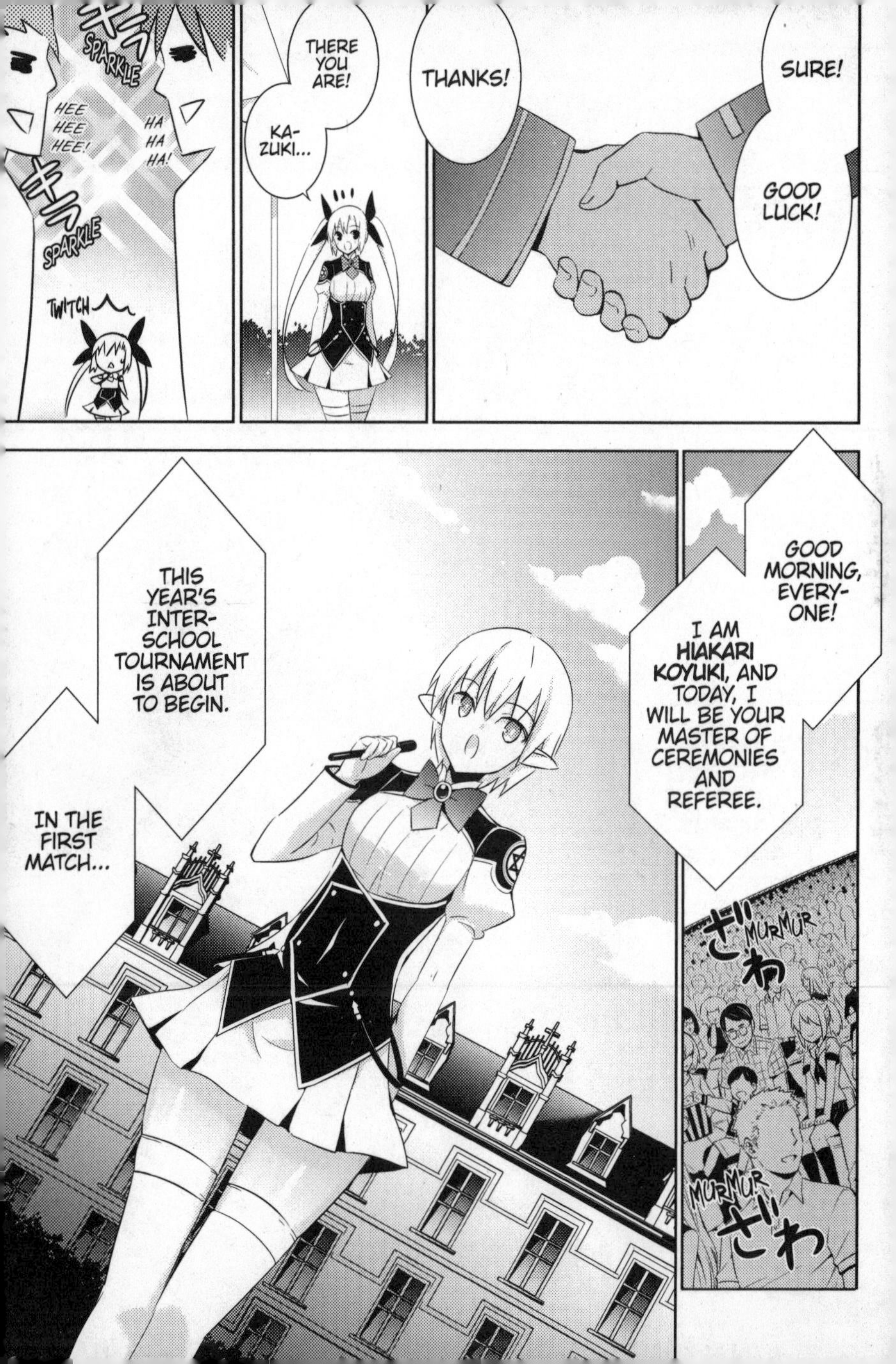
SURE!
GOOD LUCK!
THANKS!
THERE YOU ARE!
KA-ZUKI...
キラ
SPARKLE
HA HA HA!
HEE HEE HEE!
キラ
SPARKLE
TWITCH
GOOD MORNING, EVERY-ONE!
I AM HIAKARI KOYUKI, AND TODAY, I WILL BE YOUR MASTER OF CEREMONIES AND REFEREE.
ざわ
MURMUR
ざわ
MURMUR
THIS YEAR'S INTER-SCHOOL TOURNAMENT IS ABOUT TO BEGIN.
IN THE FIRST MATCH...

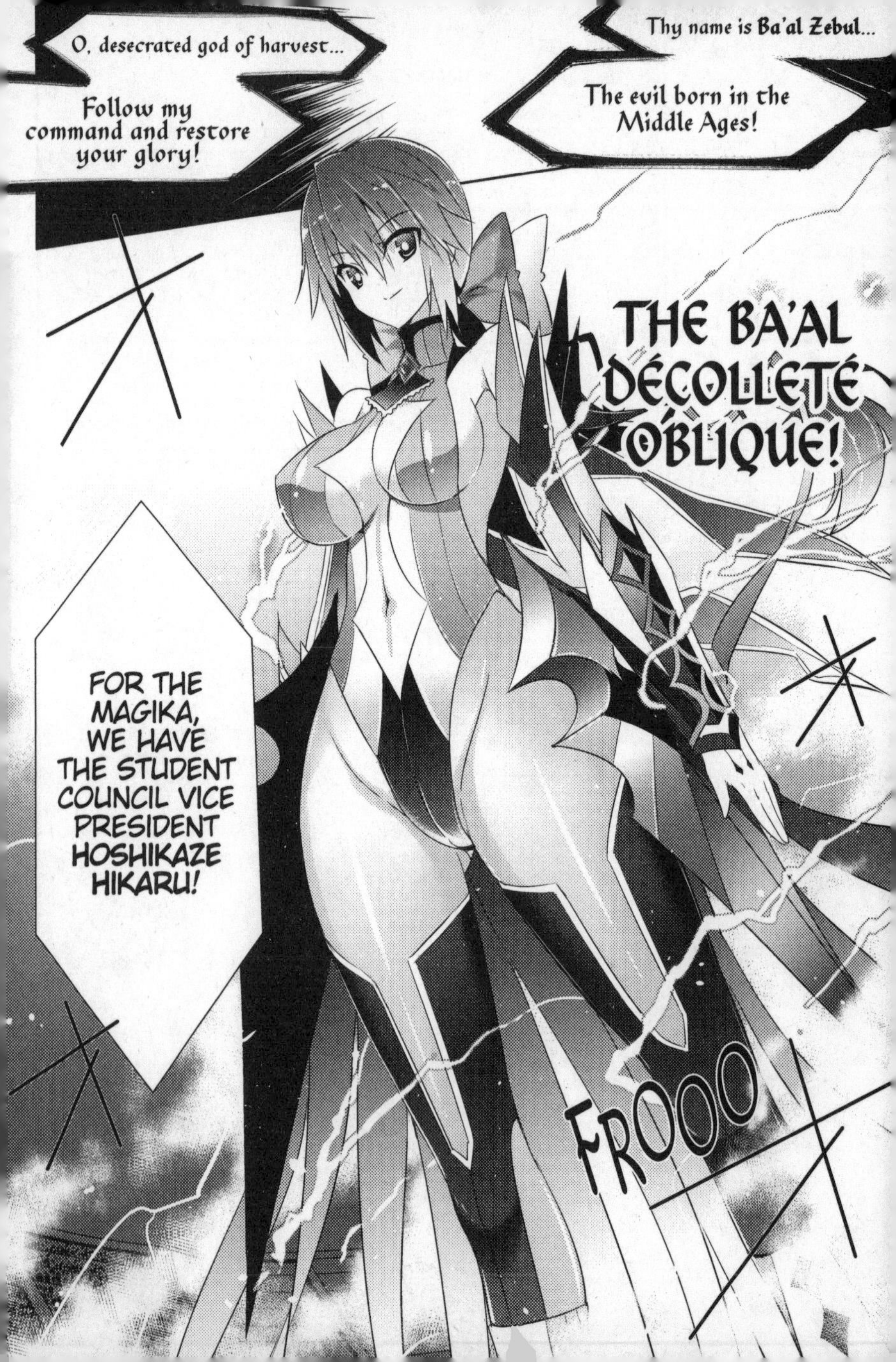
Thy name is Ba'al Zebul...
The evil born in the Middle Ages!
O, desecrated god of harvest...
Follow my command and restore your glory!
THE BA'AL DÉCOLLETÉ OBLIQUE!
FOR THE MAGIKA, WE HAVE THE STUDENT COUNCIL VICE PRESIDENT HOSHIKAZE HIKARU!
FROOO

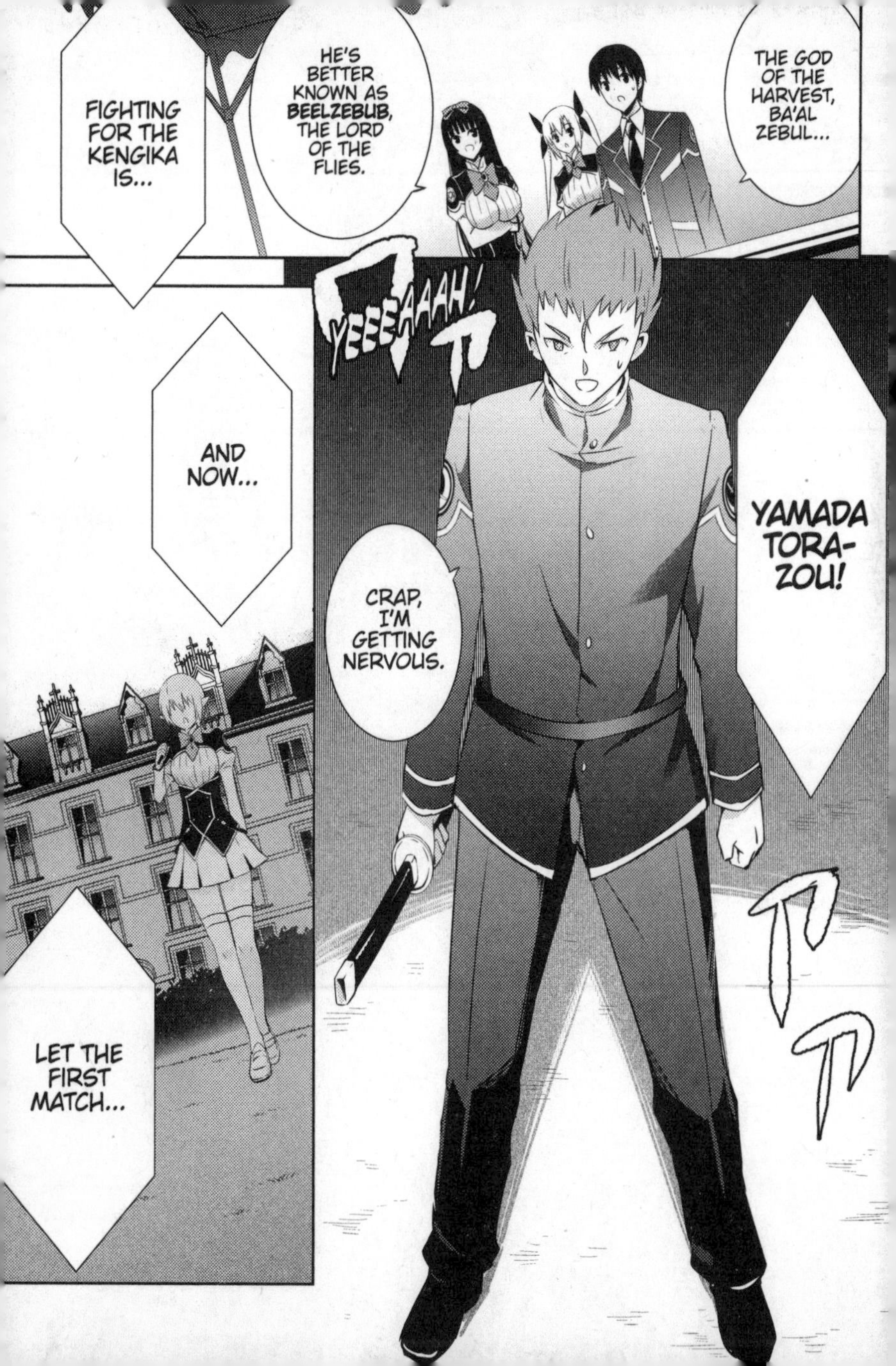
THE GOD OF THE HARVEST, BA'AL ZEBUL...
HE'S BETTER KNOWN AS BEELZEBUB, THE LORD OF THE FLIES.
FIGHTING FOR THE KENGIKA IS...
YEEEAAAH!
YAMADA TORA-ZOU!
CRAP, I'M GETTING NERVOUS.
AND NOW...
LET THE FIRST MATCH...

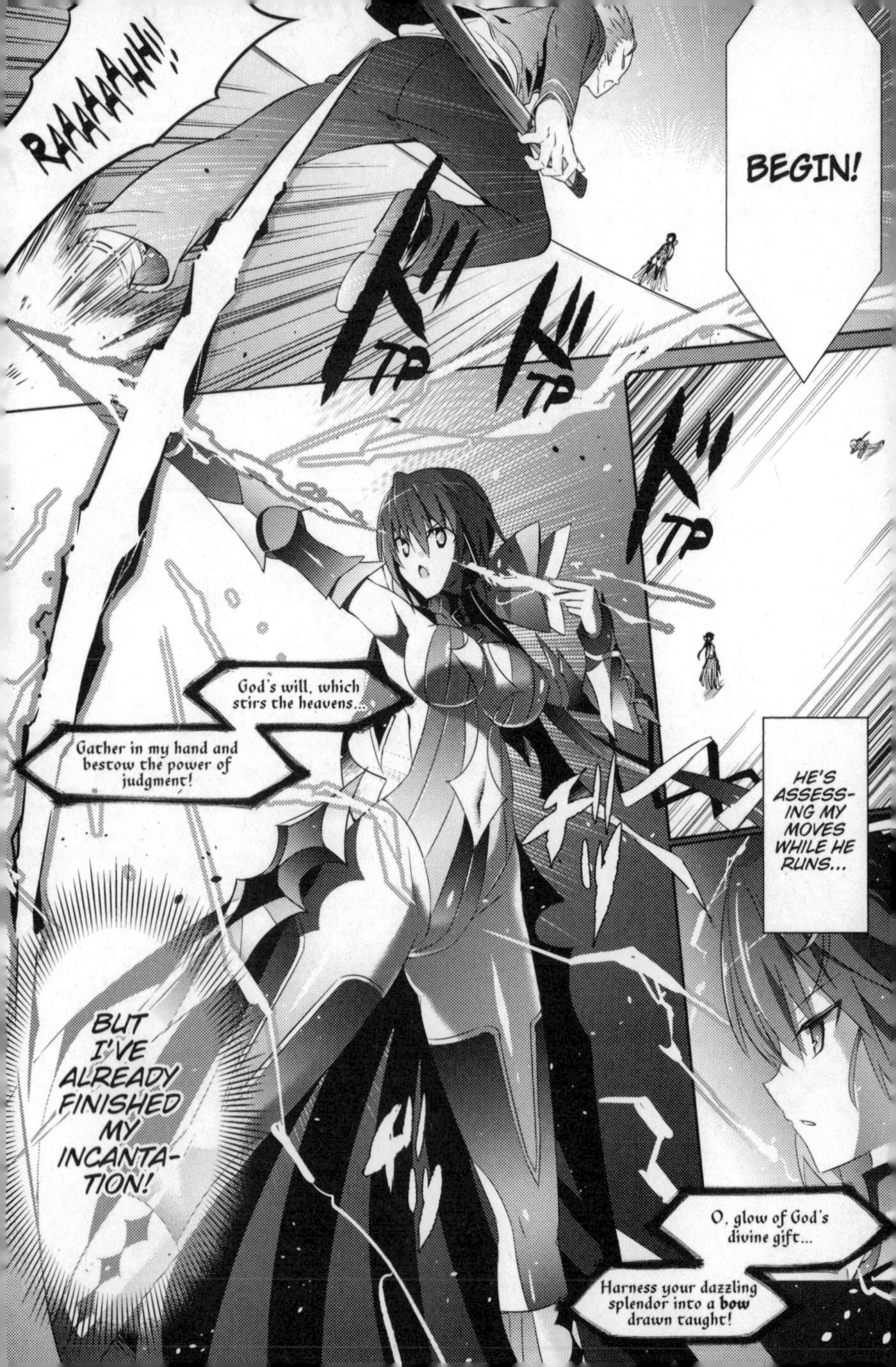
BEGIN!
RAAAAAAH!!
TP
TP
TP
HE'S ASSESSING MY MOVES WHILE HE RUNS...
God's will, which stirs the heavens...
Gather in my hand and bestow the power of judgment!
O, glow of God's divine gift...
Harness your dazzling splendor into a **bow** drawn taught!
BUT I'VE ALREADY FINISHED MY INCANTATION!

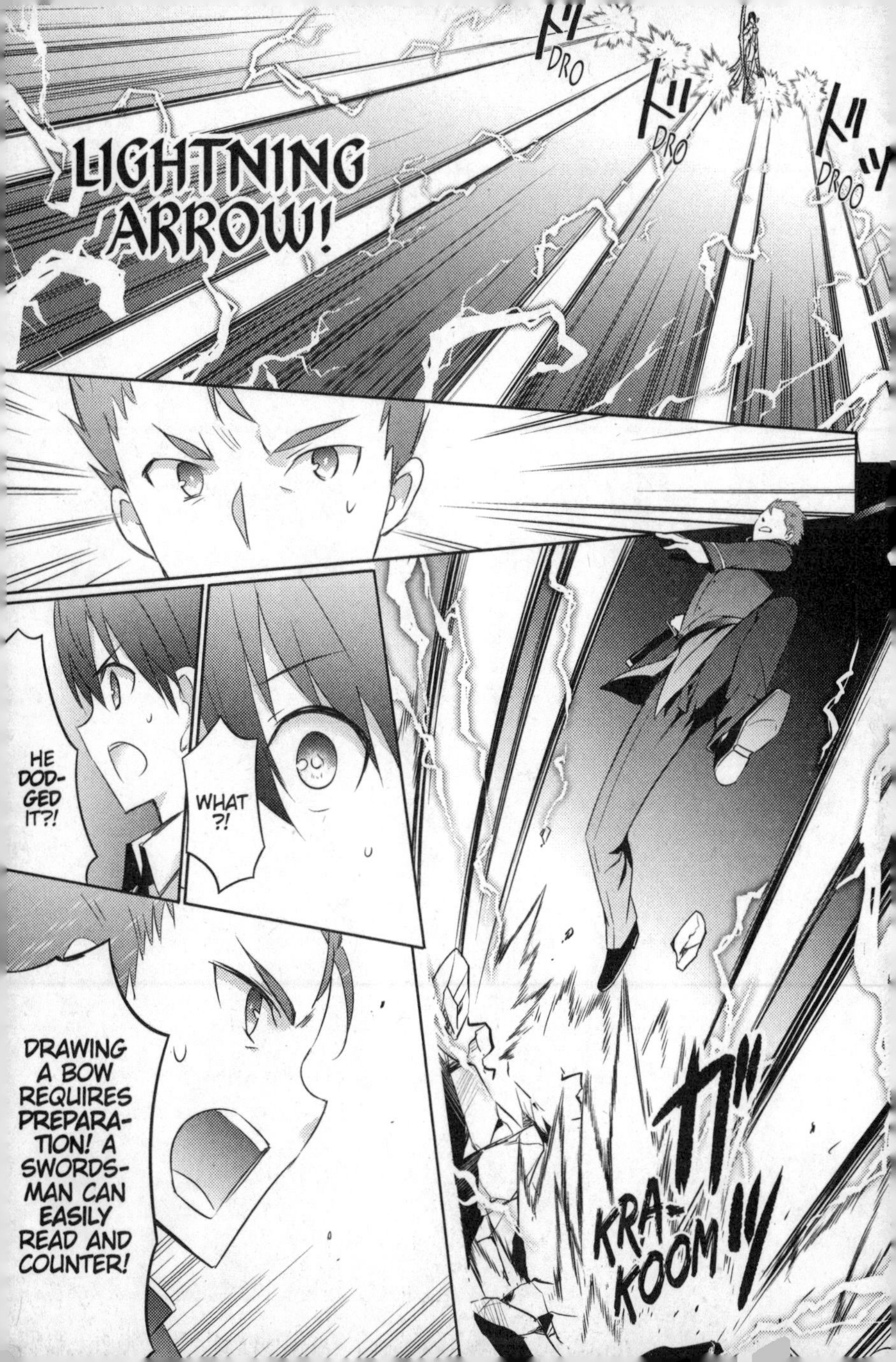
ドッ
DROO
ド
DRO
ド
DRO
LIGHTNING ARROW!
ガッ
KRA-KOOM!!
WHAT?!
HE DODGED IT?!
DRAWING A BOW REQUIRES PREPARATION! A SWORDSMAN CAN EASILY READ AND COUNTER!

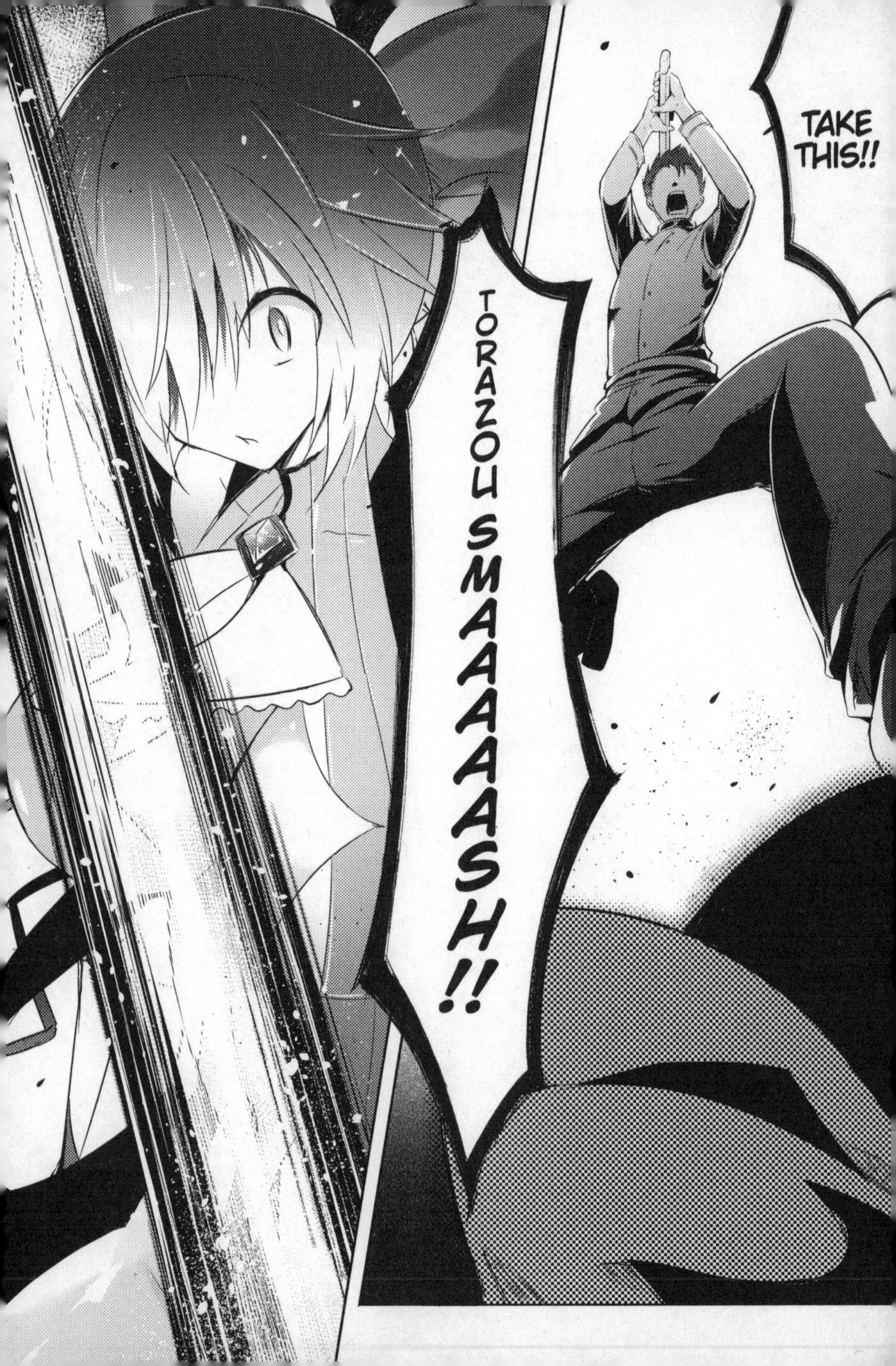
TAKE THIS!!
TORAZOU SMAAAAASH!!

Magika
SWORDSMAN
AND SUMMONER

3

魔技科の剣士と召喚魔王

3

Chapter 12

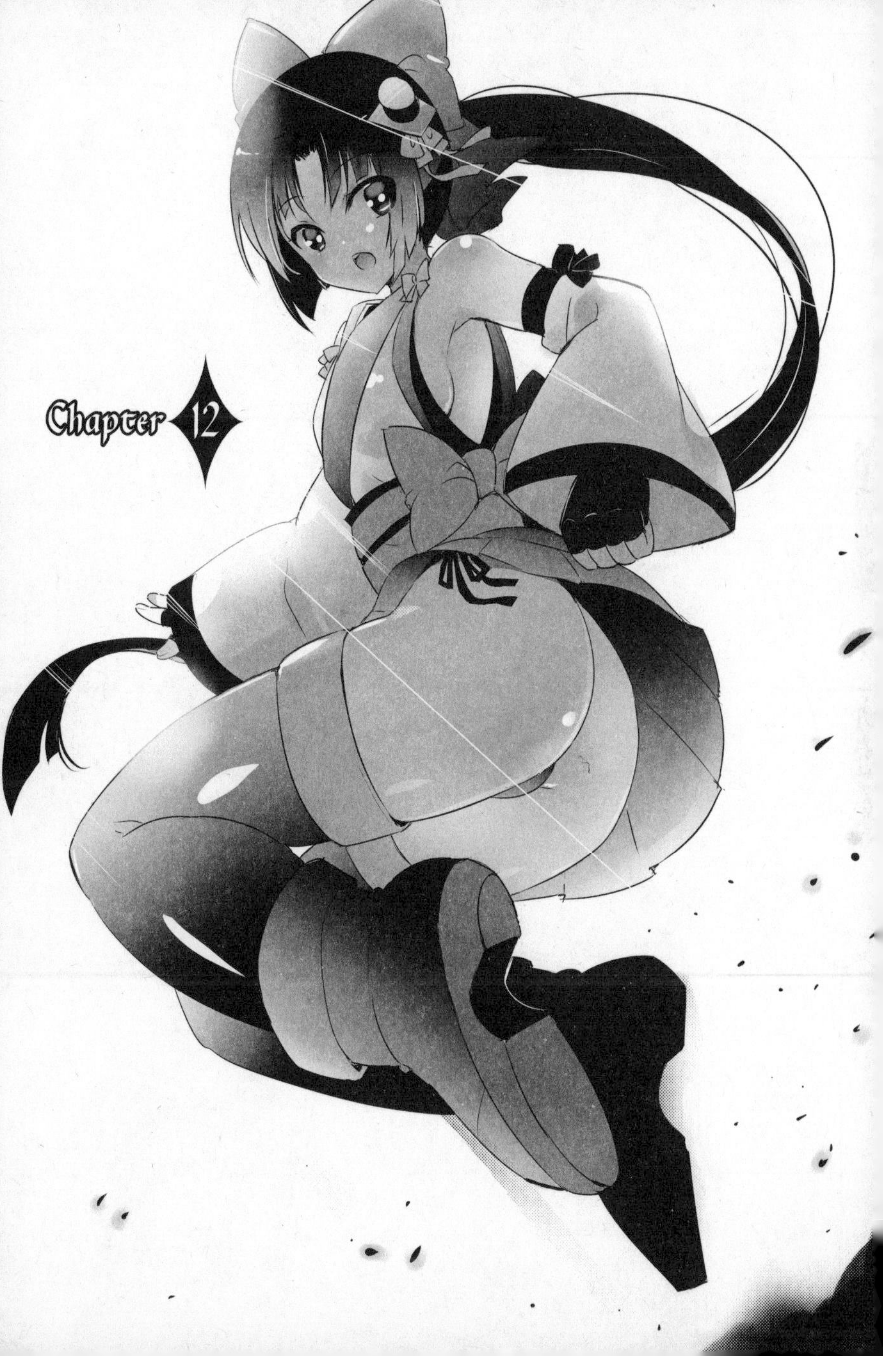

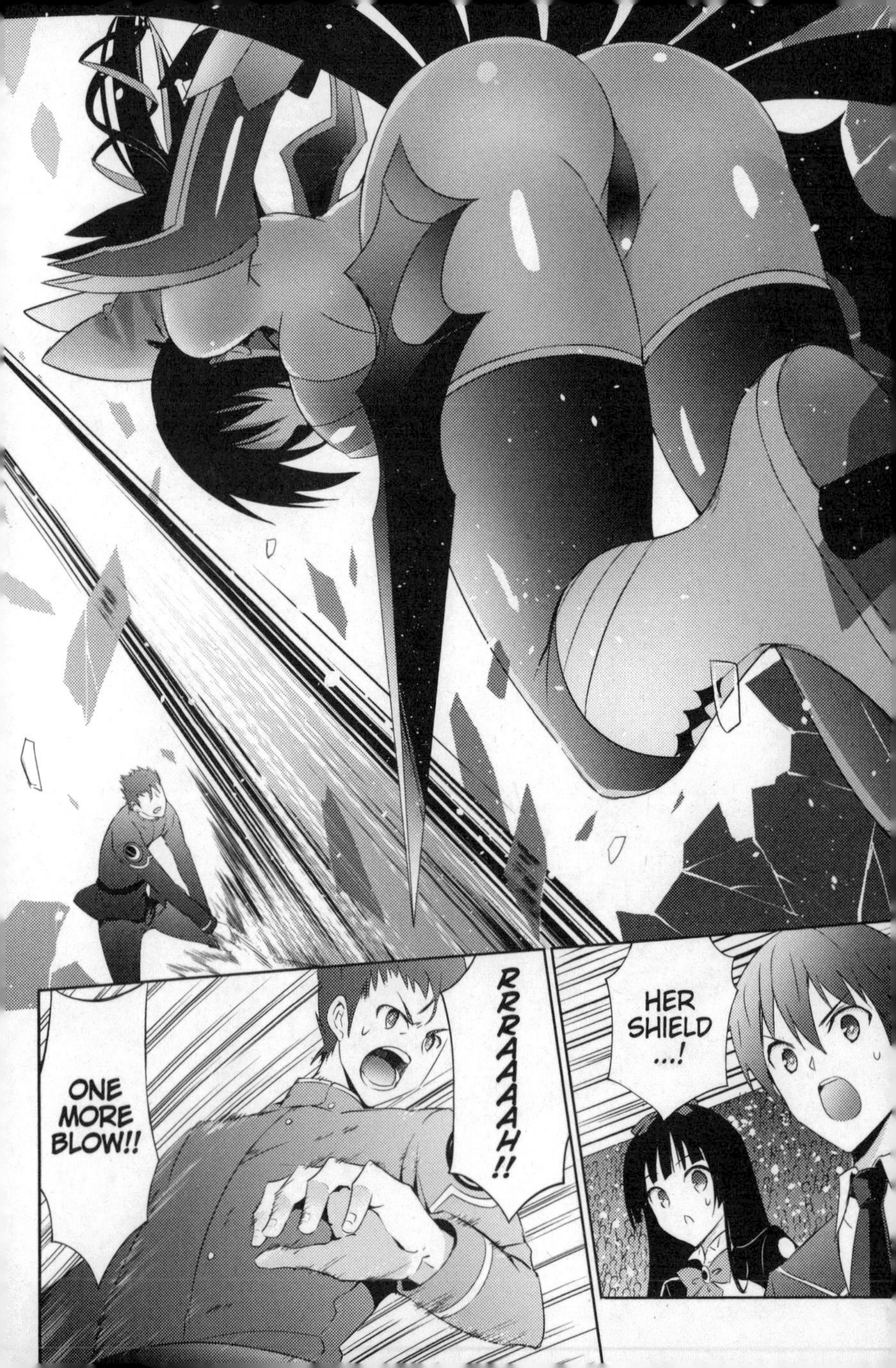
HER SHIELD ...!
RRRAAAAAH!!
ONE MORE BLOW!!

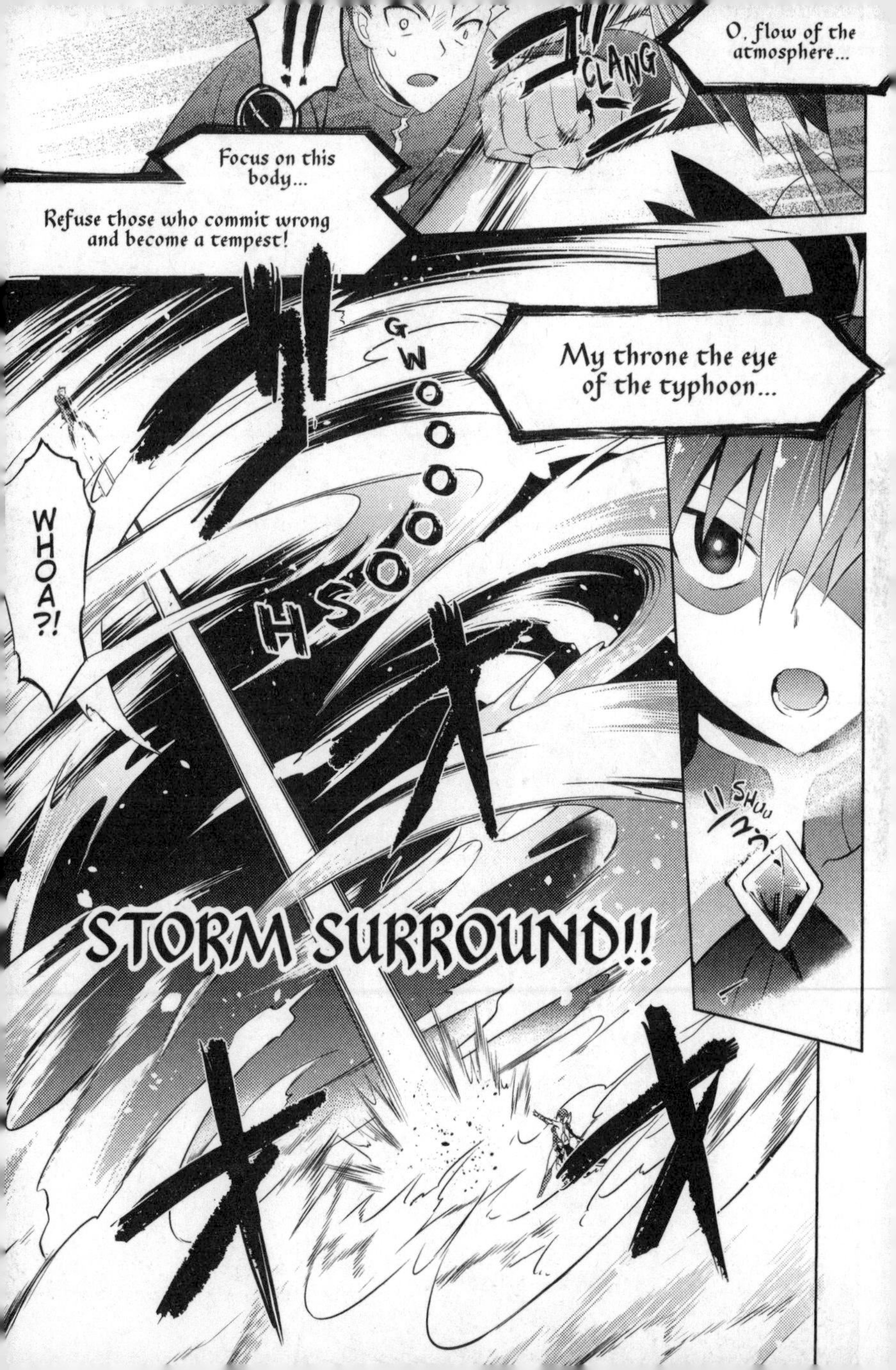

O, flow of the atmosphere...
CLANG
Focus on this body...
Refuse those who commit wrong and become a tempest!
My throne the eye of the typhoon...
SHUU
GWOOOOOSH
WHOA?!
STORM SURROUND!!

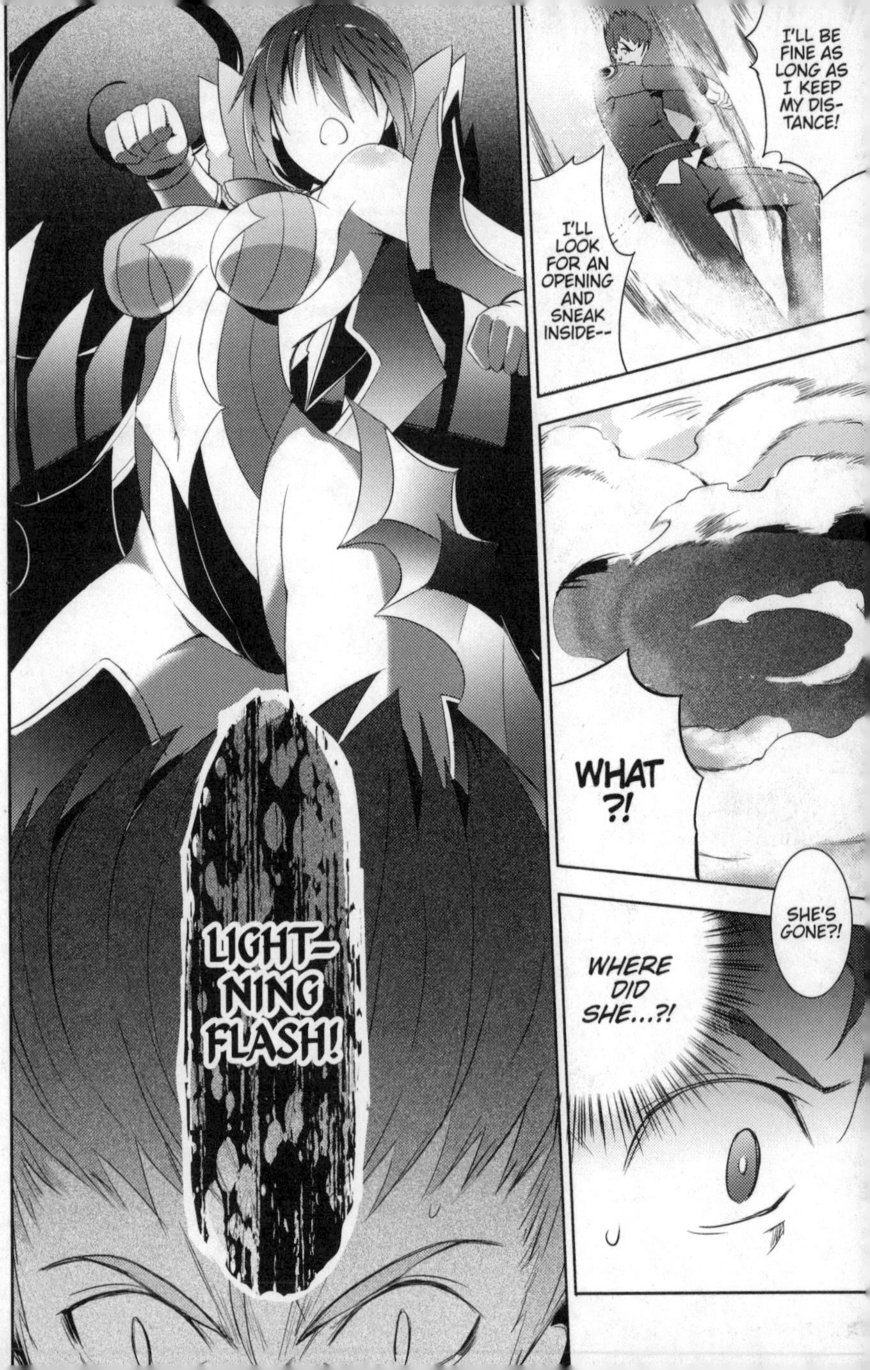
I'LL BE FINE AS LONG AS I KEEP MY DIS-TANCE!
I'LL LOOK FOR AN OPENING AND SNEAK INSIDE--
WHAT ?!
SHE'S GONE?!
WHERE DID SHE...?!
LIGHT-NING FLASH!

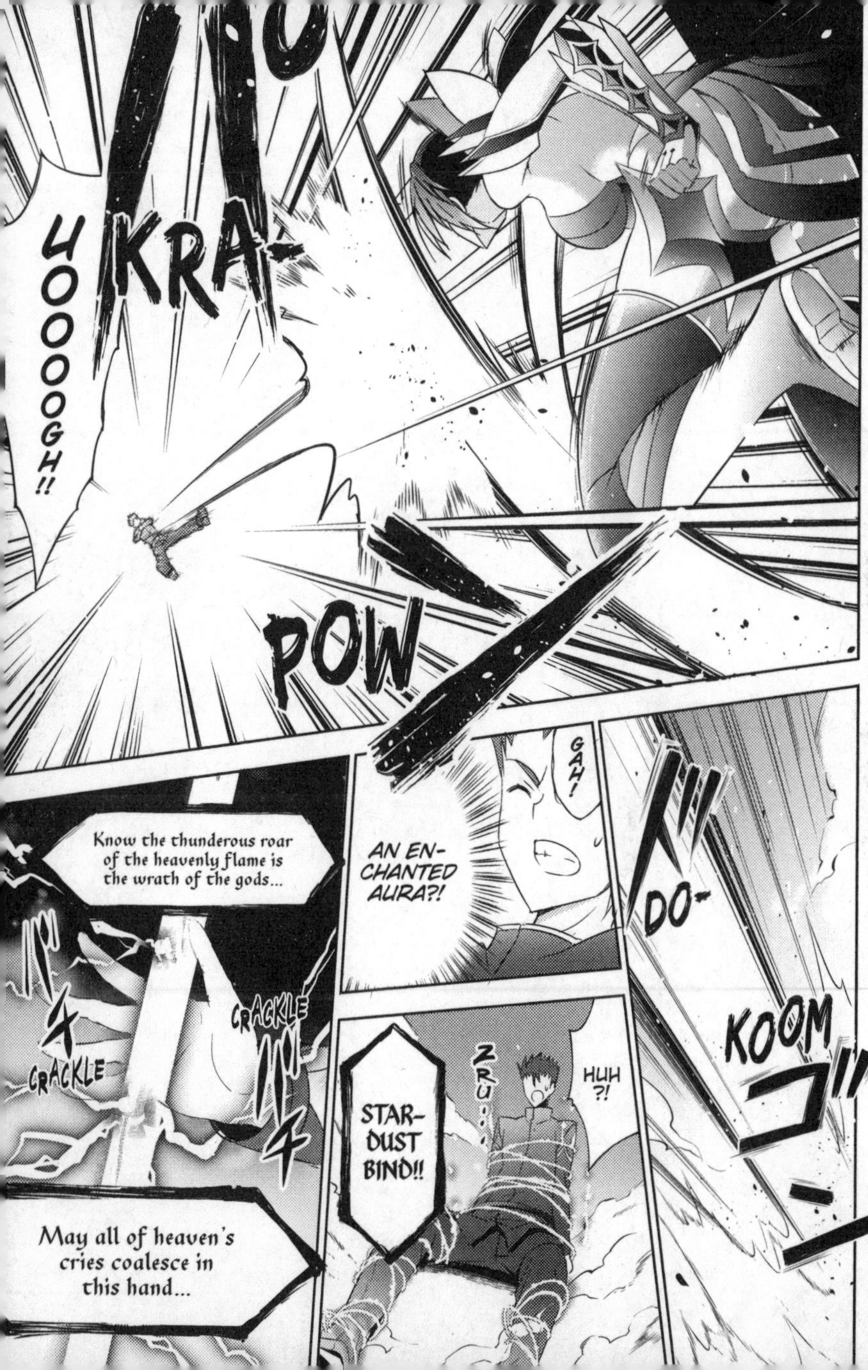
KRA-
UOOOOGH!!
POW
DO-
KOOM
GAH!
AN EN-CHANTED AURA?!
ZRU...
HUH?!
STAR-DUST BIND!!
Know the thunderous roar of the heavenly flame is the wrath of the gods...
CRACKLE
CRACKLE
May all of heaven's cries coalesce in this hand...

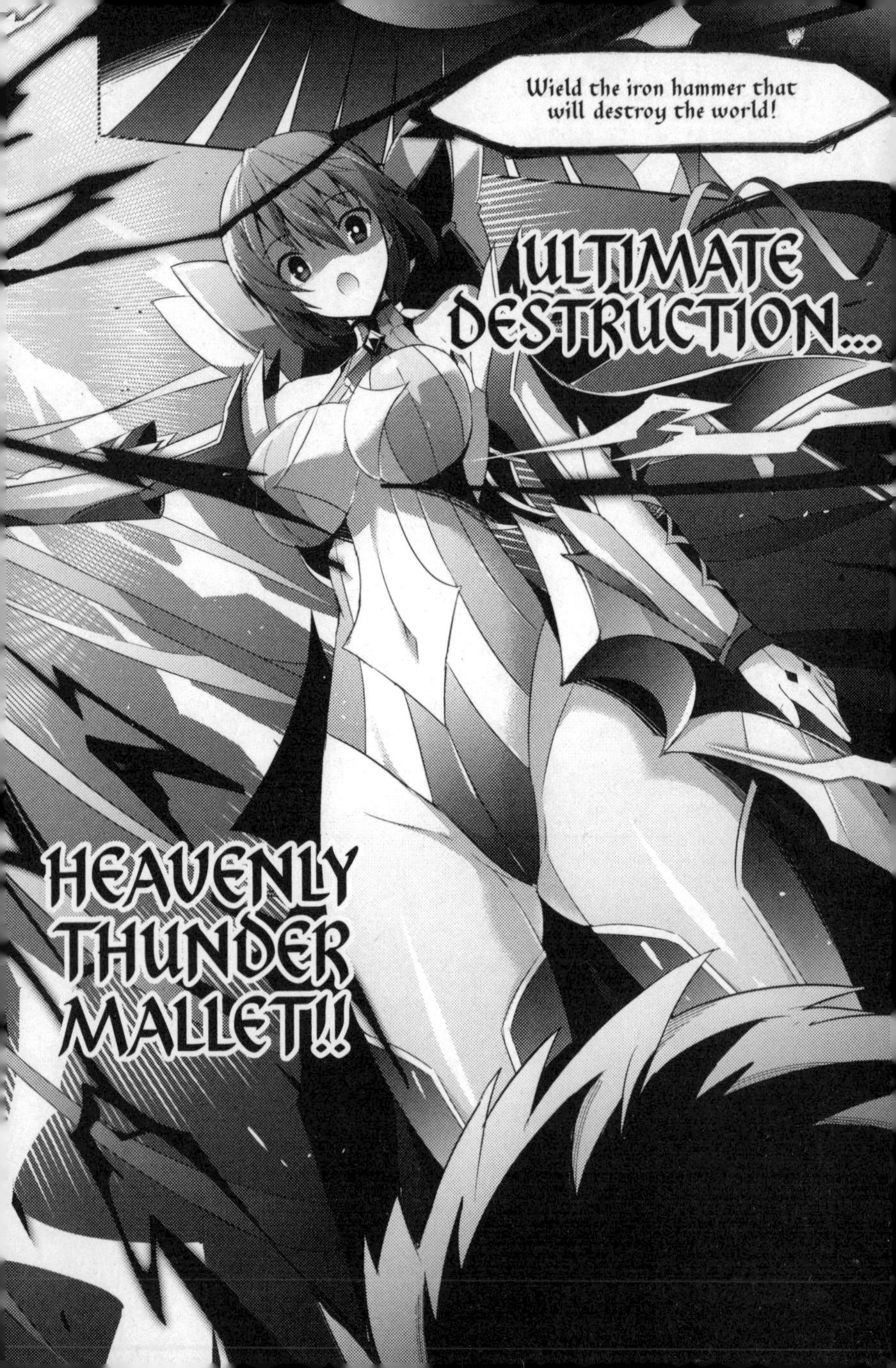
Wield the iron hammer that will destroy the world!
ULTIMATE DESTRUCTION...
HEAVENLY THUNDER MALLET!!

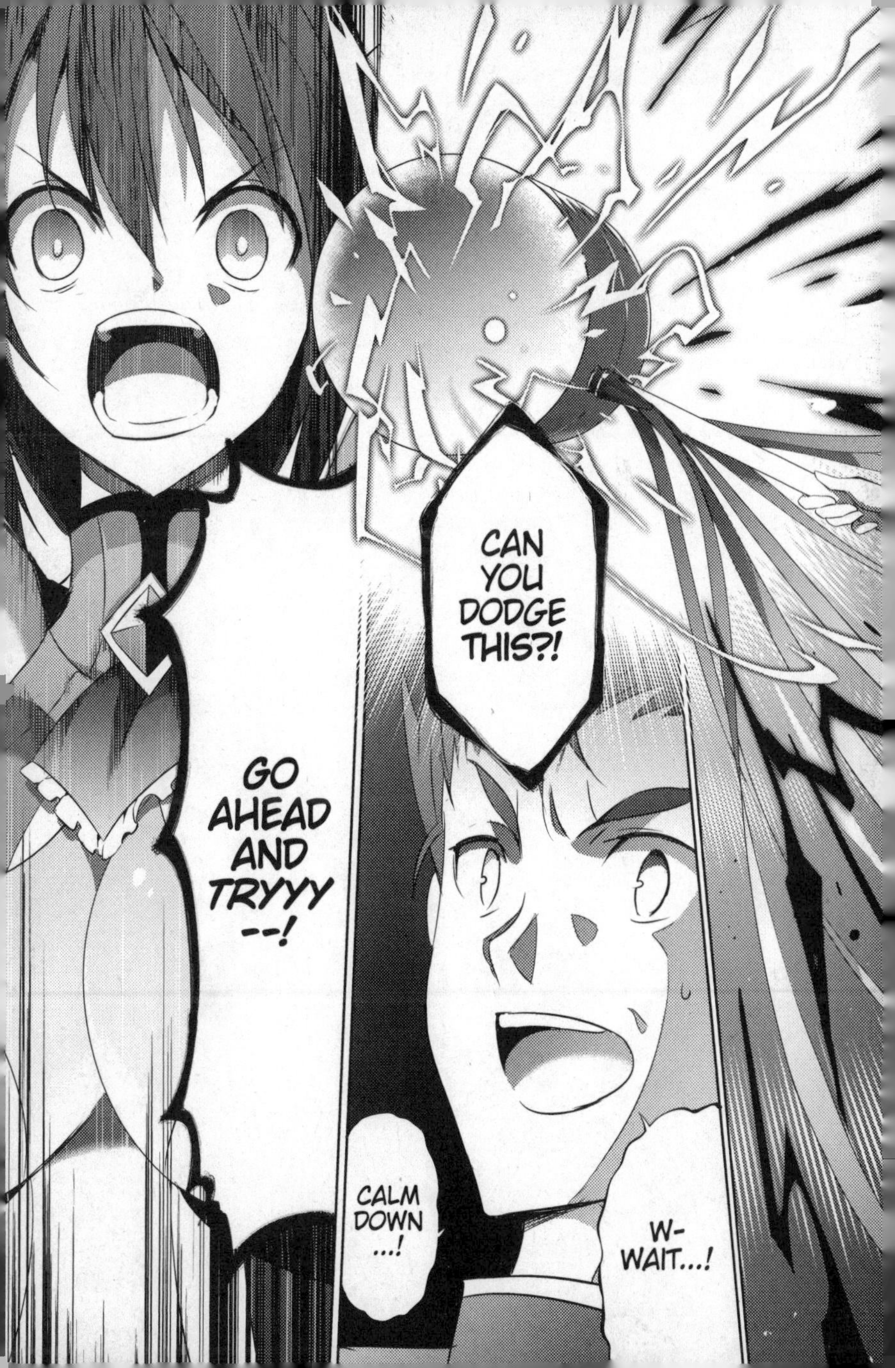
CAN YOU DODGE THIS?!
W-WAIT...!
CALM DOWN...!
GO AHEAD AND *TRYYY*--!

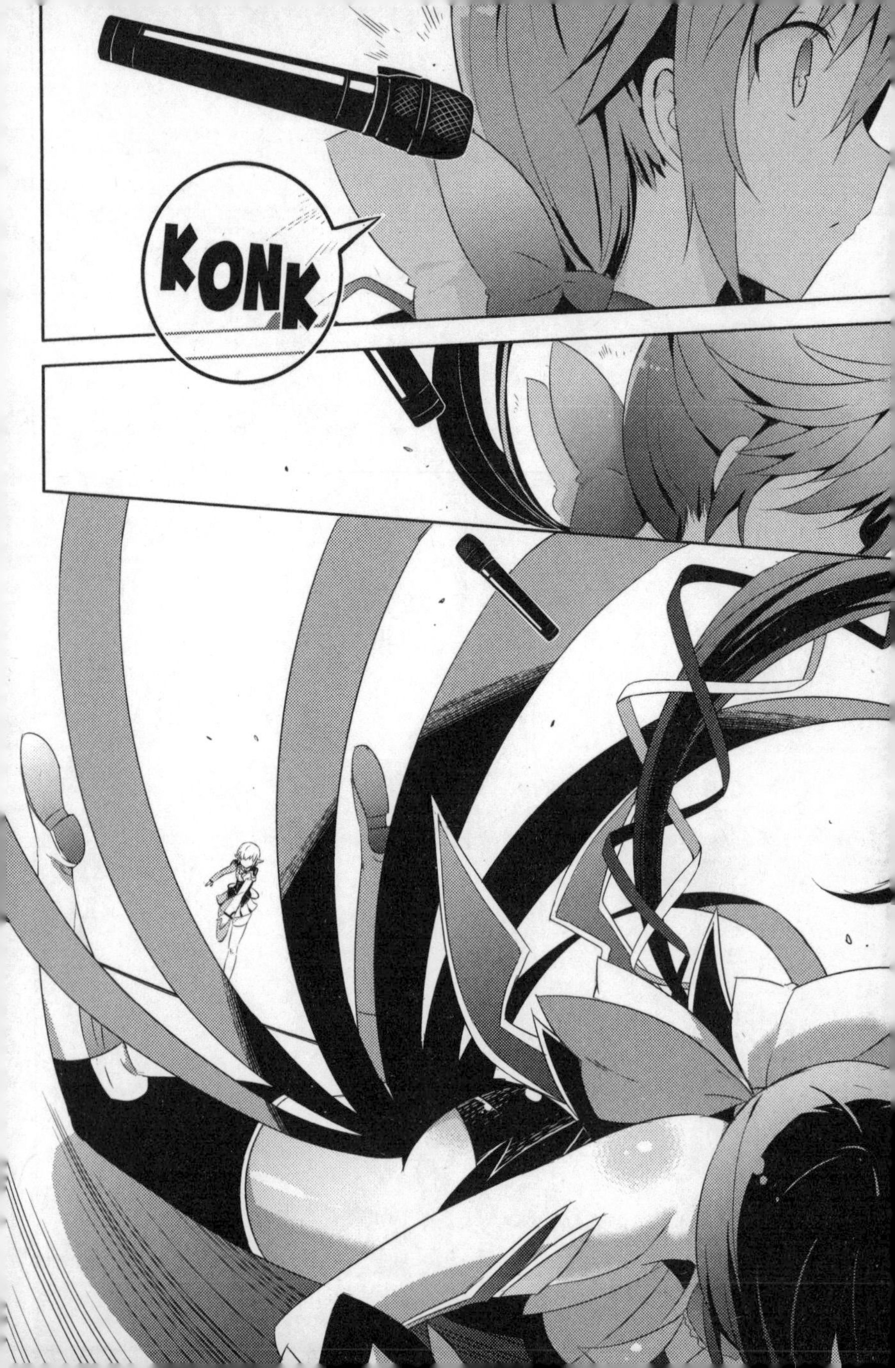
KONK

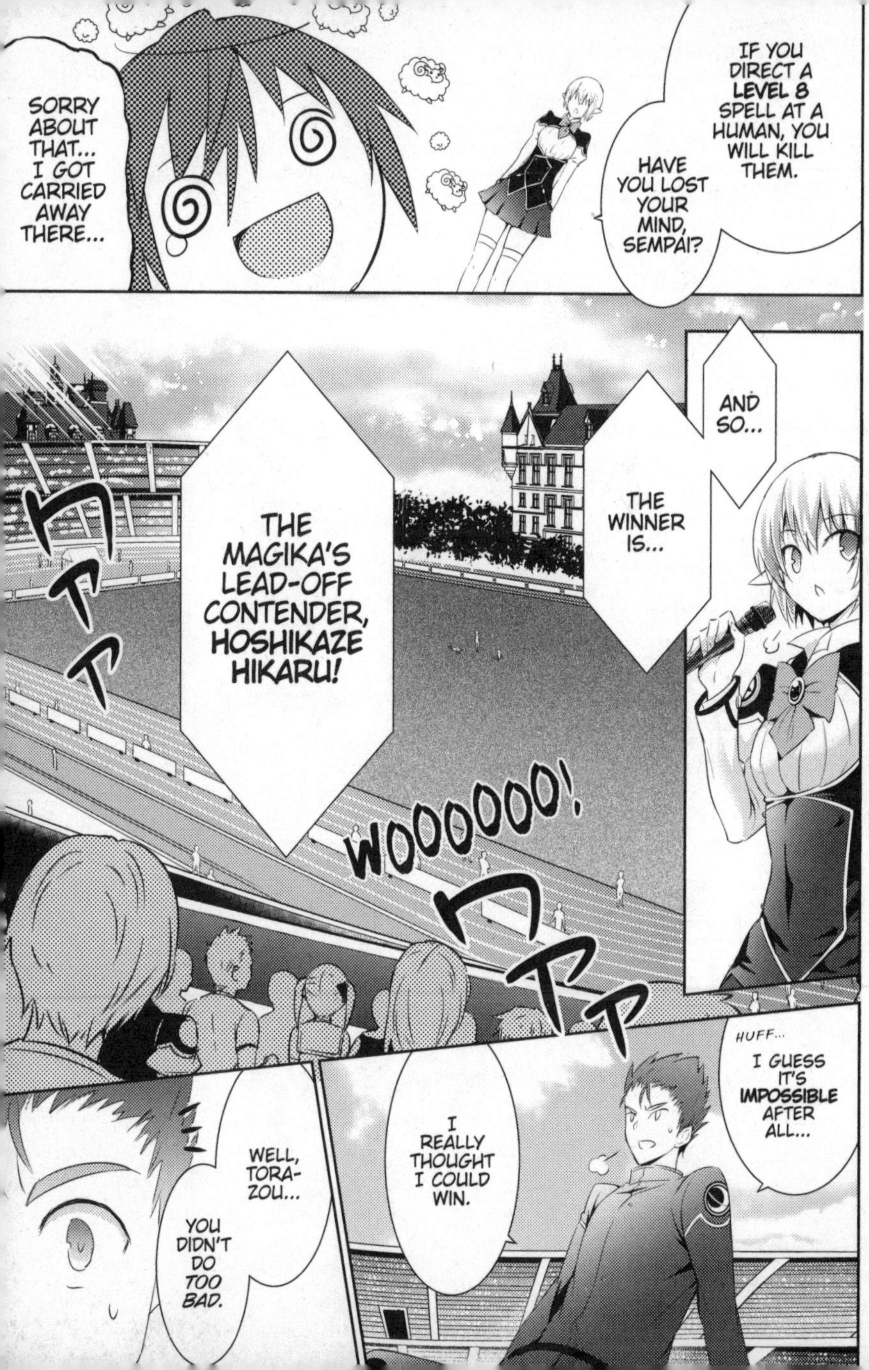
IF YOU DIRECT A LEVEL 8 SPELL AT A HUMAN, YOU WILL KILL THEM.
HAVE YOU LOST YOUR MIND, SEMPAI?
SORRY ABOUT THAT... I GOT CARRIED AWAY THERE...
AND SO...
THE WINNER IS...
THE MAGIKA'S LEAD-OFF CONTENDER, HOSHIKAZE HIKARU!
WOOOOOO!
HUFF...
I GUESS IT'S IMPOSSIBLE AFTER ALL...
I REALLY THOUGHT I COULD WIN.
WELL, TORA-ZOU...
YOU DIDN'T DO TOO BAD.

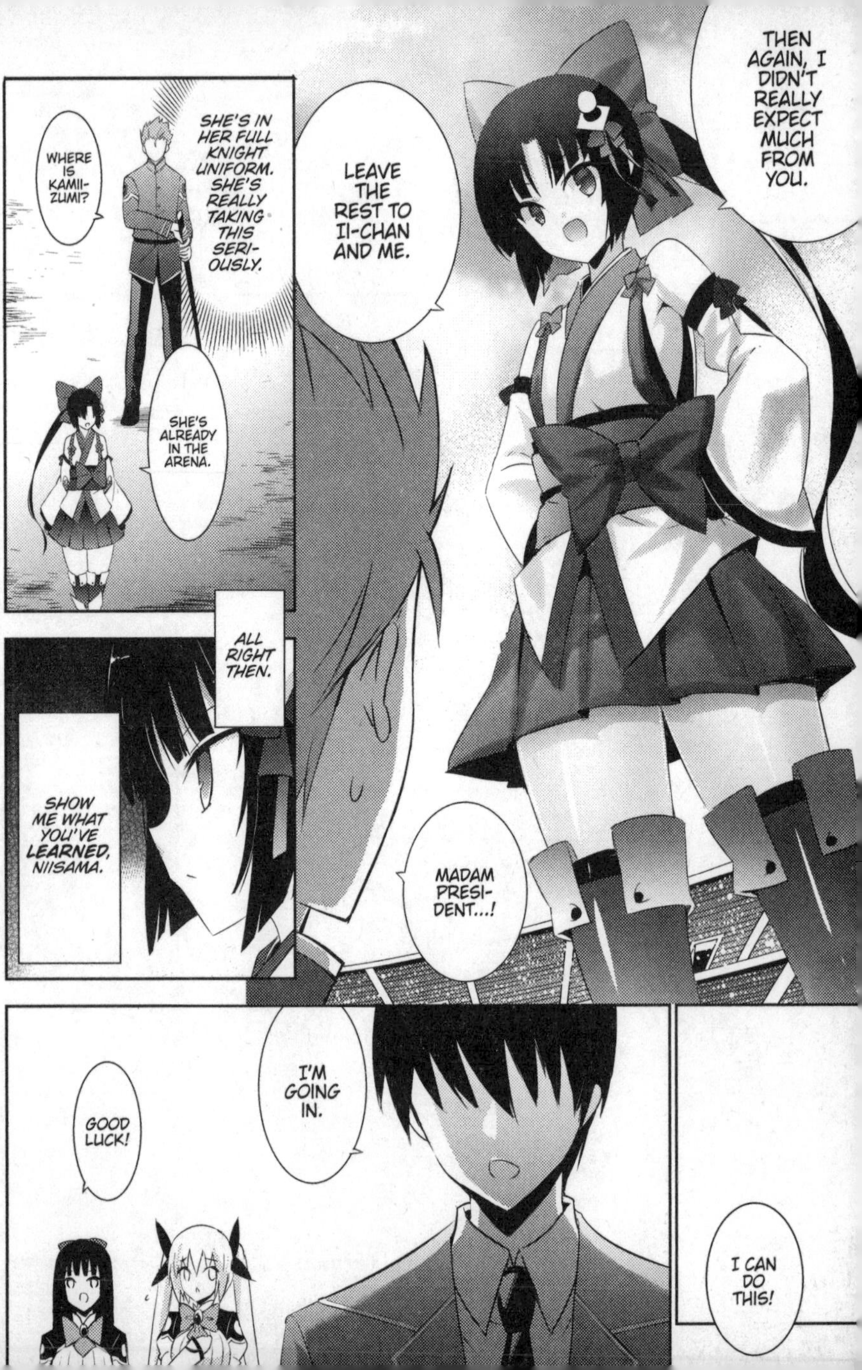
THEN AGAIN, I DIDN'T REALLY EXPECT MUCH FROM YOU.
LEAVE THE REST TO II-CHAN AND ME.
MADAM PRESIDENT...!
SHE'S IN HER FULL KNIGHT UNIFORM. SHE'S REALLY TAKING THIS SERIOUSLY.
WHERE IS KAMIIZUMI?
SHE'S ALREADY IN THE ARENA.
ALL RIGHT THEN.
SHOW ME WHAT YOU'VE LEARNED, NIISAMA.
I CAN DO THIS!
I'M GOING IN.
GOOD LUCK!

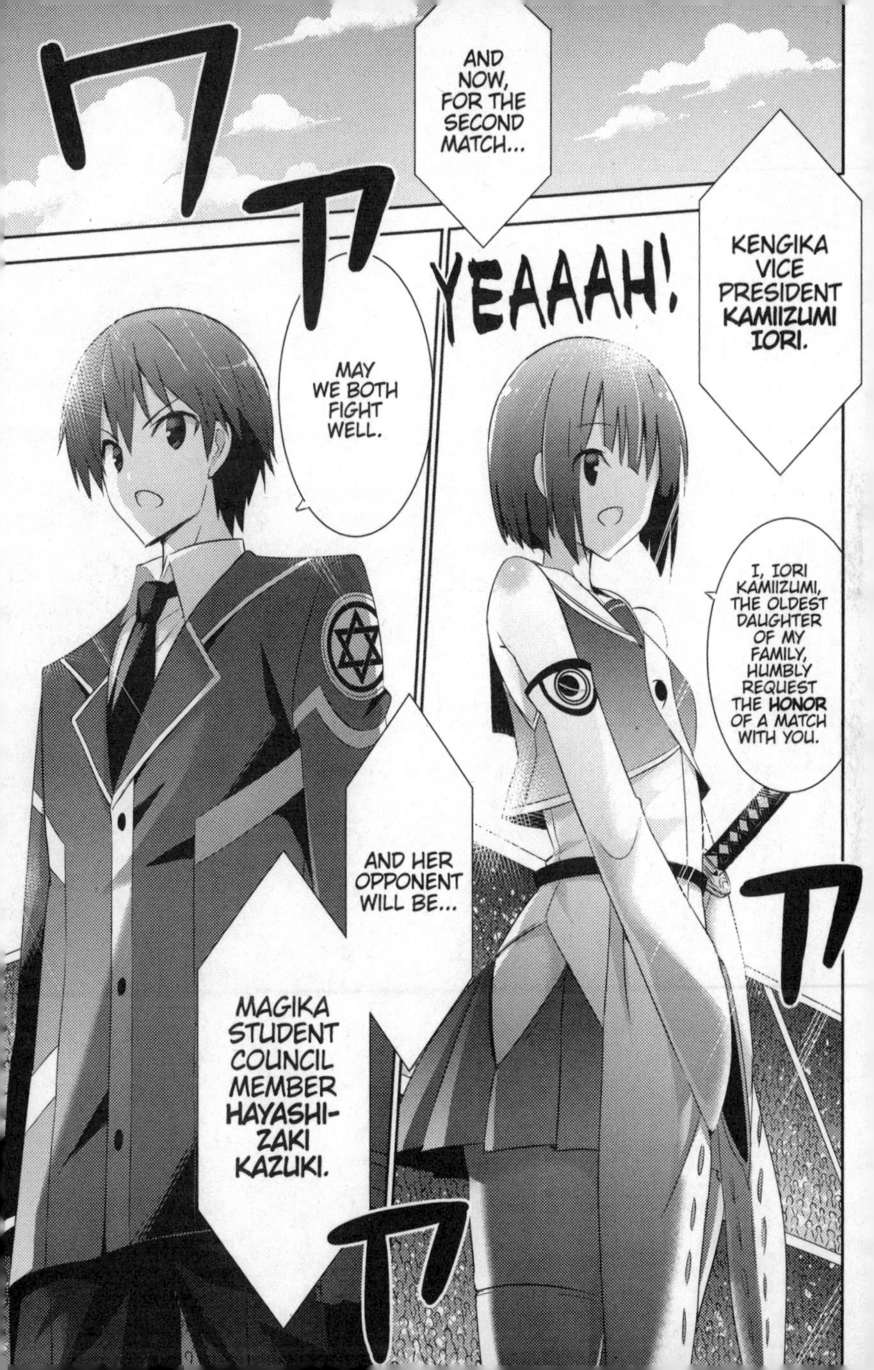
AND NOW, FOR THE SECOND MATCH...
KENGIKA VICE PRESIDENT KAMIIZUMI IORI.
ワァァァ
YEAAAH!
I, IORI KAMIIZUMI, THE OLDEST DAUGHTER OF MY FAMILY, HUMBLY REQUEST THE HONOR OF A MATCH WITH YOU.
AND HER OPPONENT WILL BE...
MAGIKA STUDENT COUNCIL MEMBER HAYASHIZAKI KAZUKI.
MAY WE BOTH FIGHT WELL.

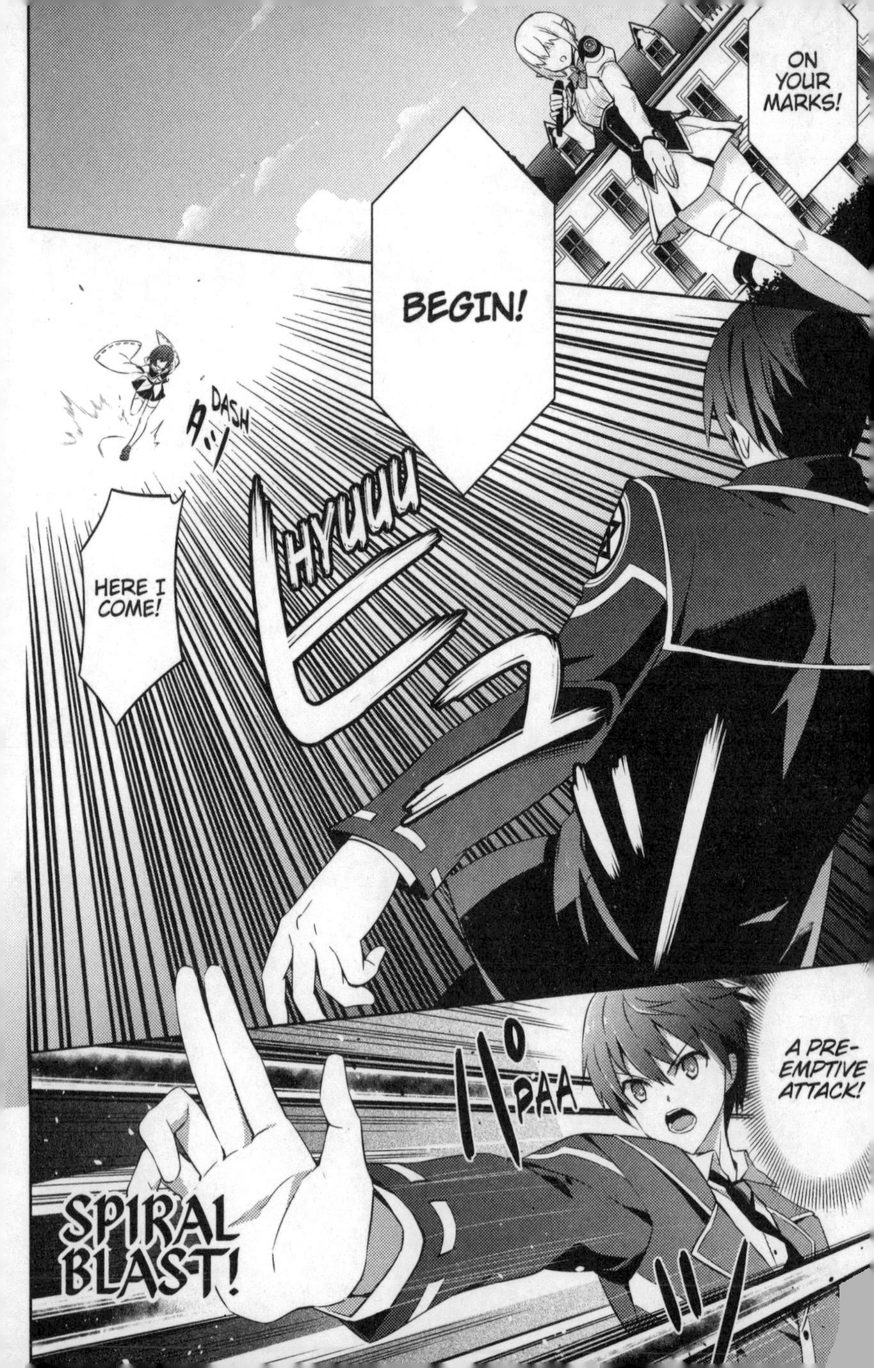
ON YOUR MARKS!
BEGIN!
HYUUU
DASH
HERE I COME!
A PRE-EMPTIVE ATTACK!
PAA
SPIRAL BLAST!

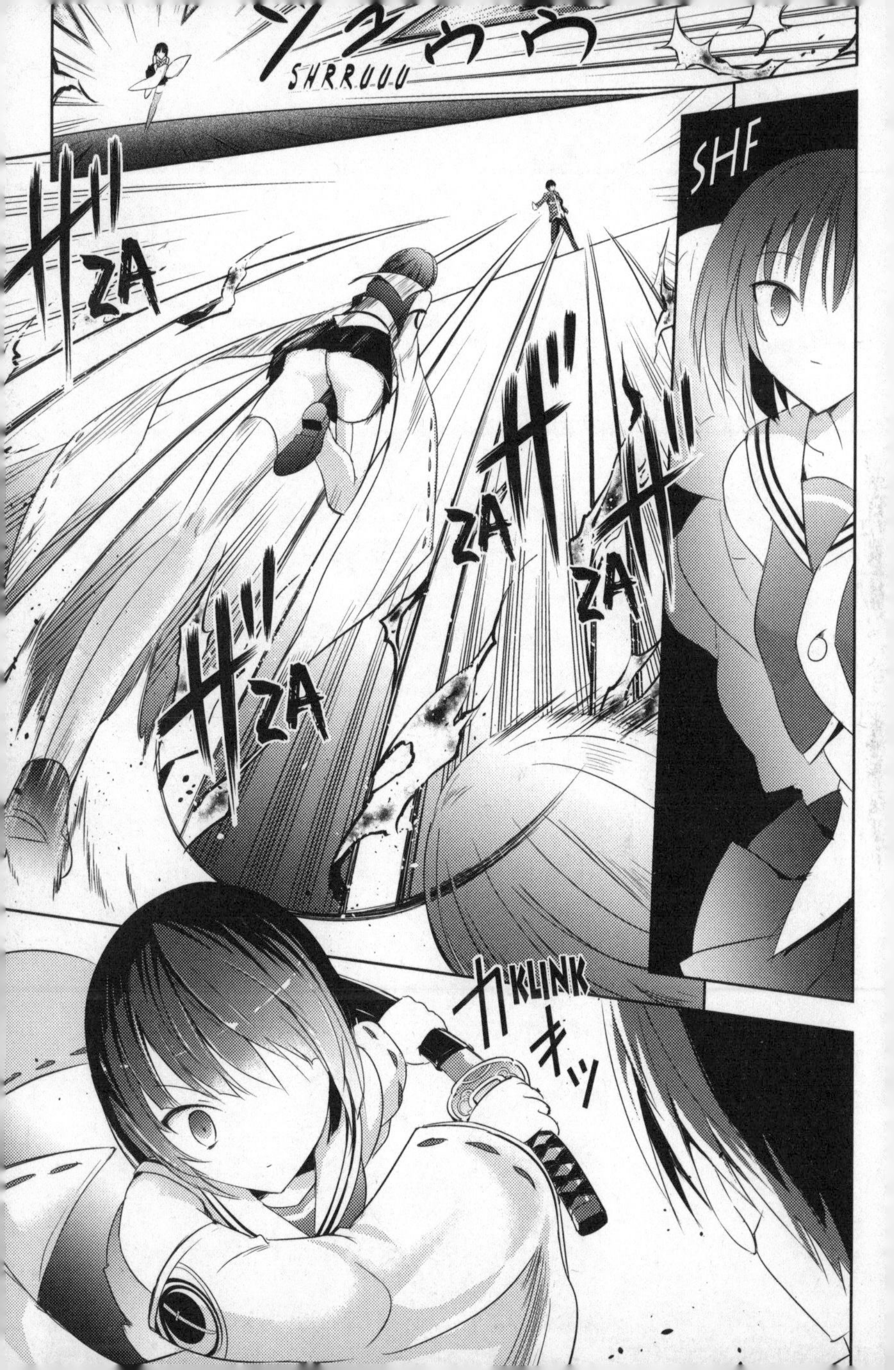
SHRRUUU
ZA
ZA
ZA
ZA
SHF
KLINK

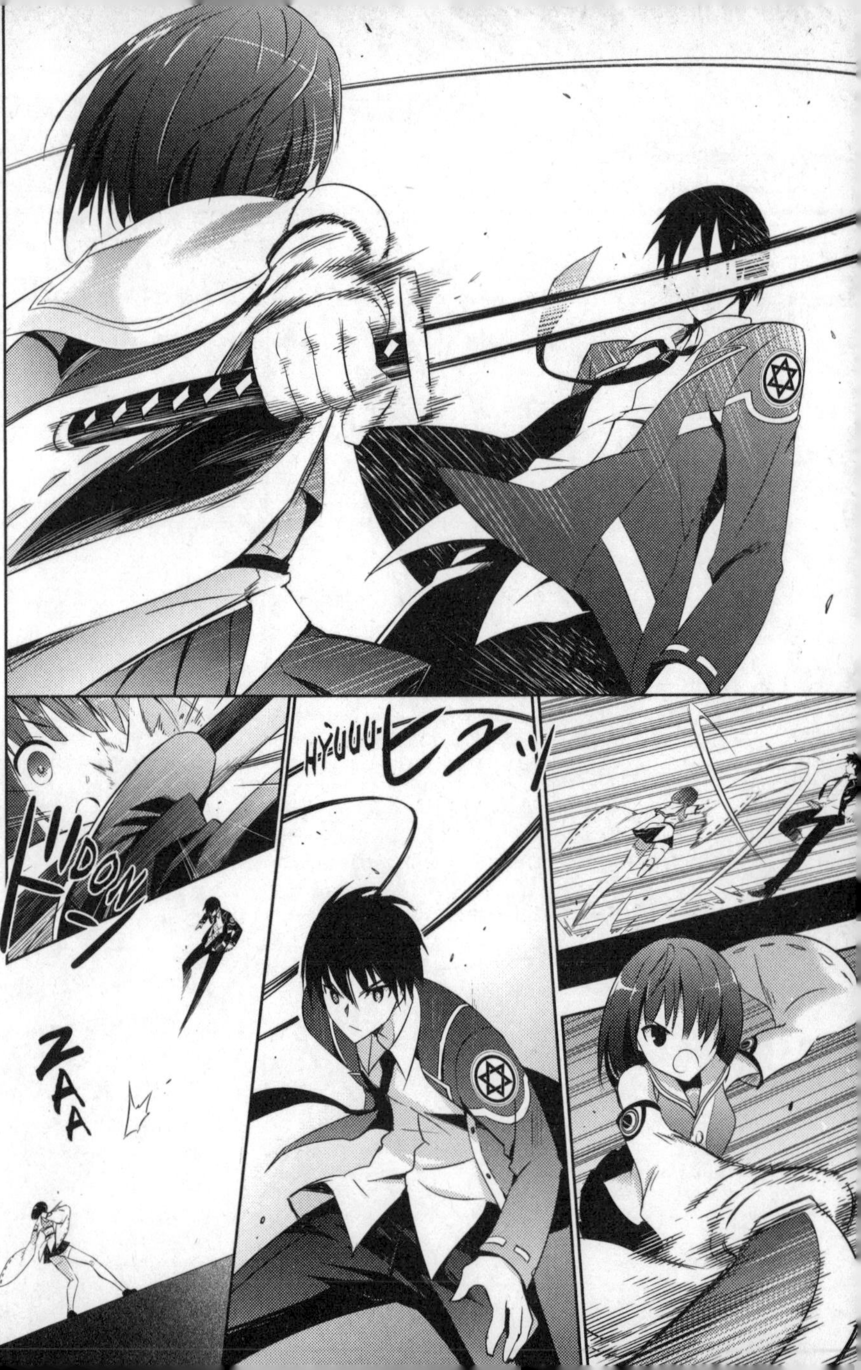
HYUUU
DON
ZAA

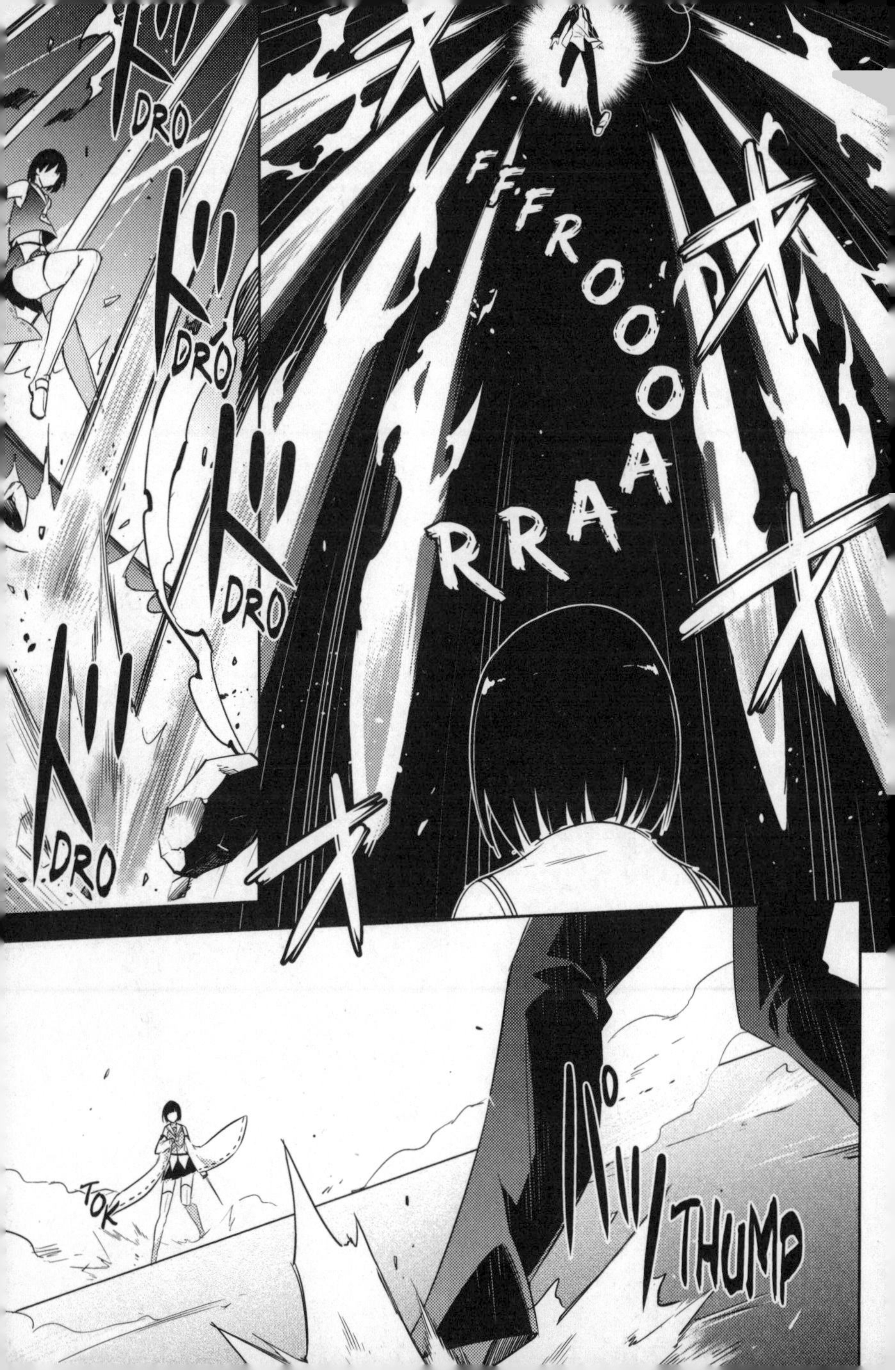
FFFROOOOARRAA
DRO
DRO
DRO
DRO
THUMP
TOK

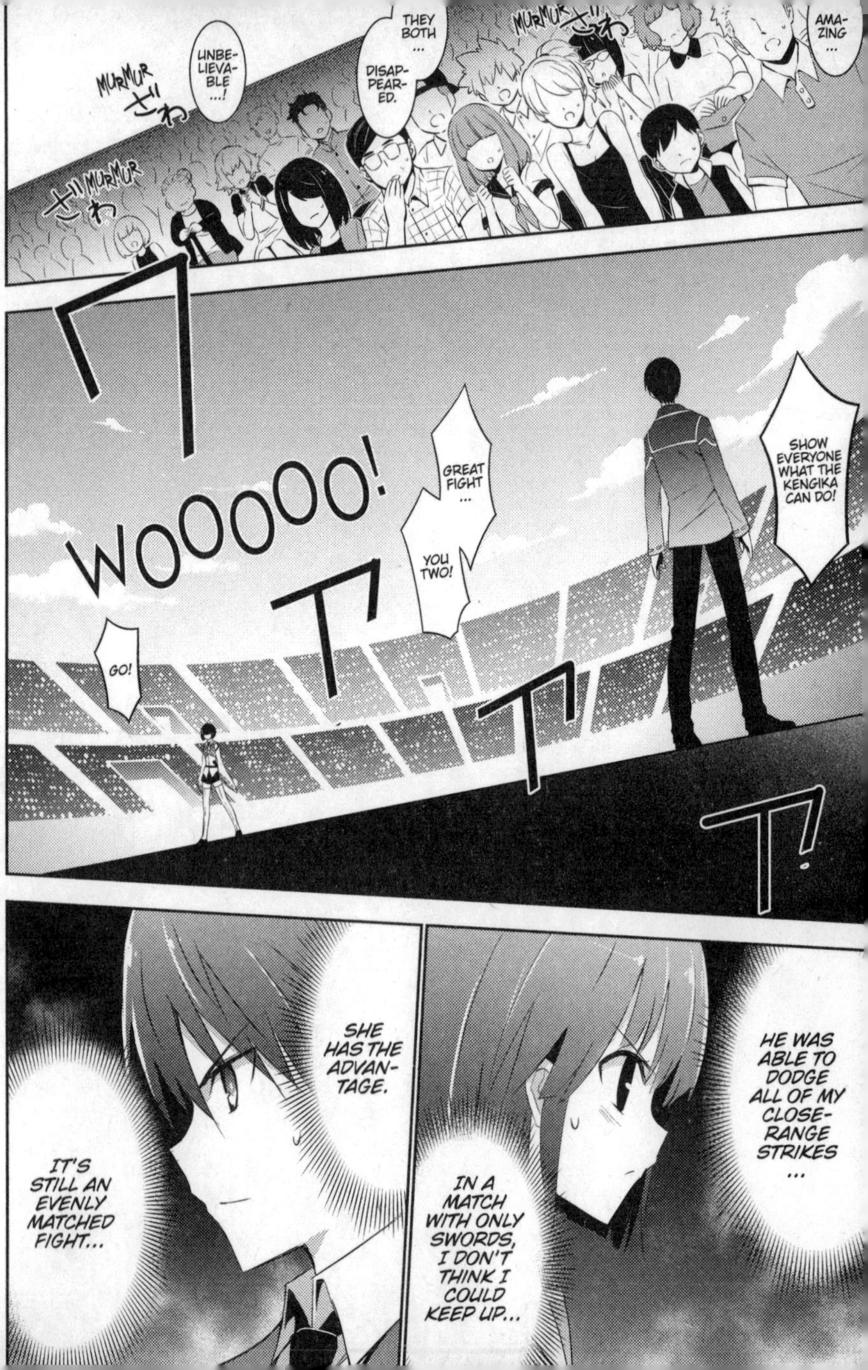

AMAZING...
MURMUR ざわ
THEY BOTH... DISAPPEARED.
UNBELIEVABLE...!
MURMUR ざわ
ざわ MURMUR
SHOW EVERYONE WHAT THE KENGIKA CAN DO!
GREAT FIGHT... YOU TWO!
GO!
WOOOOO!
HE WAS ABLE TO DODGE ALL OF MY CLOSE-RANGE STRIKES...
IN A MATCH WITH ONLY SWORDS, I DON'T THINK I COULD KEEP UP...
SHE HAS THE ADVANTAGE.
IT'S STILL AN EVENLY MATCHED FIGHT...

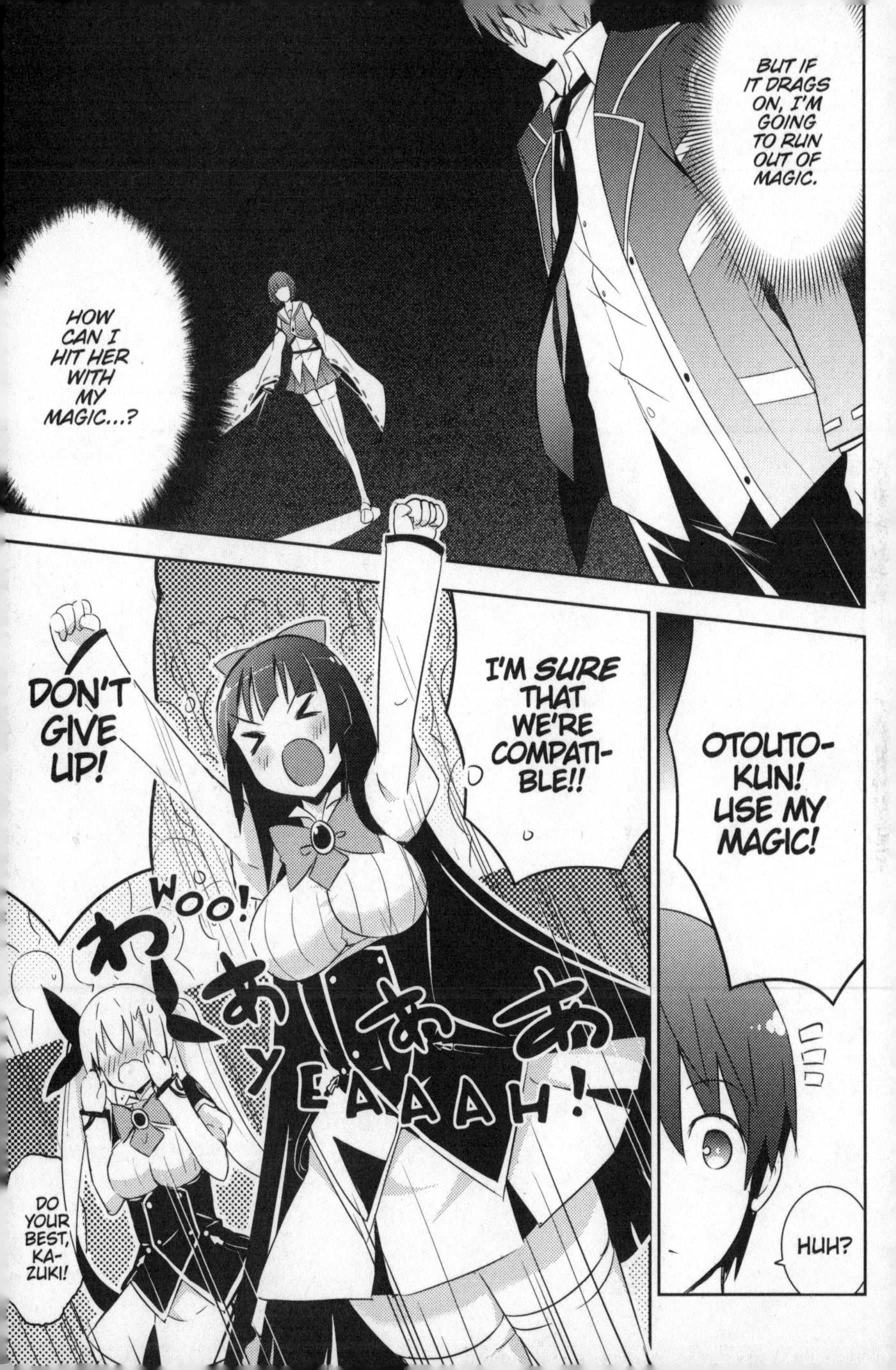
BUT IF IT DRAGS ON, I'M GOING TO RUN OUT OF MAGIC.
HOW CAN I HIT HER WITH MY MAGIC...?
OTOUTO-KUN! USE MY MAGIC!
HUH?
I'M *SURE* THAT WE'RE COMPATI-BLE!!
DON'T GIVE UP!
WOO!
わあああ
YEAAAAH!
DO YOUR BEST, KAZUKI!

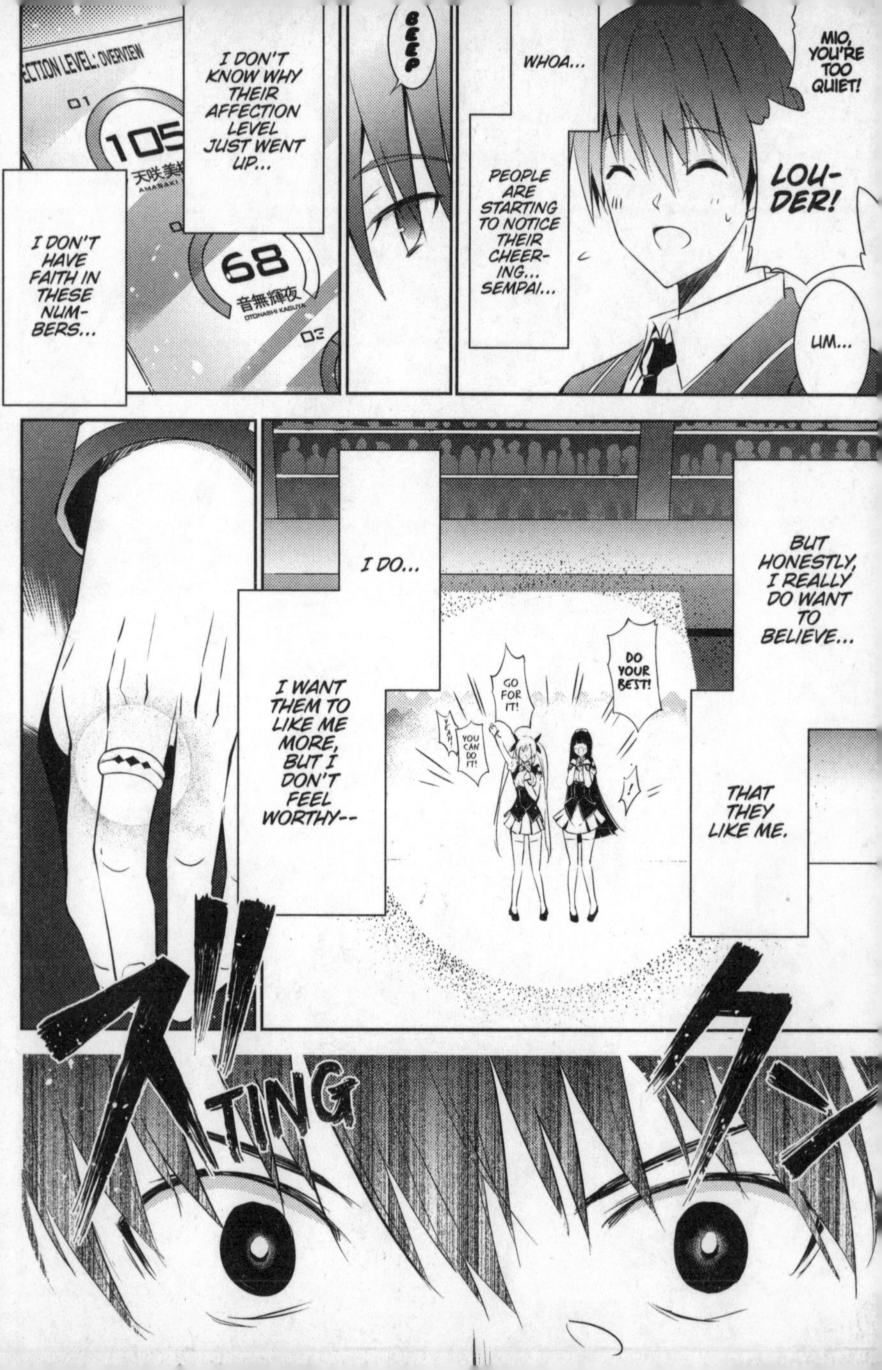
MIO, YOU'RE TOO QUIET!
LOUDER!
UM...
WHOA...
PEOPLE ARE STARTING TO NOTICE THEIR CHEERING... SEMPAI...
BEEP
I DON'T KNOW WHY THEIR AFFECTION LEVEL JUST WENT UP...
ECTION LEVEL: OVERVIEW
01
105
AMASAKI
68
音無輝夜
OTONASHI KAGUYA
03
I DON'T HAVE FAITH IN THESE NUMBERS...
BUT HONESTLY, I REALLY DO WANT TO BELIEVE...
THAT THEY LIKE ME.
DO YOUR BEST!
!
GO FOR IT!
YOU CAN DO IT!
YEAH!
I DO...
I WANT THEM TO LIKE ME MORE, BUT I DON'T FEEL WORTHY--
TING

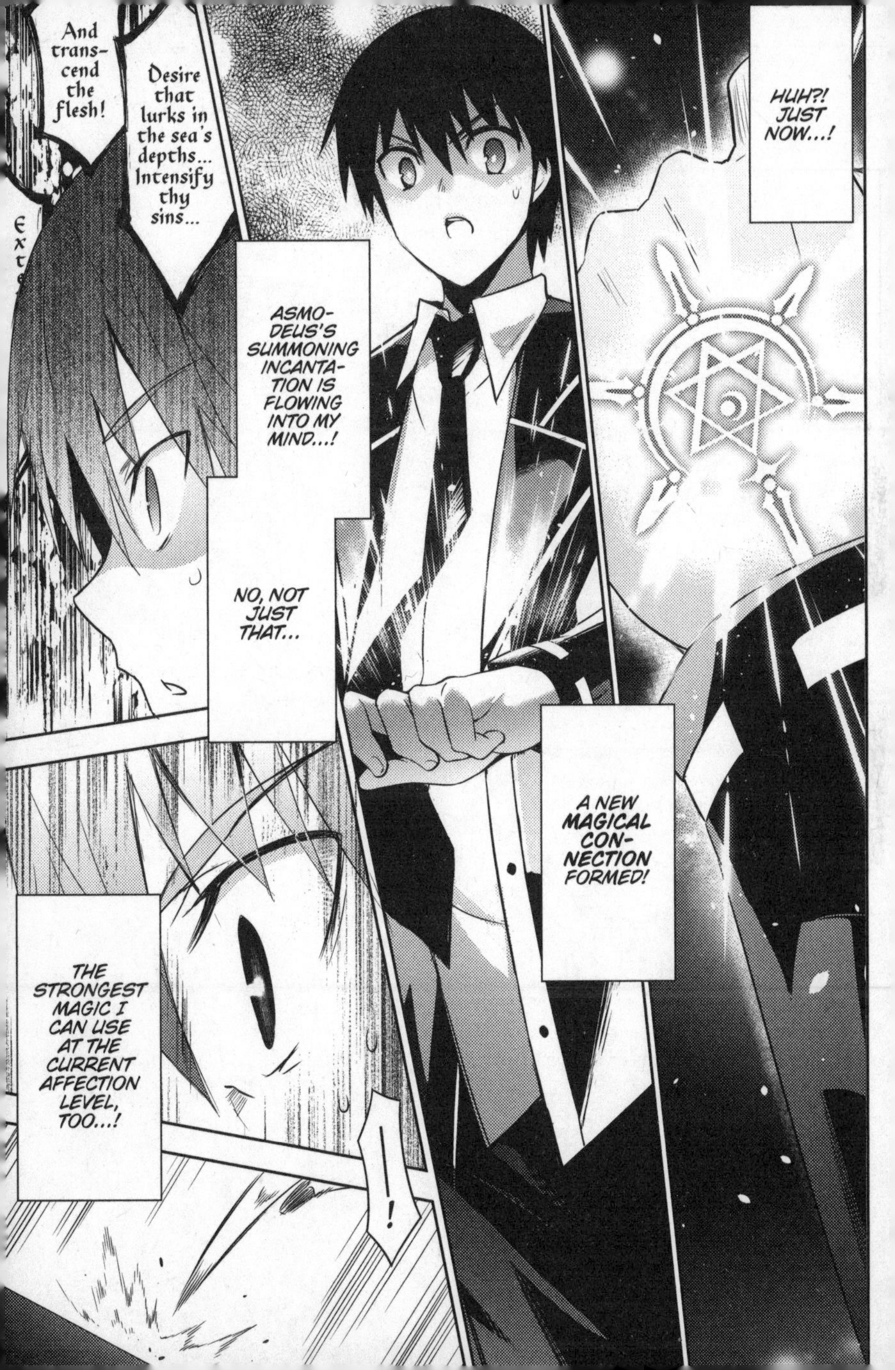
HUH?! JUST NOW...!
ASMO-DEUS'S SUMMONING INCANTA-TION IS FLOWING INTO MY MIND...!
Desire that lurks in the sea's depths... Intensify thy sins...
And trans-cend the flesh!
NO, NOT JUST THAT...
A NEW MAGICAL CON-NECTION FORMED!
THE STRONGEST MAGIC I CAN USE AT THE CURRENT AFFECTION LEVEL, TOO...!
!

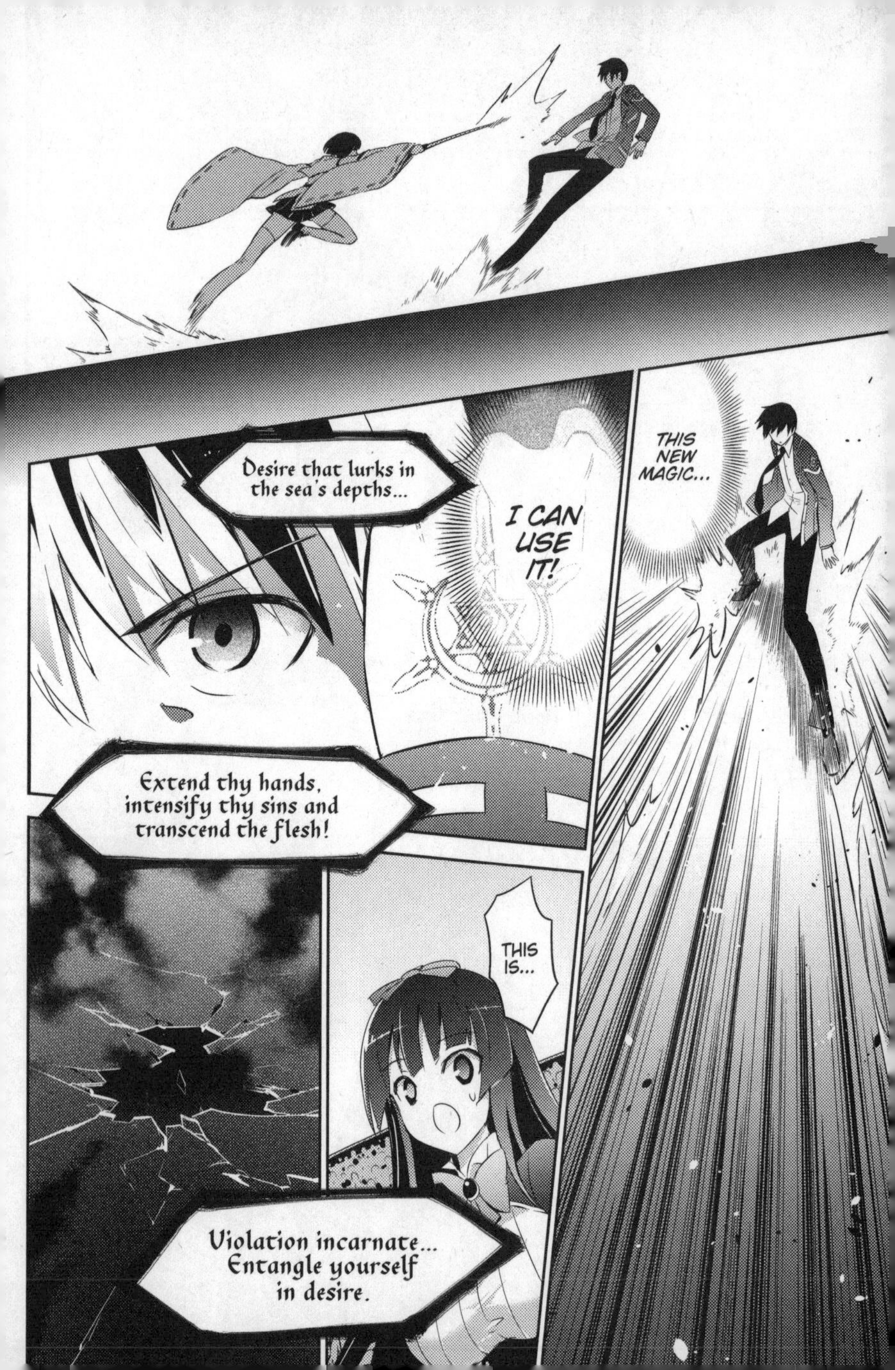
THIS NEW MAGIC...
I CAN USE IT!
Desire that lurks in the sea's depths...
Extend thy hands, intensify thy sins and transcend the flesh!
THIS IS...
Violation incarnate... Entangle yourself in desire.

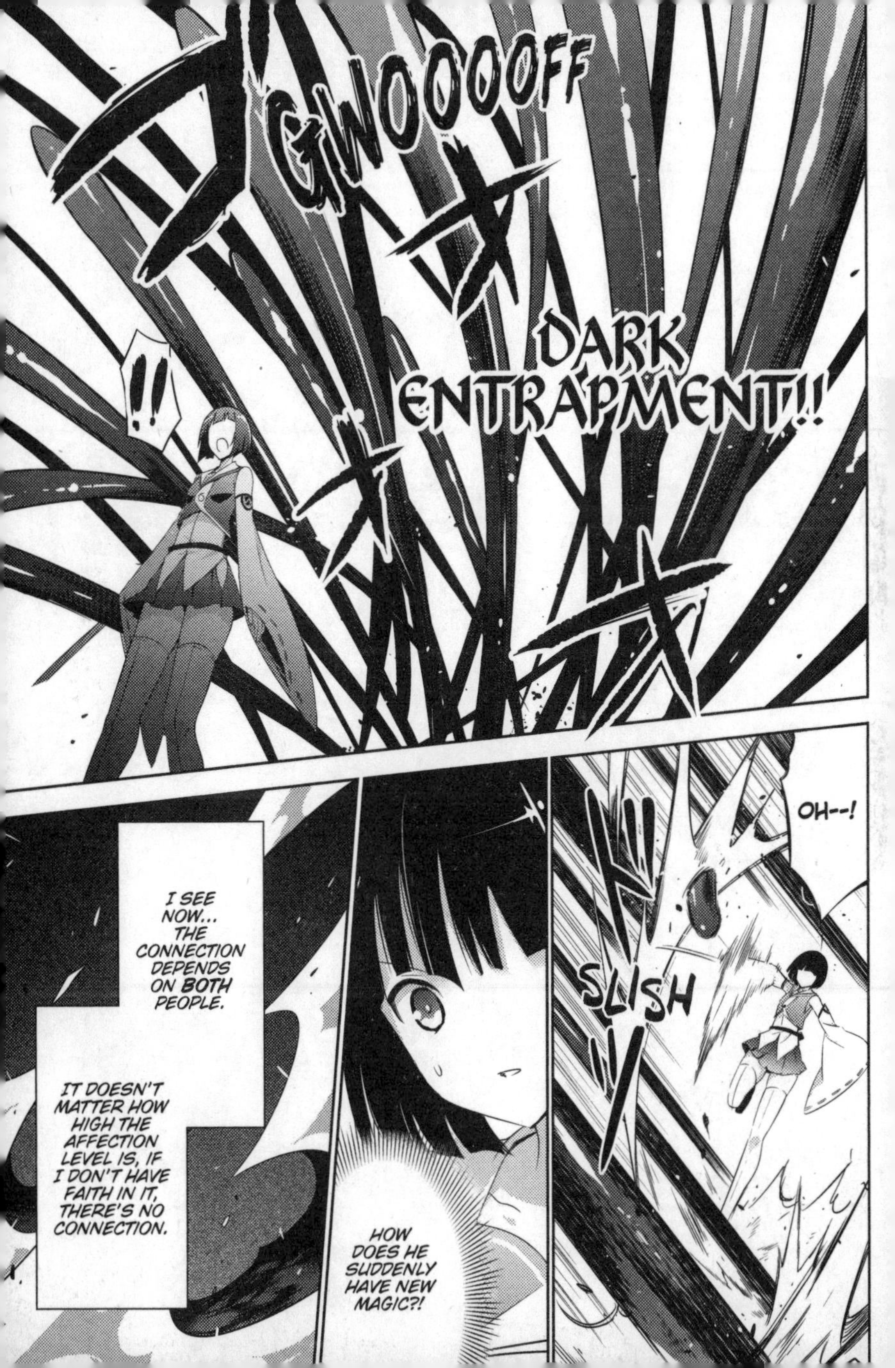
GWOOOOFF
DARK ENTRAPMENT!!
!!
OH--!
SLISH
HOW DOES HE SUDDENLY HAVE NEW MAGIC?!
I SEE NOW... THE CONNECTION DEPENDS ON BOTH PEOPLE.
IT DOESN'T MATTER HOW HIGH THE AFFECTION LEVEL IS, IF I DON'T HAVE FAITH IN IT, THERE'S NO CONNECTION.

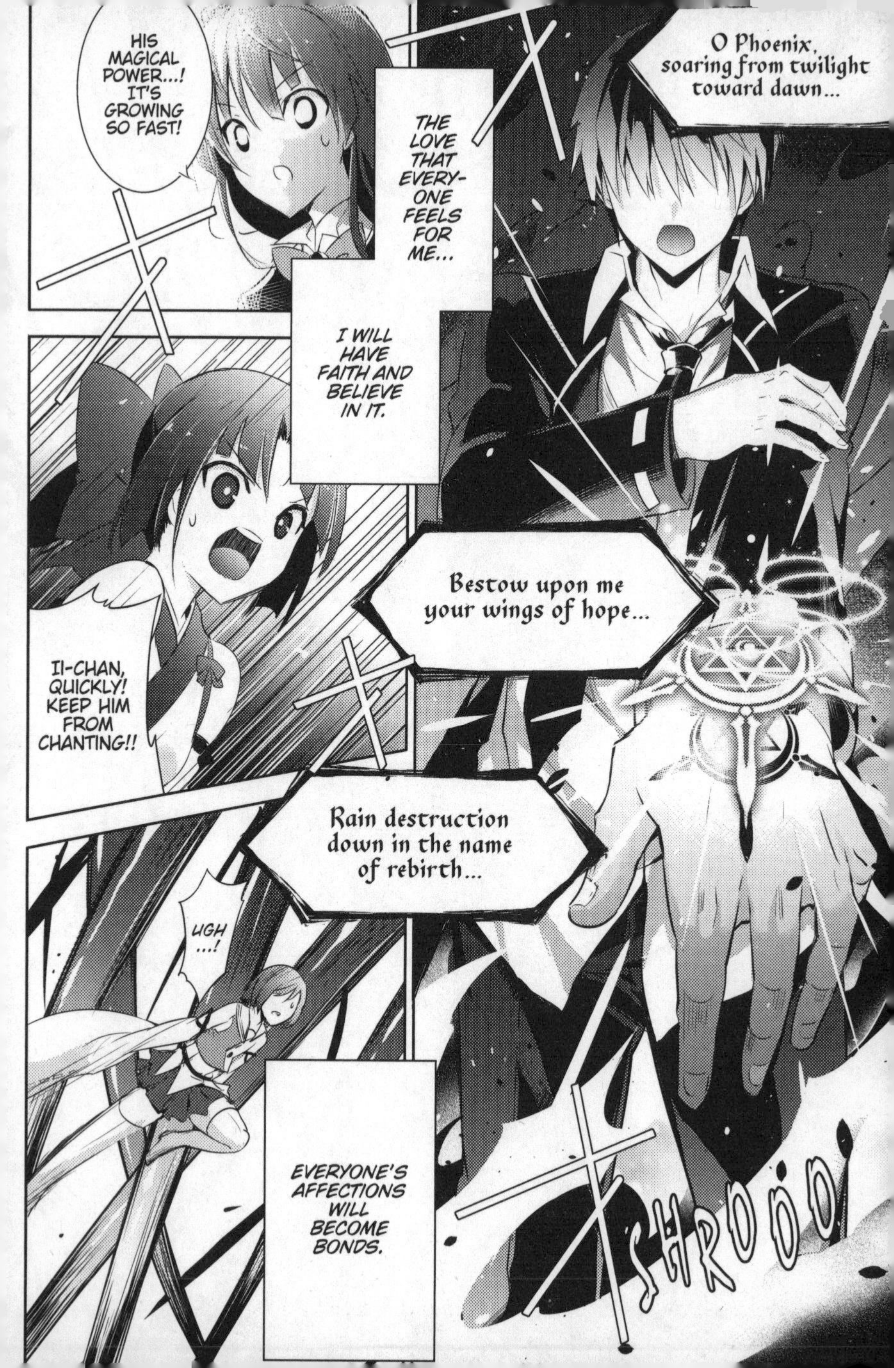
O Phoenix, soaring from twilight toward dawn...
THE LOVE THAT EVERY-ONE FEELS FOR ME...
I WILL HAVE FAITH AND BELIEVE IN IT.
Bestow upon me your wings of hope...
Rain destruction down in the name of rebirth...
EVERYONE'S AFFECTIONS WILL BECOME BONDS.
SHROOO
HIS MAGICAL POWER...! IT'S GROWING SO FAST!
II-CHAN, QUICKLY! KEEP HIM FROM CHANTING!!
UGH ...!

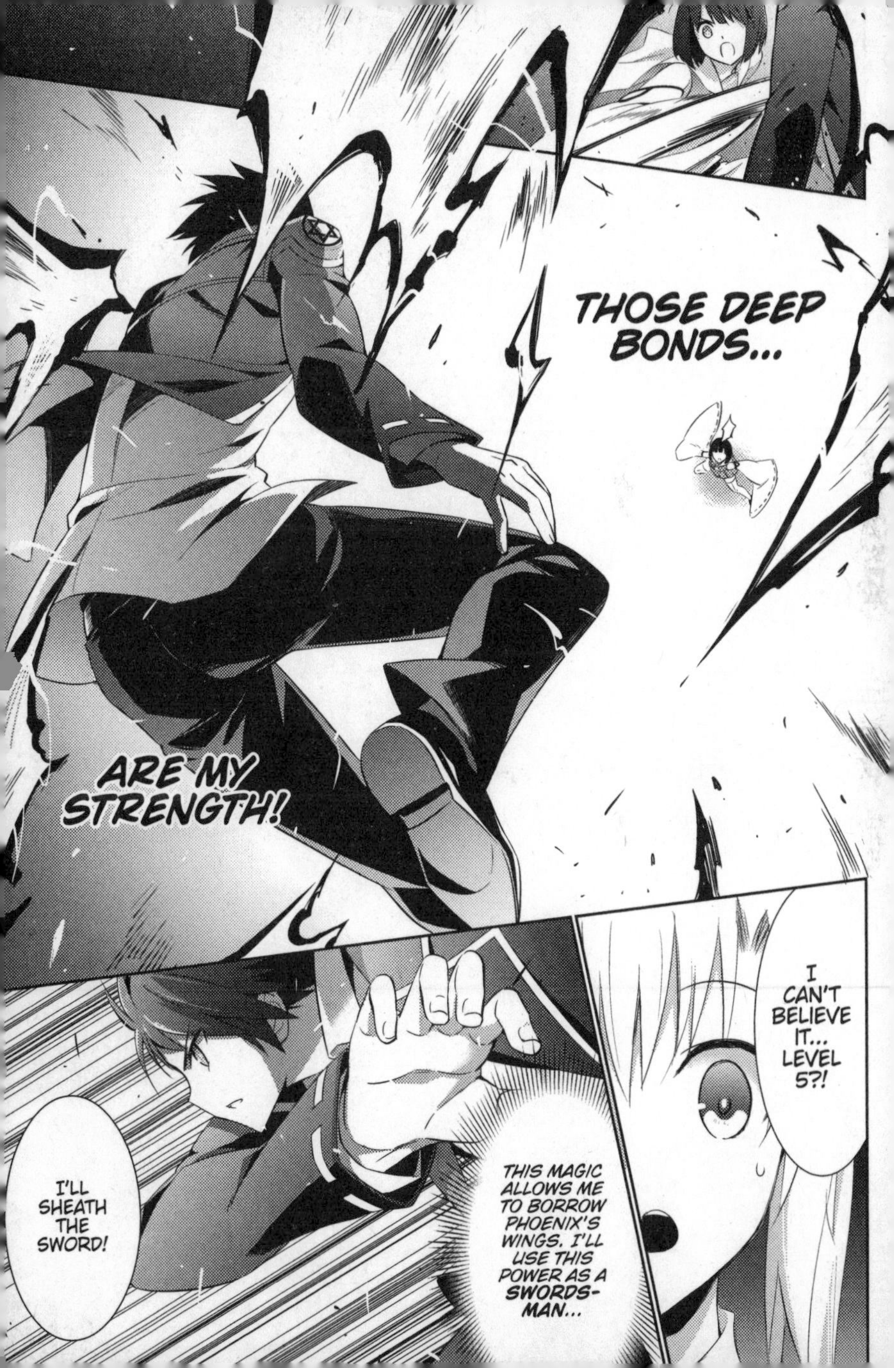
THOSE DEEP BONDS...
ARE MY STRENGTH!
I CAN'T BELIEVE IT... LEVEL 5?!
THIS MAGIC ALLOWS ME TO BORROW PHOENIX'S WINGS. I'LL USE THIS POWER AS A SWORDS-MAN...
I'LL SHEATH THE SWORD!

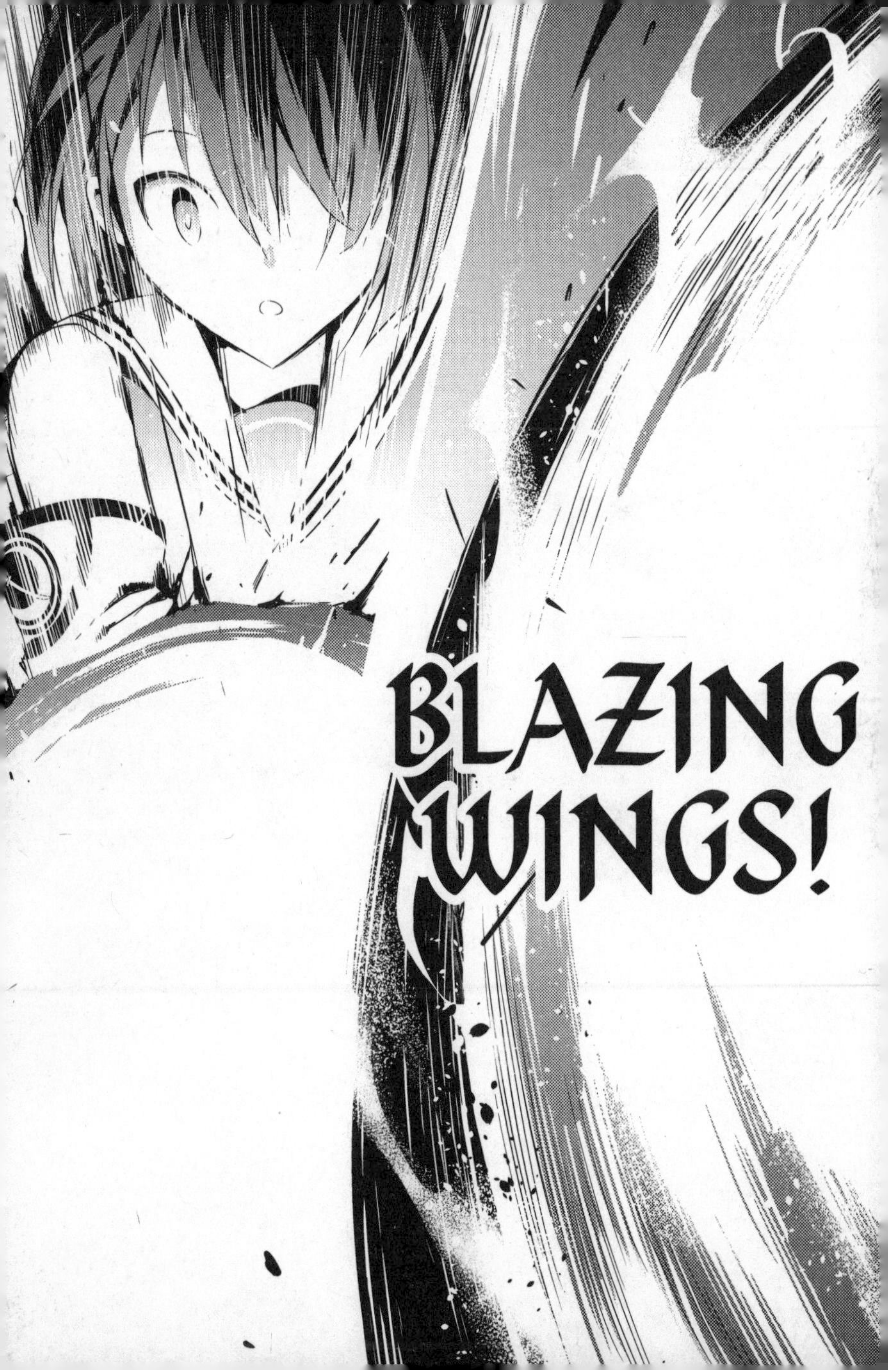
BLAZING WINGS!

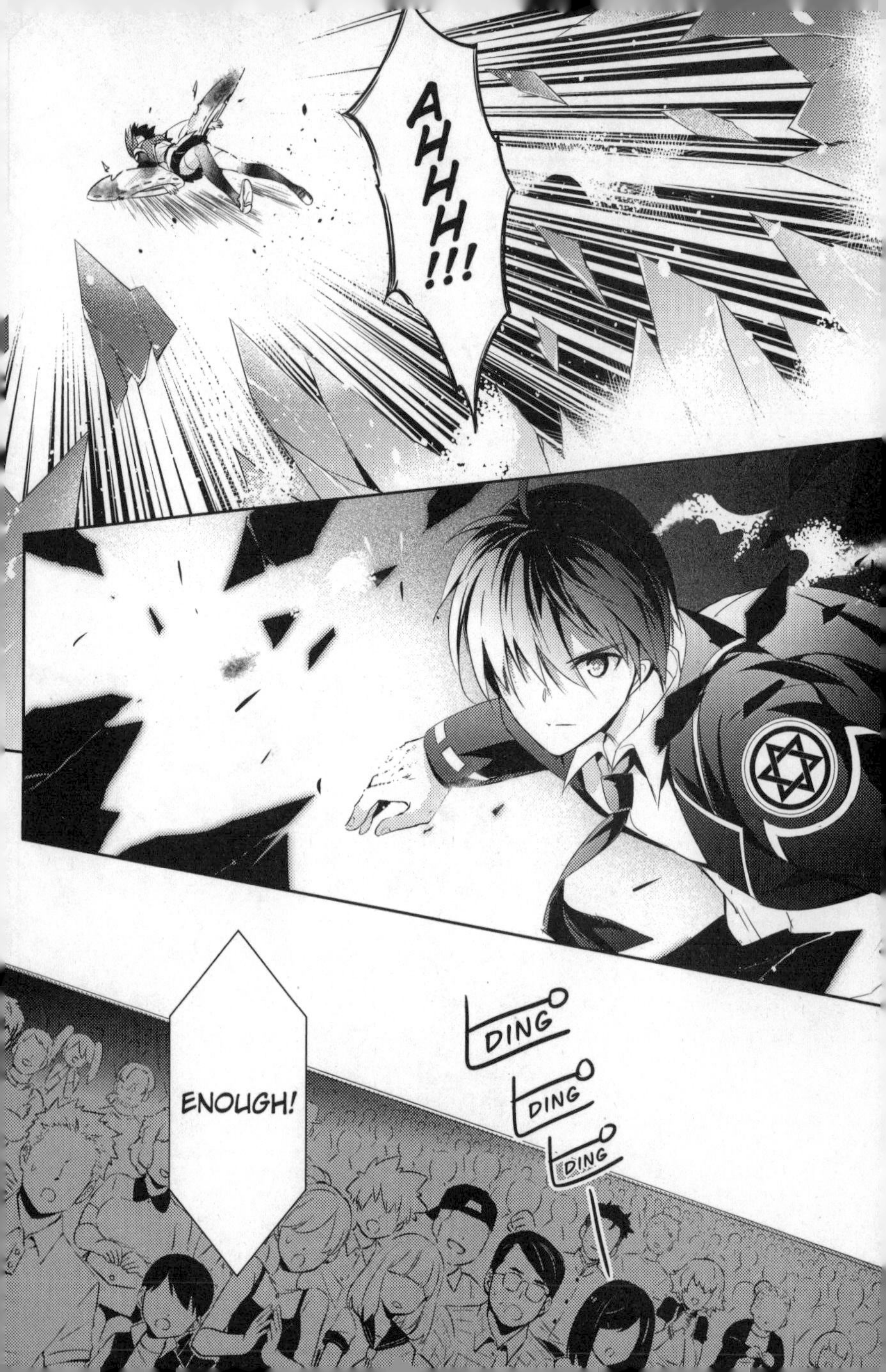
AHHH!!!
DING
DING
DING
ENOUGH!

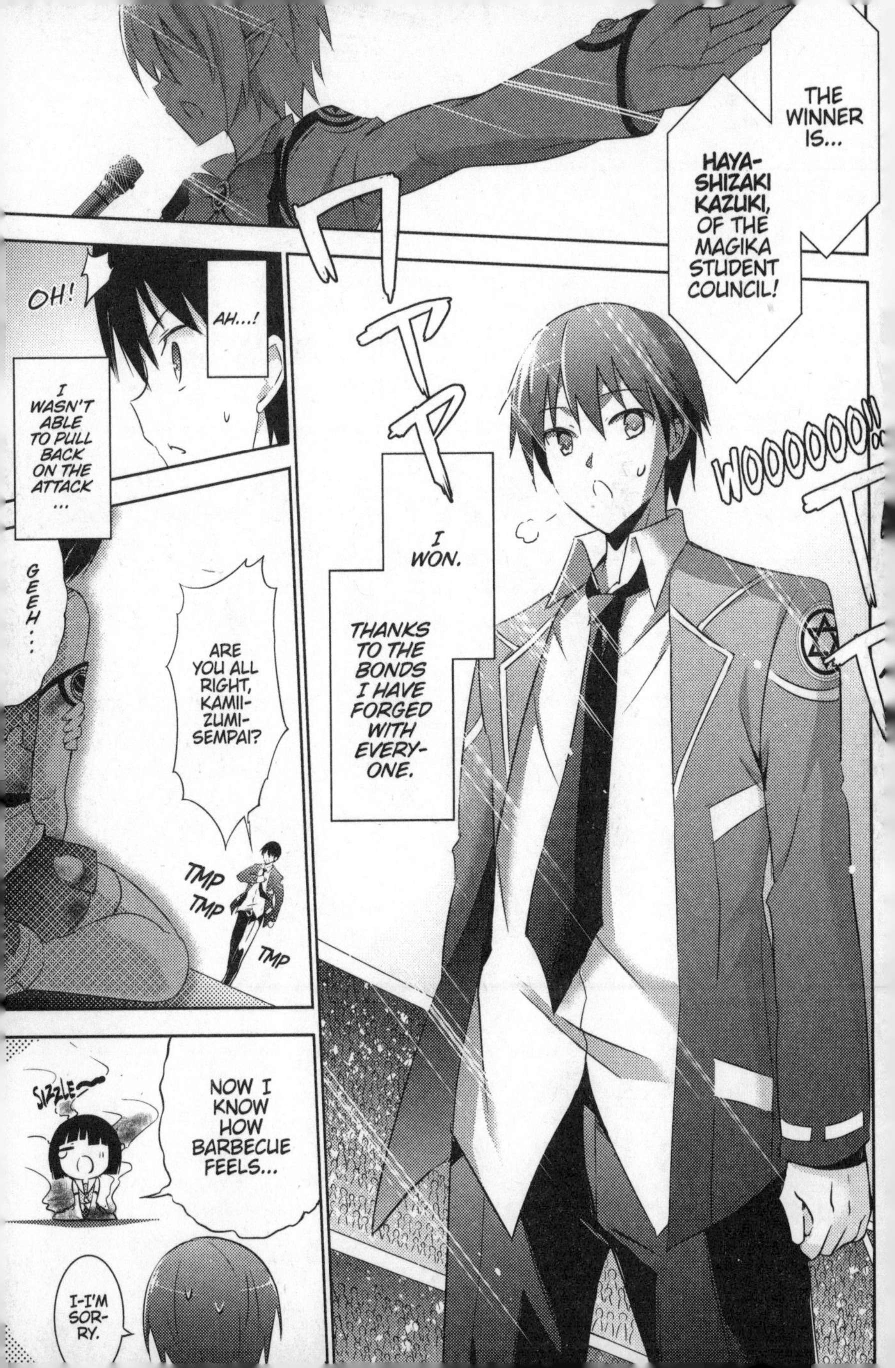
THE WINNER IS...
HAYA-SHIZAKI KAZUKI, OF THE MAGIKA STUDENT COUNCIL!
WOOOOOO!!
I WON.
THANKS TO THE BONDS I HAVE FORGED WITH EVERY-ONE.
OH!
AH...!
I WASN'T ABLE TO PULL BACK ON THE ATTACK...
ARE YOU ALL RIGHT, KAMII-ZUMI-SEMPAI?
GEEH...
TMP
TMP
TMP
NOW I KNOW HOW BARBECUE FEELS...
SIZZLE~
I-I'M SORRY.

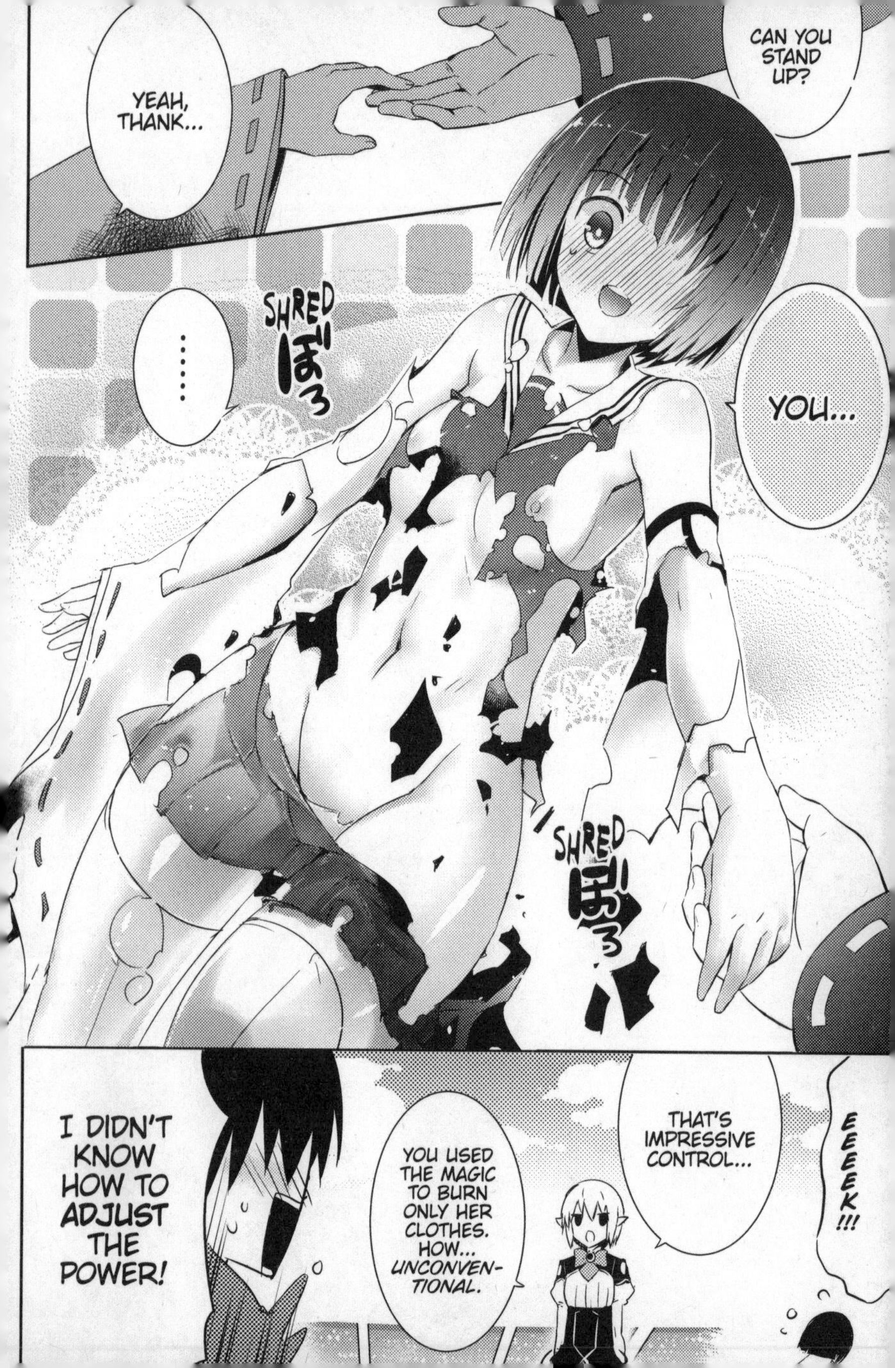
CAN YOU STAND UP?
YEAH, THANK...
YOU...
SHRED ぼろ
......
SHRED ぼろ
EEEEK!!!
THAT'S IMPRESSIVE CONTROL...
YOU USED THE MAGIC TO BURN ONLY HER CLOTHES. HOW... *UNCONVENTIONAL.*
I DIDN'T KNOW HOW TO ADJUST THE POWER!

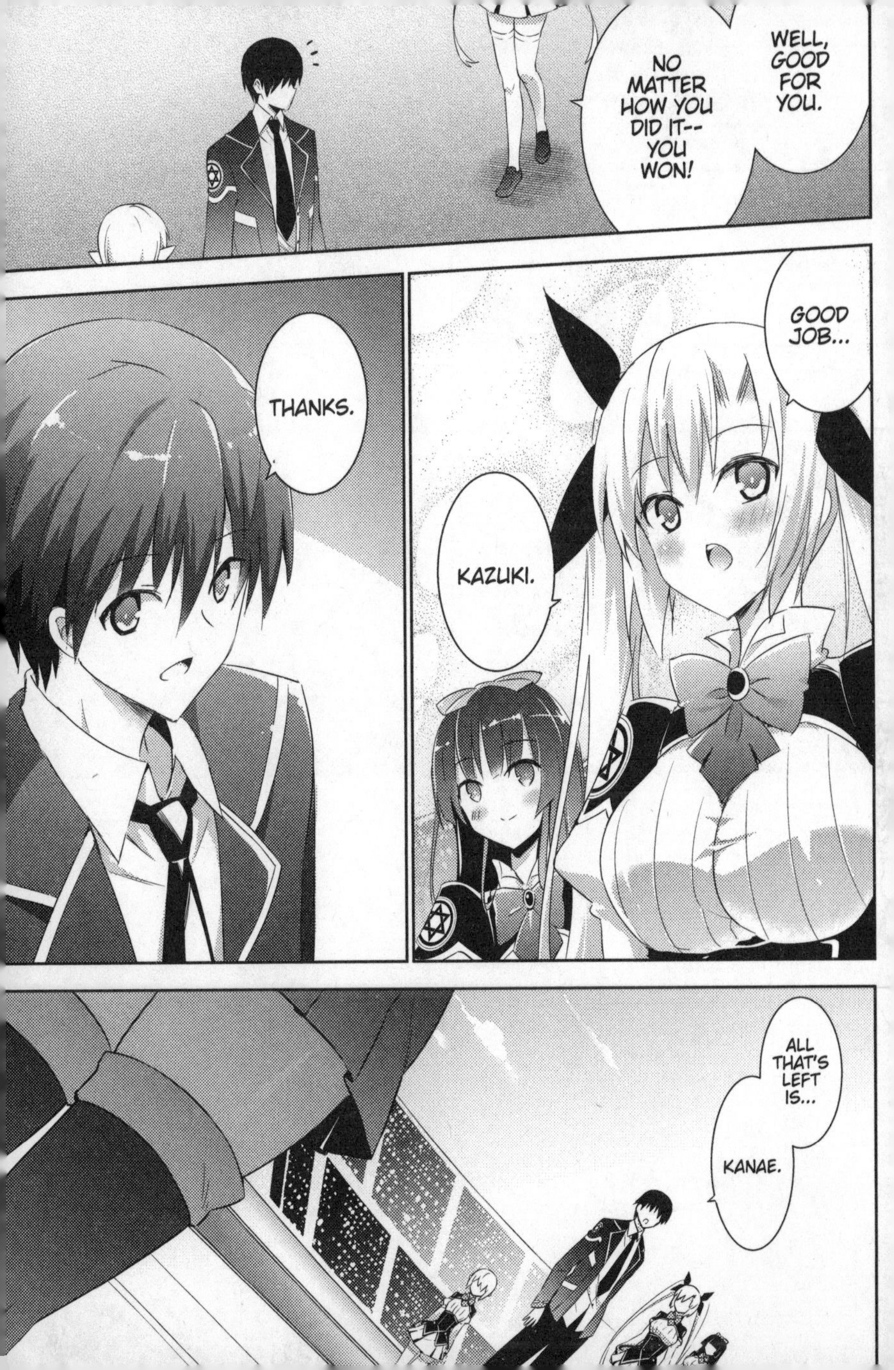
WELL, GOOD FOR YOU.
NO MATTER HOW YOU DID IT-- YOU WON!
GOOD JOB...
KAZUKI.
THANKS.
ALL THAT'S LEFT IS...
KANAE.

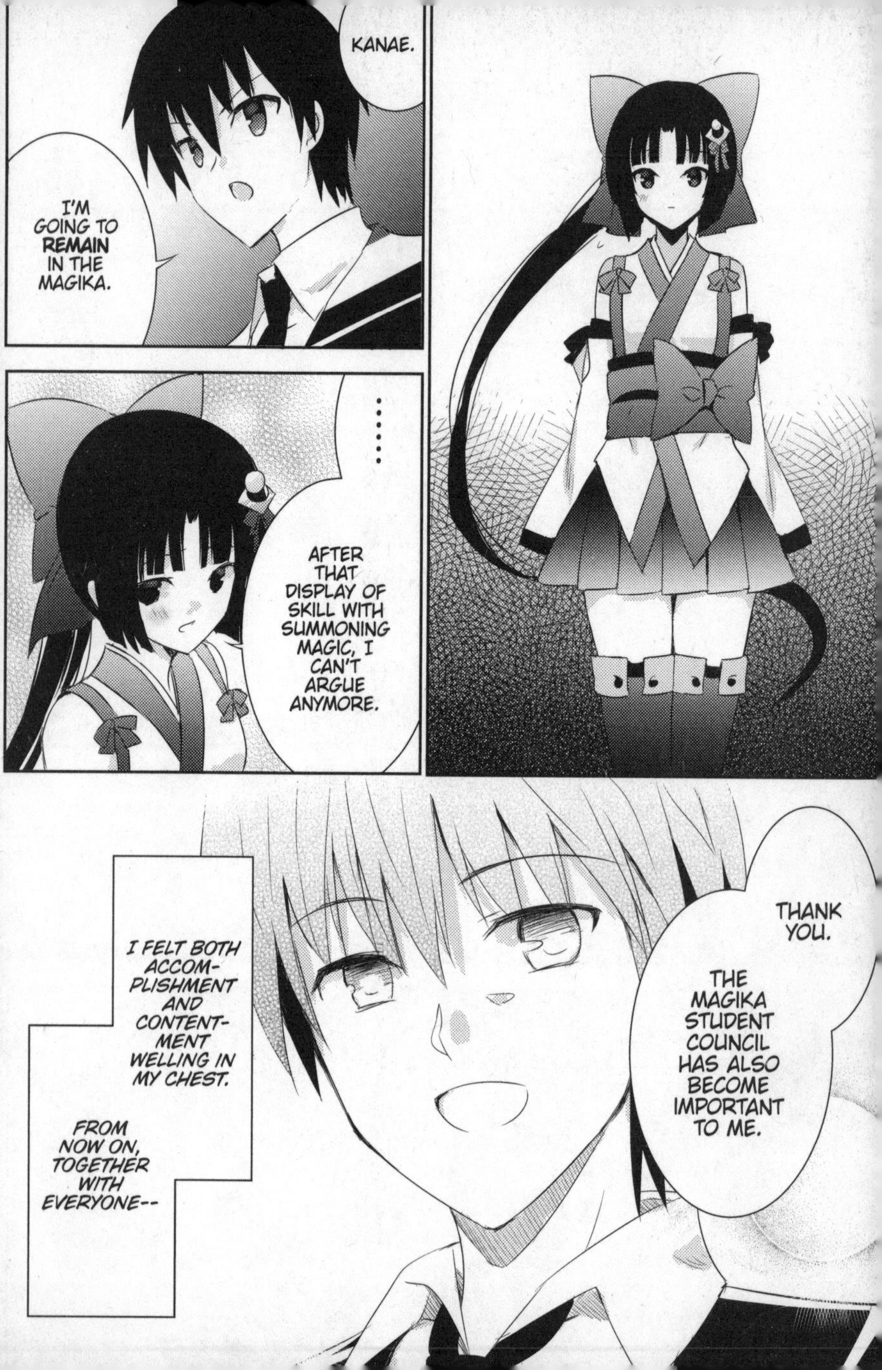
KANAE.
I'M GOING TO REMAIN IN THE MAGIKA.
......
AFTER THAT DISPLAY OF SKILL WITH SUMMONING MAGIC, I CAN'T ARGUE ANYMORE.
THANK YOU.
THE MAGIKA STUDENT COUNCIL HAS ALSO BECOME IMPORTANT TO ME.
I FELT BOTH ACCOM-PLISHMENT AND CONTENT-MENT WELLING IN MY CHEST.
FROM NOW ON, TOGETHER WITH EVERYONE--

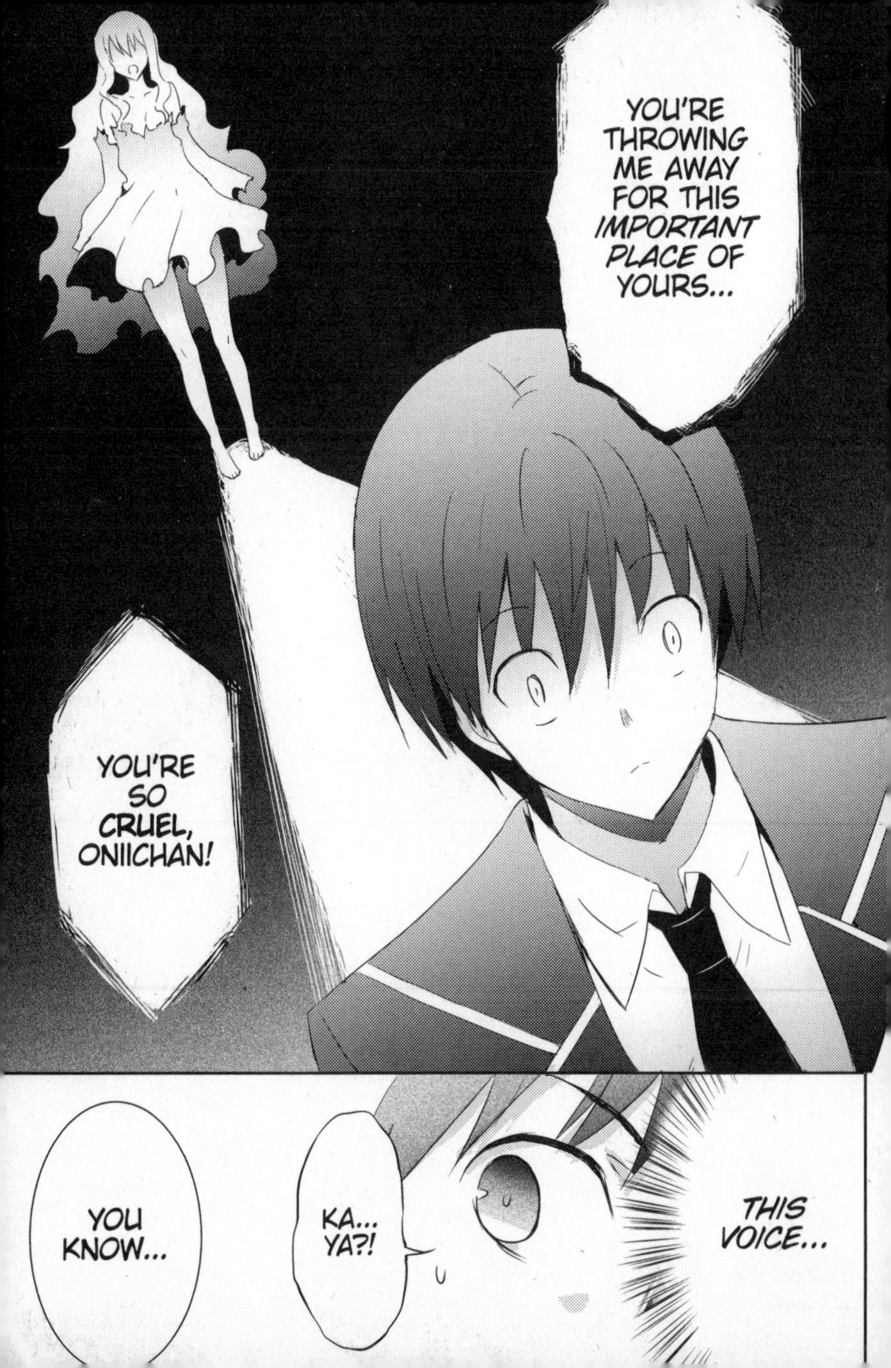
YOU'RE THROWING ME AWAY FOR THIS *IMPORTANT* PLACE OF YOURS...
YOU'RE SO CRUEL, ONIICHAN!
THIS VOICE...
KA... YA?!
YOU KNOW...

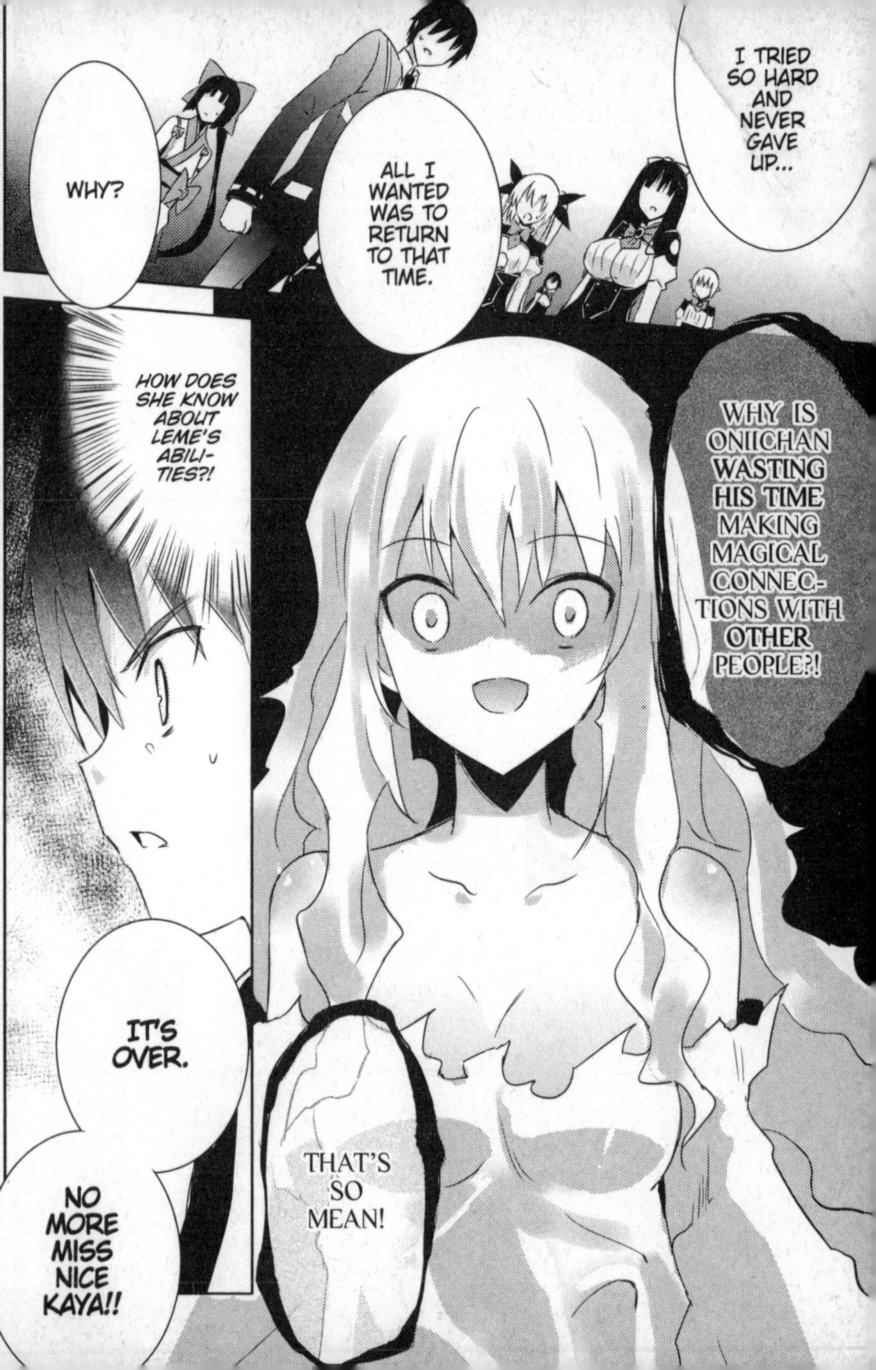
I TRIED SO HARD AND NEVER GAVE UP...
ALL I WANTED WAS TO RETURN TO THAT TIME.
WHY?
WHY IS ONIICHAN WASTING HIS TIME MAKING MAGICAL CONNEC-TIONS WITH OTHER PEOPLE?!
THAT'S SO MEAN!
HOW DOES SHE KNOW ABOUT LEME'S ABILI-TIES?!
IT'S OVER.
NO MORE MISS NICE KAYA!!

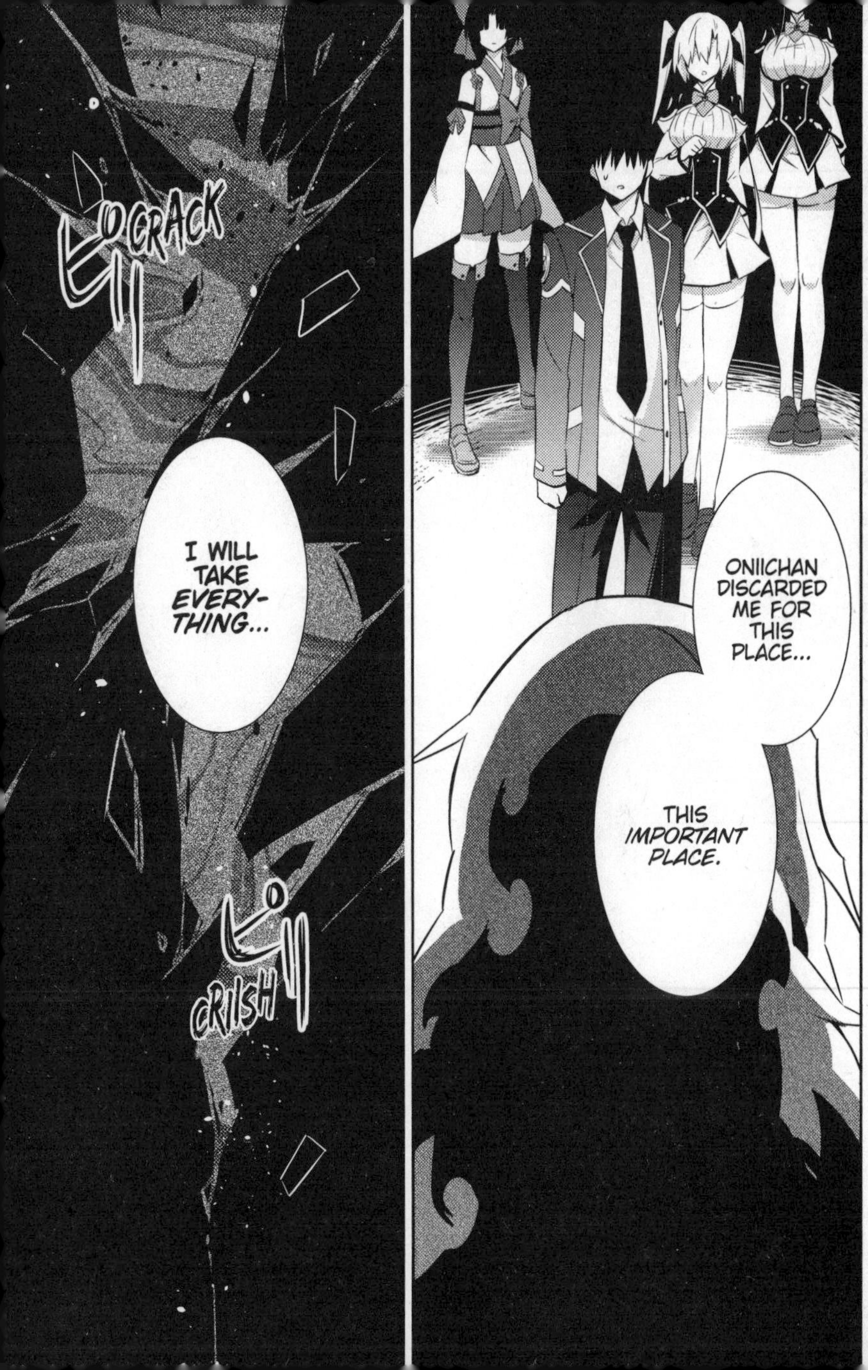
ONIICHAN DISCARDED ME FOR THIS PLACE...
THIS IMPORTANT PLACE.
CRACK
I WILL TAKE EVERY-THING...
CRISH

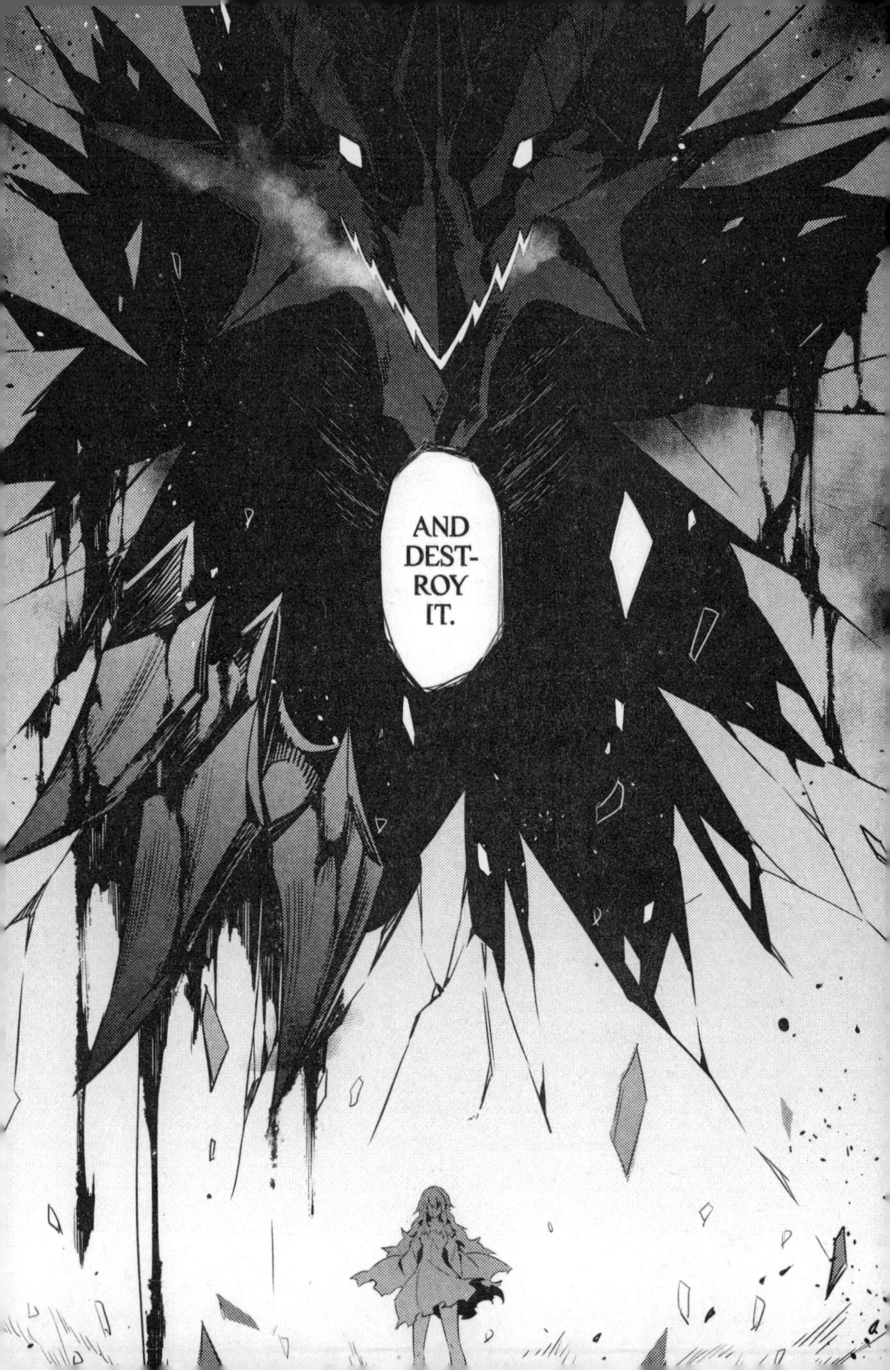
AND DEST-ROY IT.

Magika
SWORDSMAN
AND SUMMONER

3

魔技科の剣士と召喚魔王

3

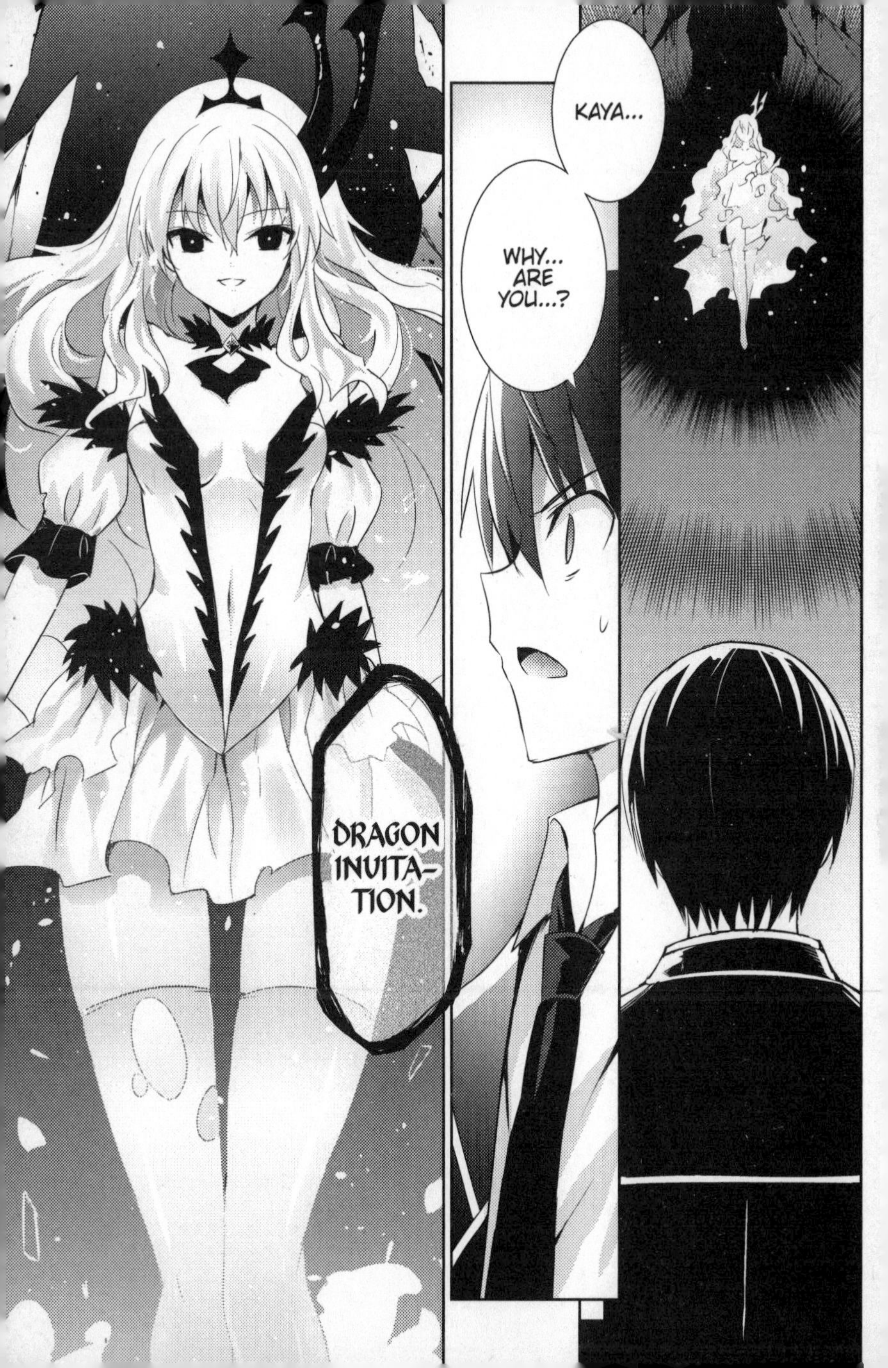
KAYA...
WHY... ARE YOU...?
DRAGON INVITA-TION.

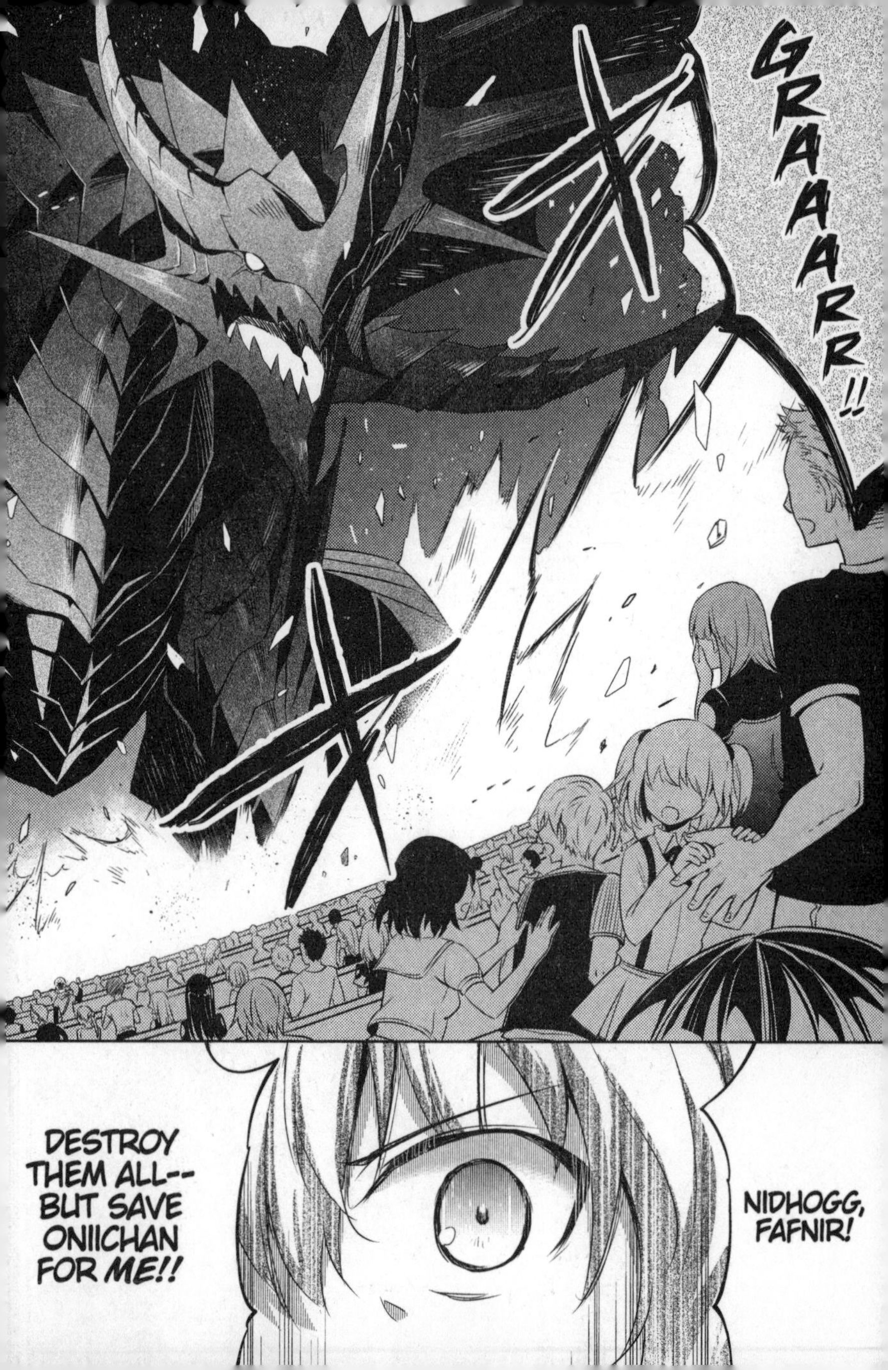
GRAAARR!!
NIDHOGG, FAFNIR!
DESTROY THEM ALL-- BUT SAVE ONIICHAN FOR *ME*!!

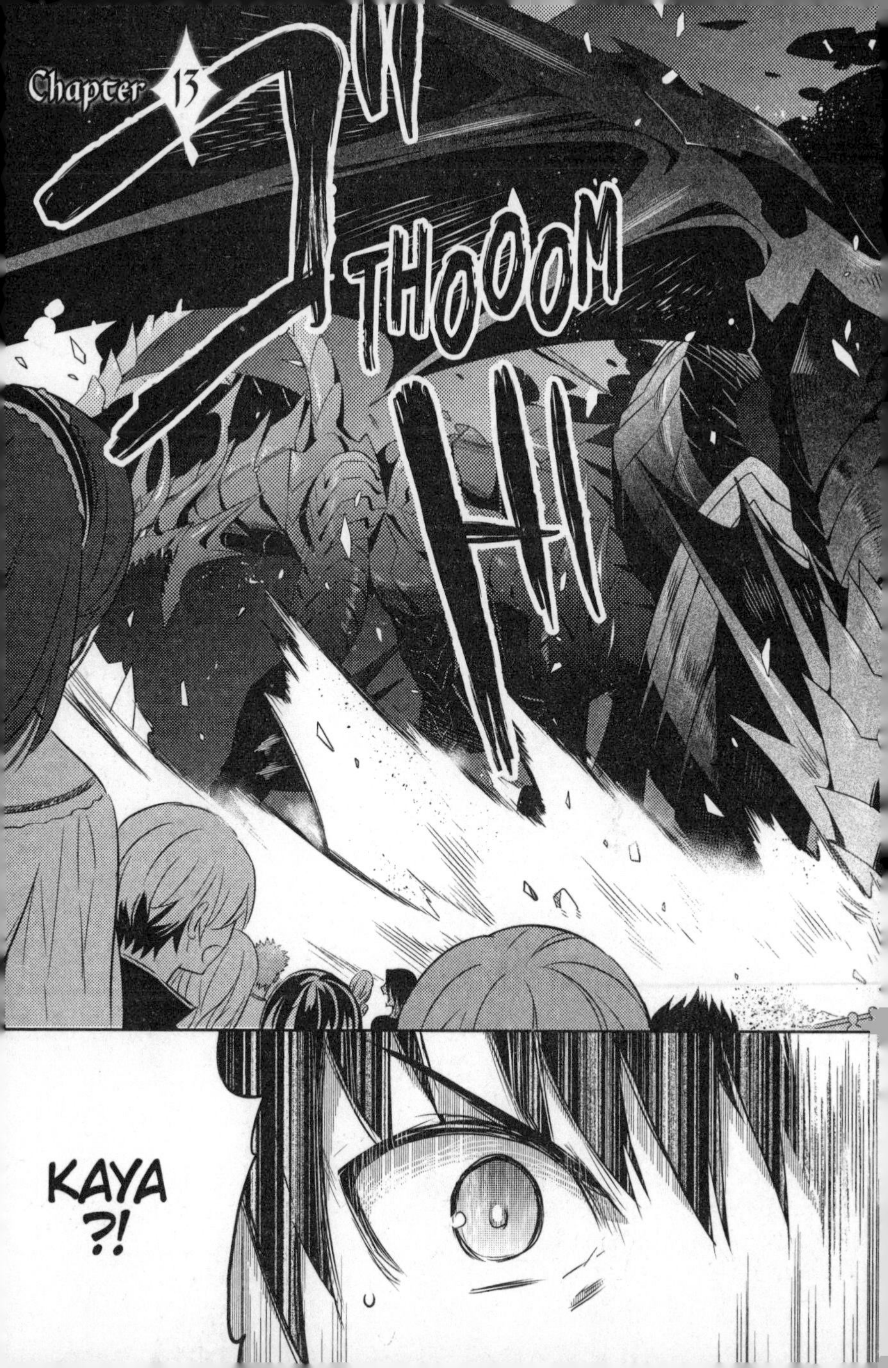
Chapter 13
THOOOM
KAYA ?!

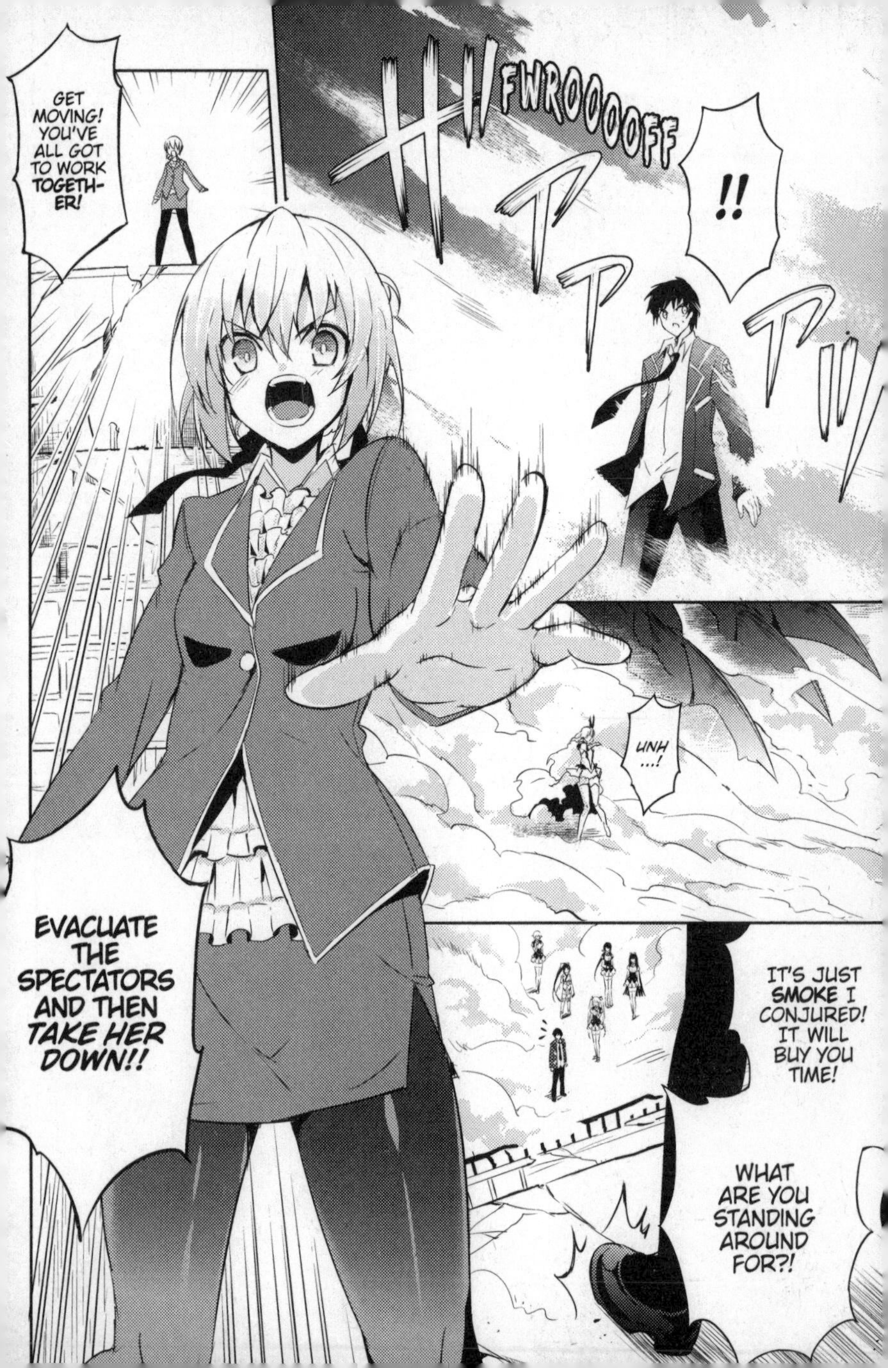
FWROOOOOFF
!!
UNH ...!
IT'S JUST SMOKE I CONJURED! IT WILL BUY YOU TIME!
WHAT ARE YOU STANDING AROUND FOR?!
GET MOVING! YOU'VE ALL GOT TO WORK TOGETH-ER!
EVACUATE THE SPECTATORS AND THEN *TAKE HER DOWN!!*

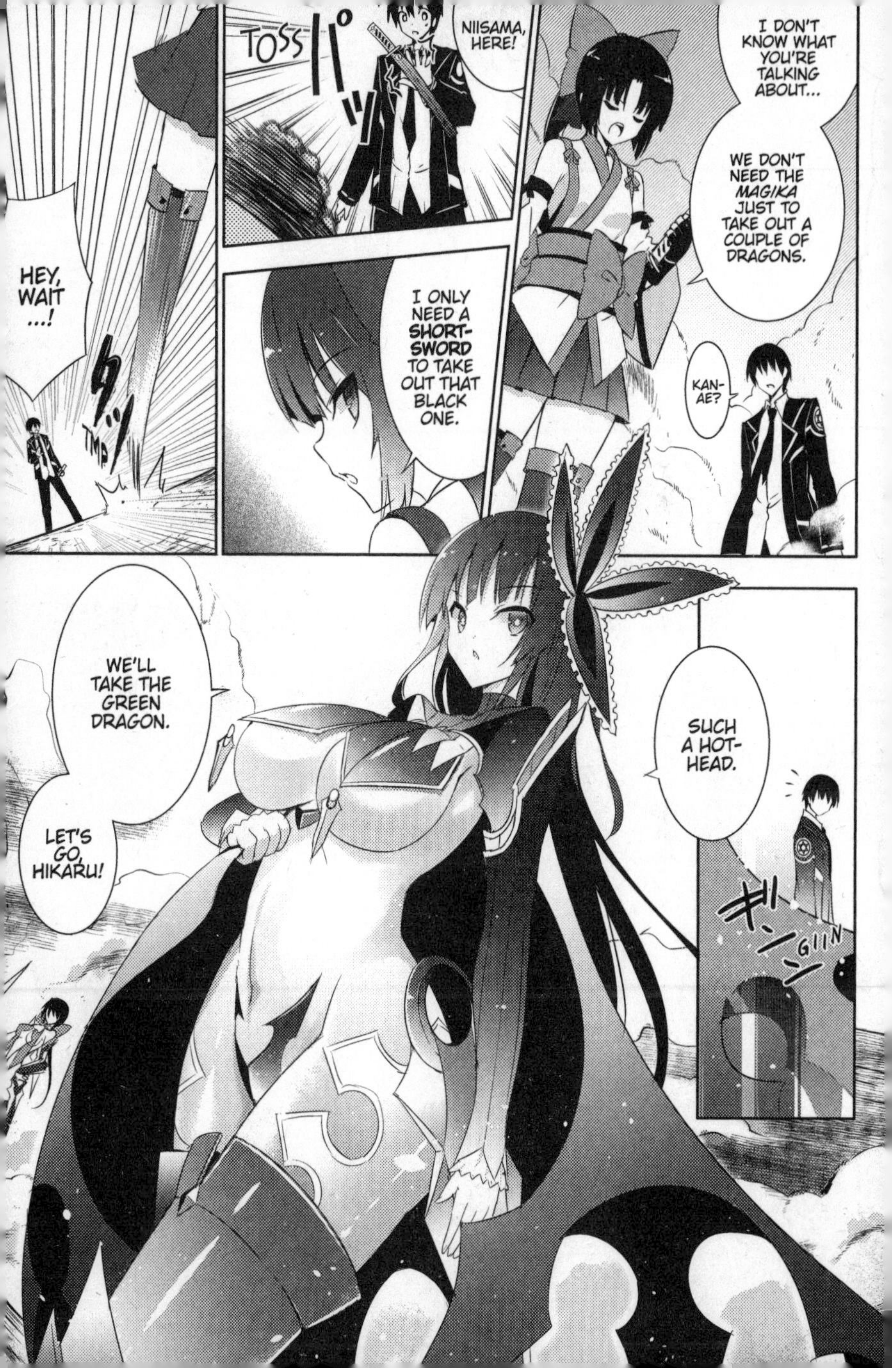
I DON'T KNOW WHAT YOU'RE TALKING ABOUT...
WE DON'T NEED THE *MAGIKA* JUST TO TAKE OUT A COUPLE OF DRAGONS.
KAN-AE?
NIISAMA, HERE!
TOSS
I ONLY NEED A **SHORT-SWORD** TO TAKE OUT THAT BLACK ONE.
HEY, WAIT...!
TMP
SUCH A HOT-HEAD.
GIIN
WE'LL TAKE THE GREEN DRAGON.
LET'S GO, HIKARU!

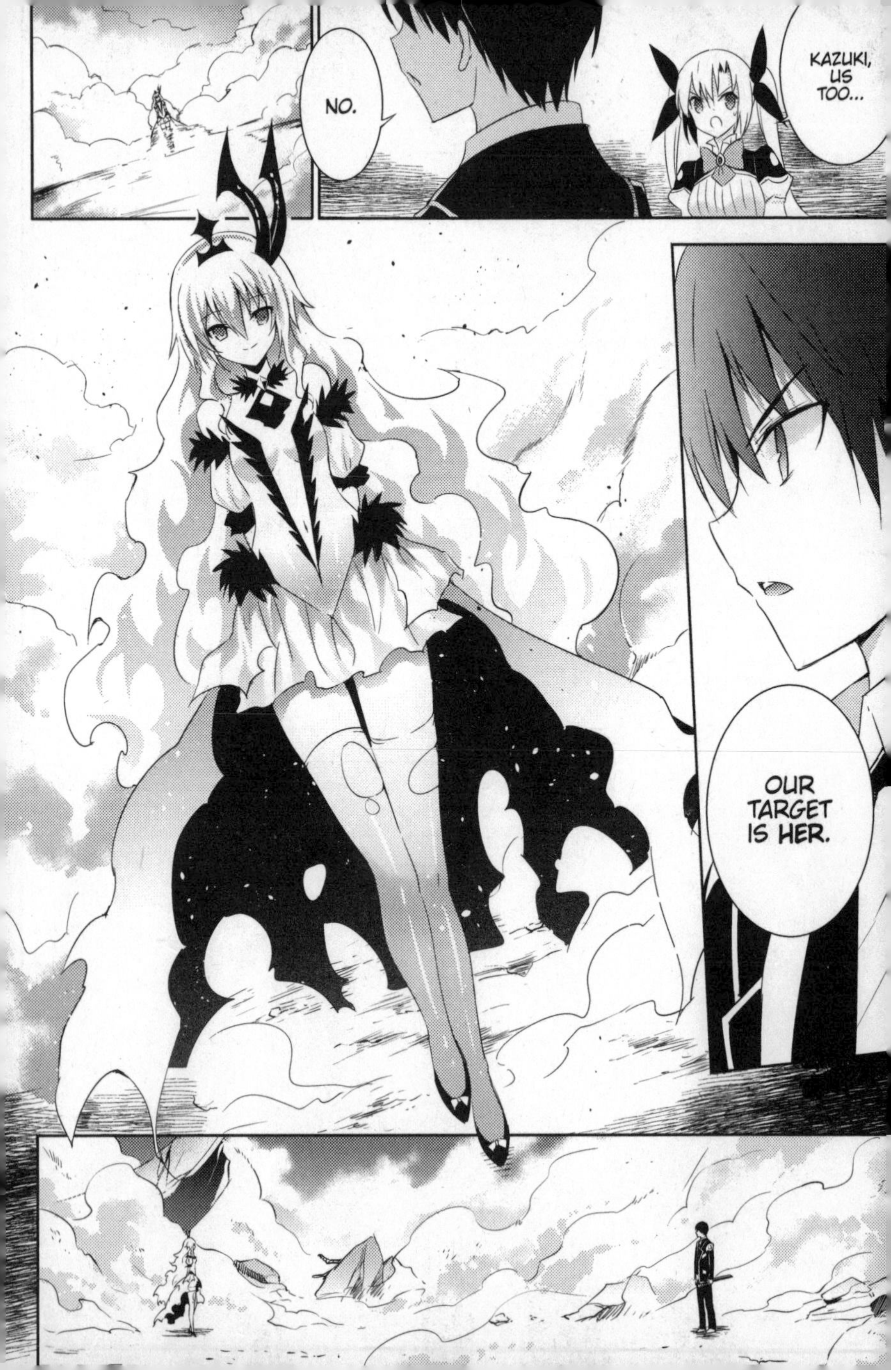
KAZUKI, US TOO...
NO.
OUR TARGET IS HER.

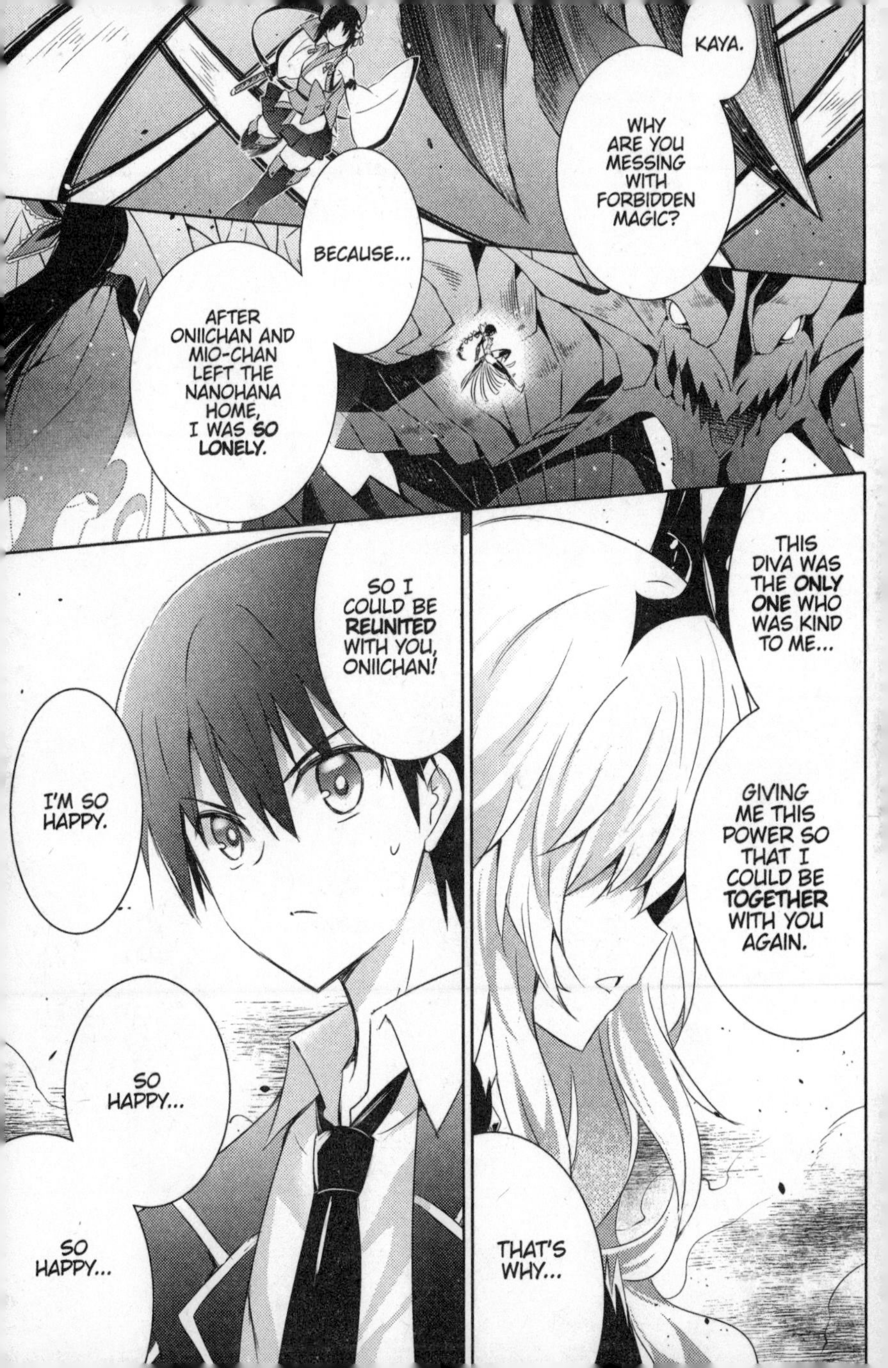
KAYA.
WHY ARE YOU MESSING WITH FORBIDDEN MAGIC?
BECAUSE...
AFTER ONIICHAN AND MIO-CHAN LEFT THE NANOHANA HOME, I WAS SO LONELY.
THIS DIVA WAS THE ONLY ONE WHO WAS KIND TO ME...
GIVING ME THIS POWER SO THAT I COULD BE TOGETHER WITH YOU AGAIN.
THAT'S WHY...
SO I COULD BE REUNITED WITH YOU, ONIICHAN!
I'M SO HAPPY.
SO HAPPY...
SO HAPPY...

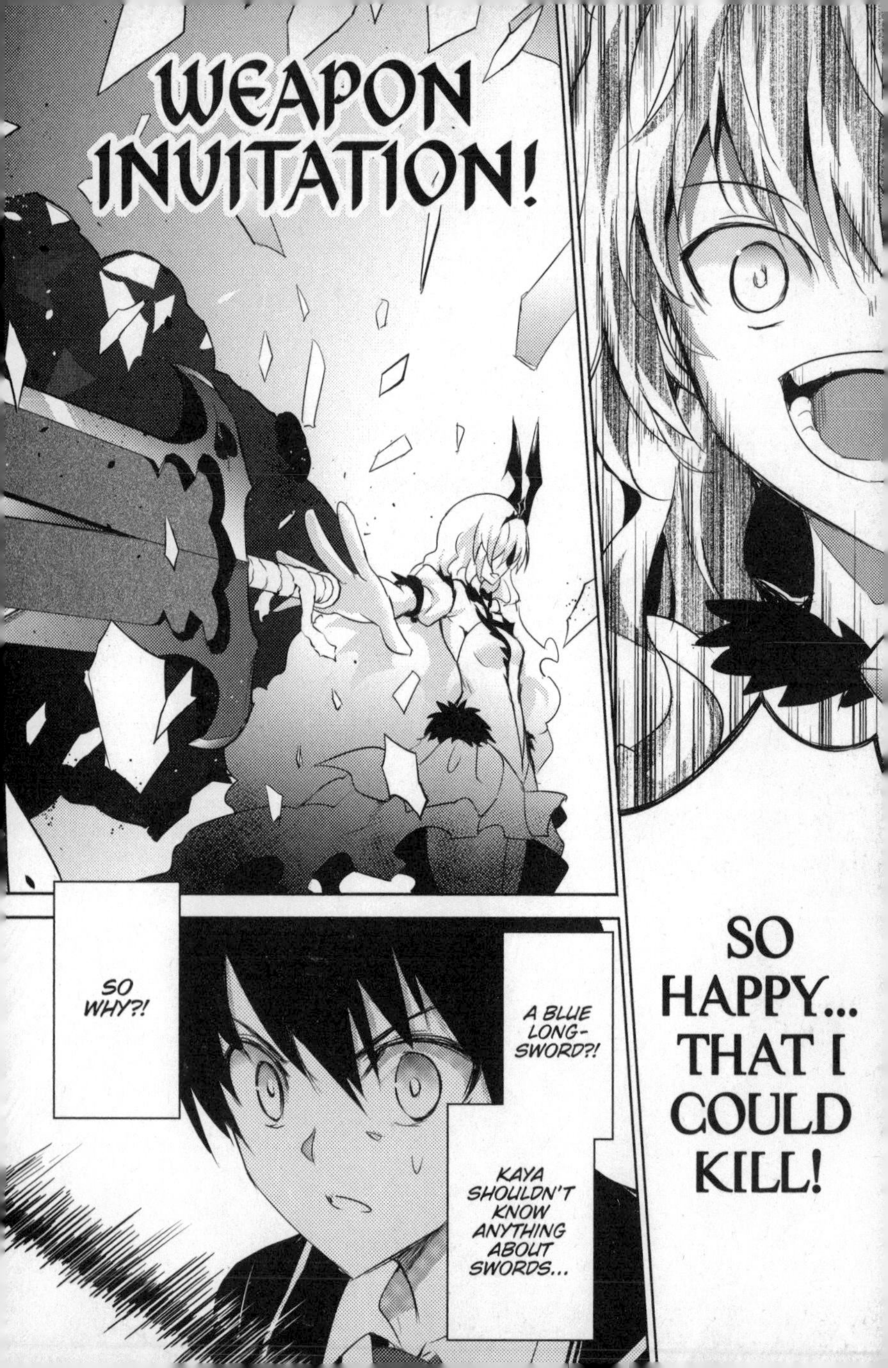
SO HAPPY... THAT I COULD KILL!
WEAPON INVITATION!
A BLUE LONG-SWORD?!
KAYA SHOULDN'T KNOW ANYTHING ABOUT SWORDS...
SO WHY?!

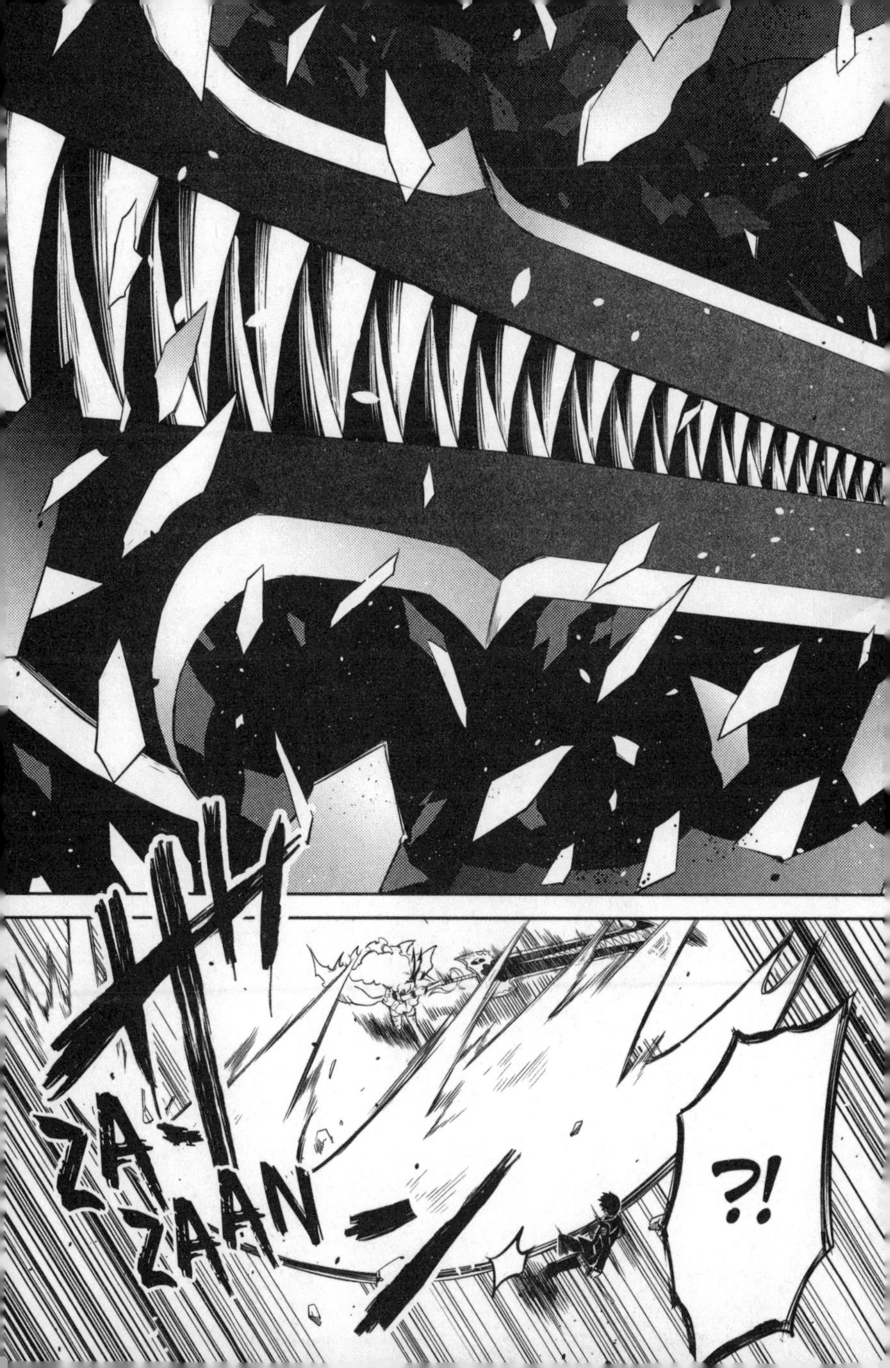
?!
ZA ZAAN

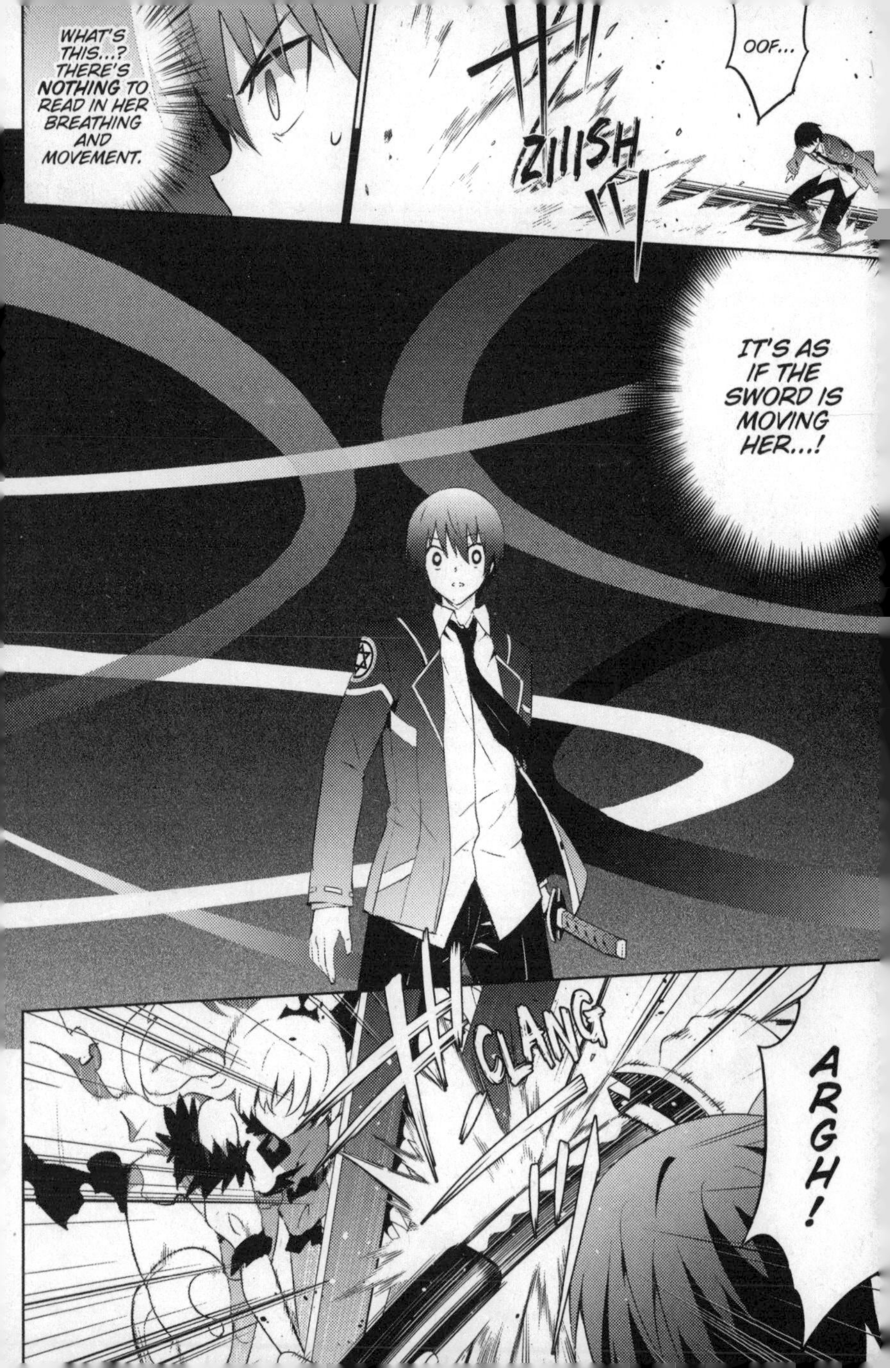

OOF...
ZIIISH
WHAT'S THIS...? THERE'S NOTHING TO READ IN HER BREATHING AND MOVEMENT.
IT'S AS IF THE SWORD IS MOVING HER...!
ARGH!
CLANG

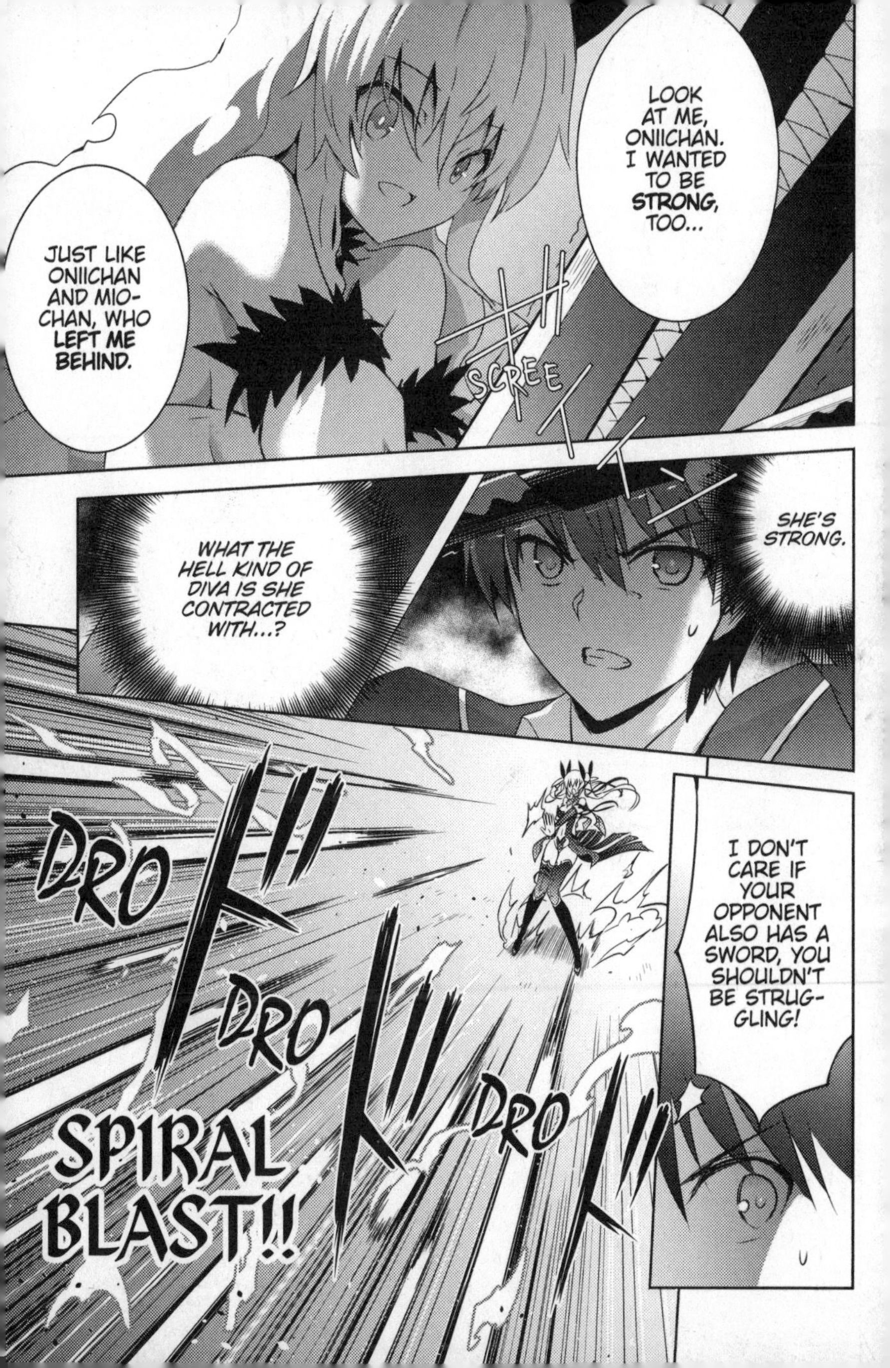
LOOK AT ME, ONIICHAN. I WANTED TO BE STRONG, TOO...
JUST LIKE ONIICHAN AND MIO-CHAN, WHO LEFT ME BEHIND.
SCREE
SHE'S STRONG.
WHAT THE HELL KIND OF DIVA IS SHE CONTRACTED WITH...?
I DON'T CARE IF YOUR OPPONENT ALSO HAS A SWORD, YOU SHOULDN'T BE STRUG-GLING!
DROK!!
DROK!!
DROK!!
SPIRAL BLAST!!

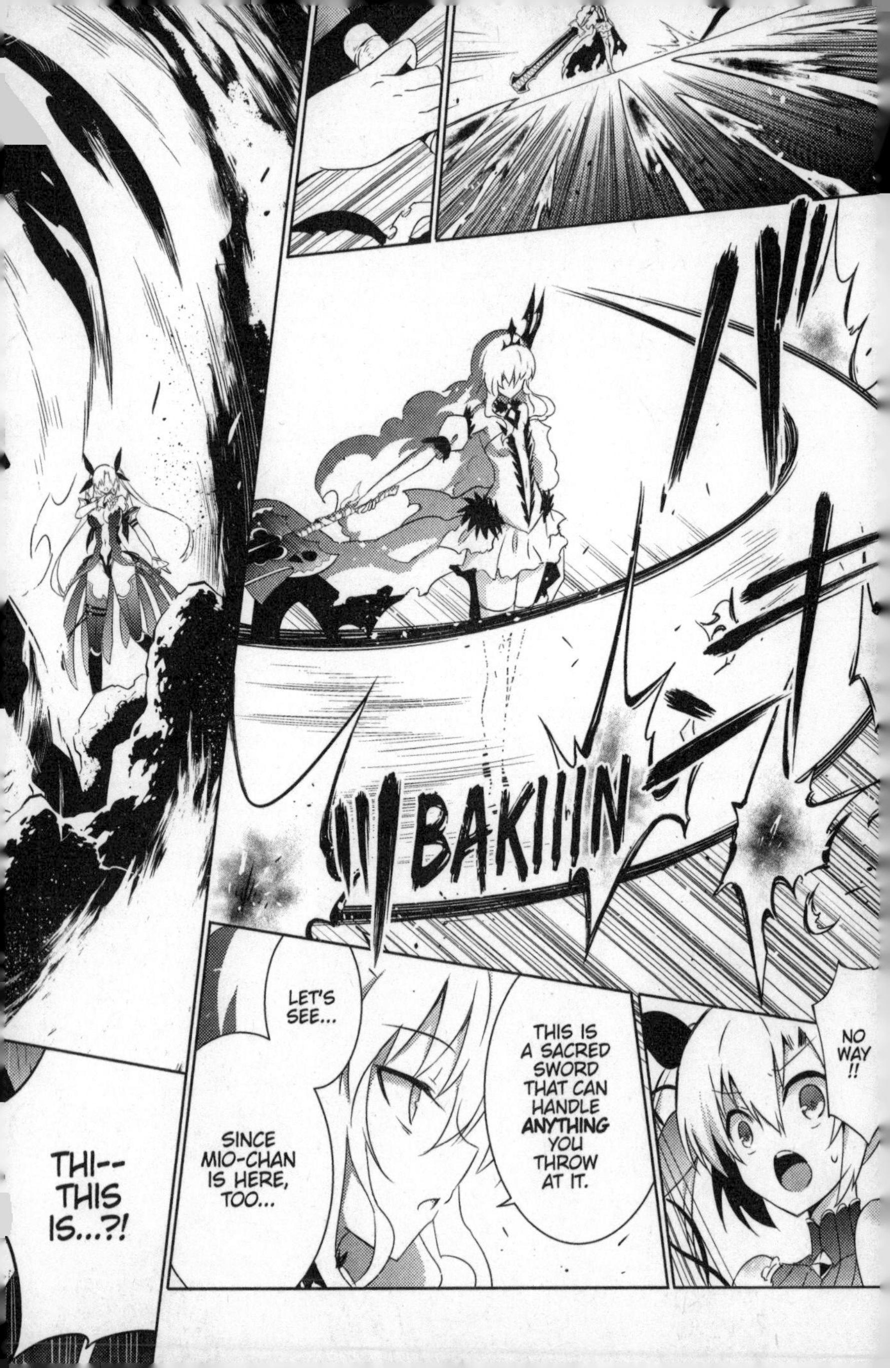
BAKIIIN
NO WAY!!
THIS IS A SACRED SWORD THAT CAN HANDLE ANYTHING YOU THROW AT IT.
LET'S SEE...
SINCE MIO-CHAN IS HERE, TOO...
THI-- THIS IS...?!

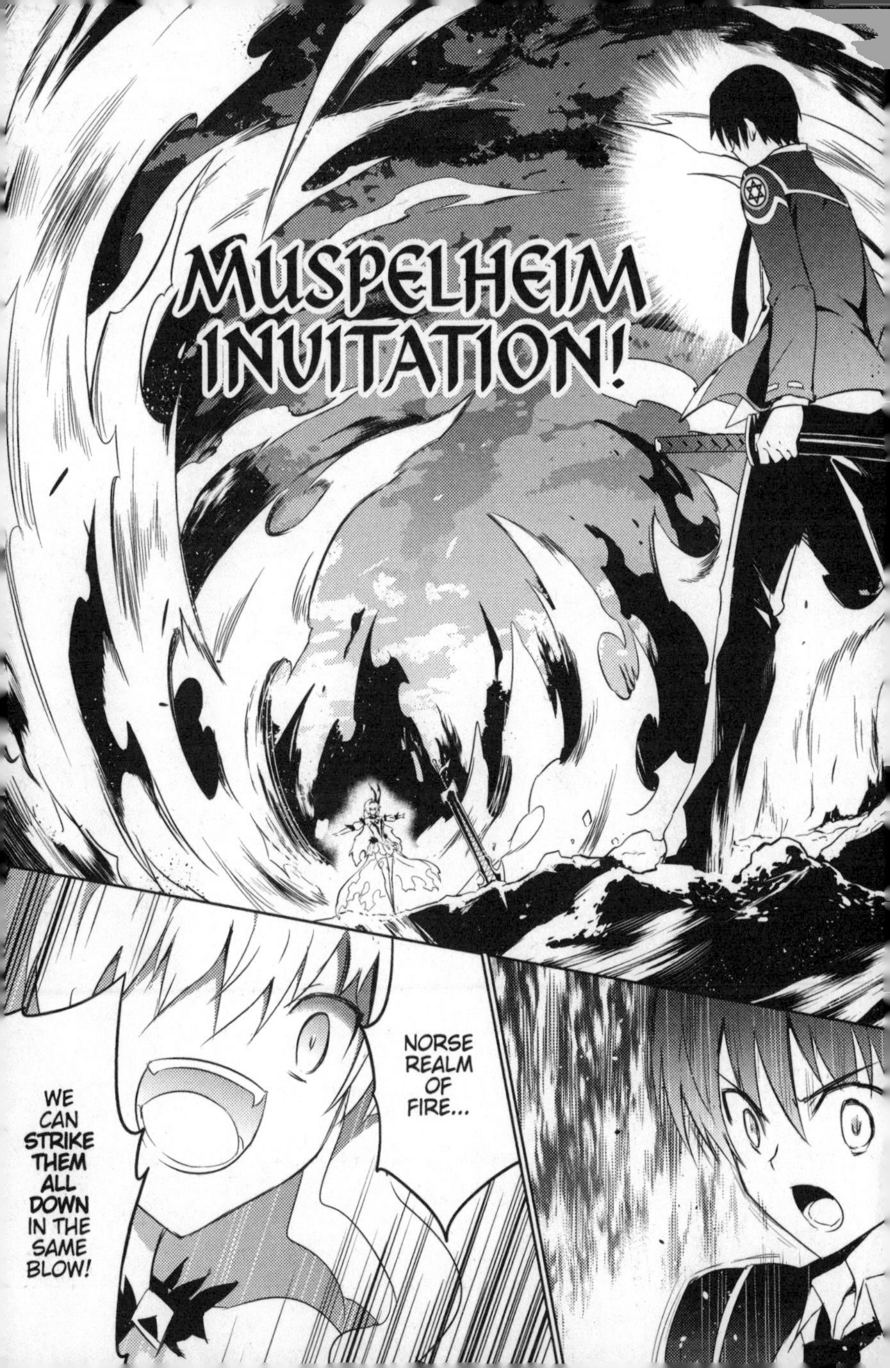
MUSPELHEIM INUITATION!
NORSE REALM OF FIRE...
WE CAN STRIKE THEM ALL DOWN IN THE SAME BLOW!

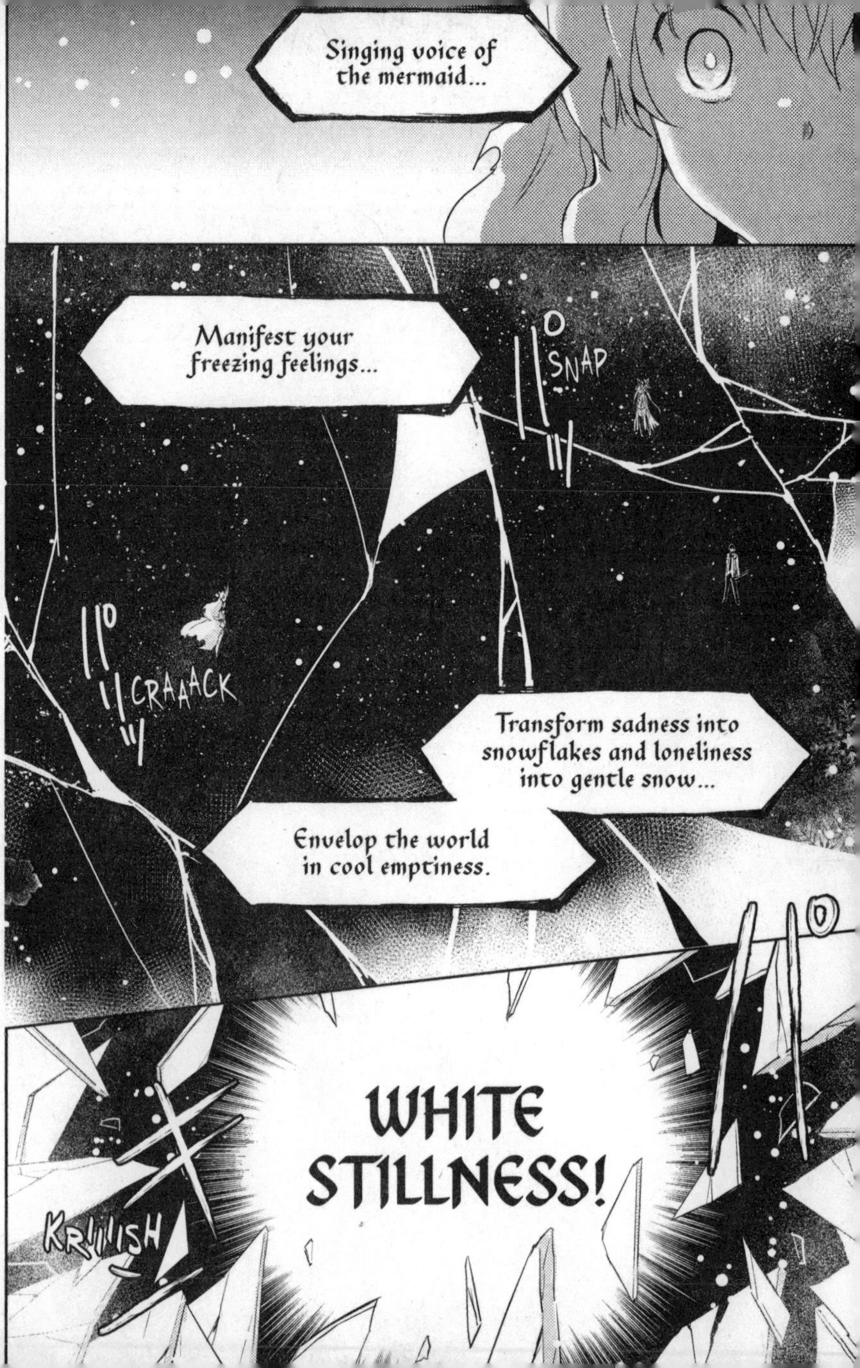
Singing voice of the mermaid...
SNAP
Manifest your freezing feelings...
CRAAACK
Transform sadness into snowflakes and loneliness into gentle snow...
Envelop the world in cool emptiness.
WHITE STILLNESS!
KRIIIISH

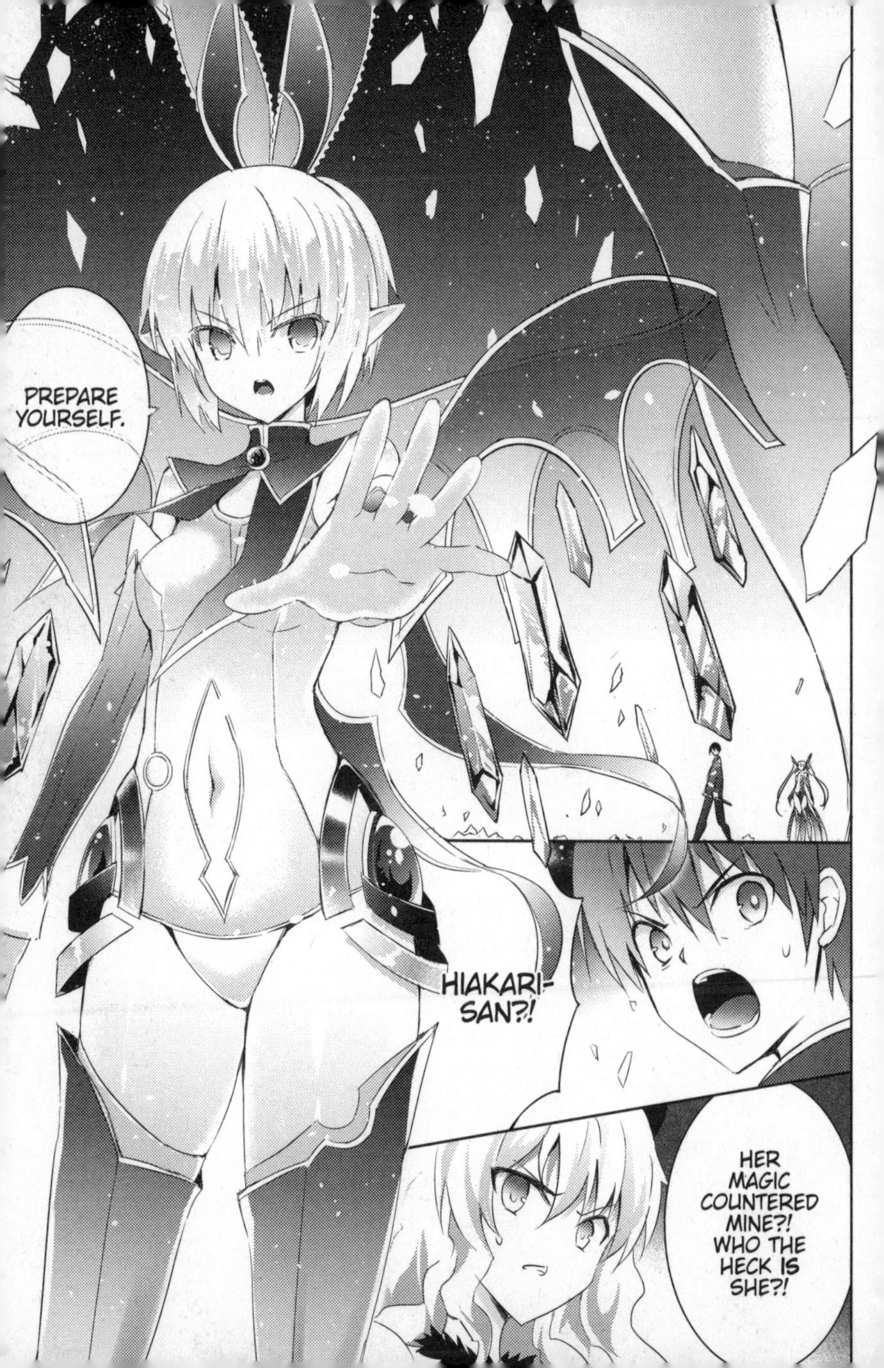
PREPARE YOURSELF.
HIAKARI-SAN?!
HER MAGIC COUNTERED MINE?! WHO THE HECK IS SHE?!

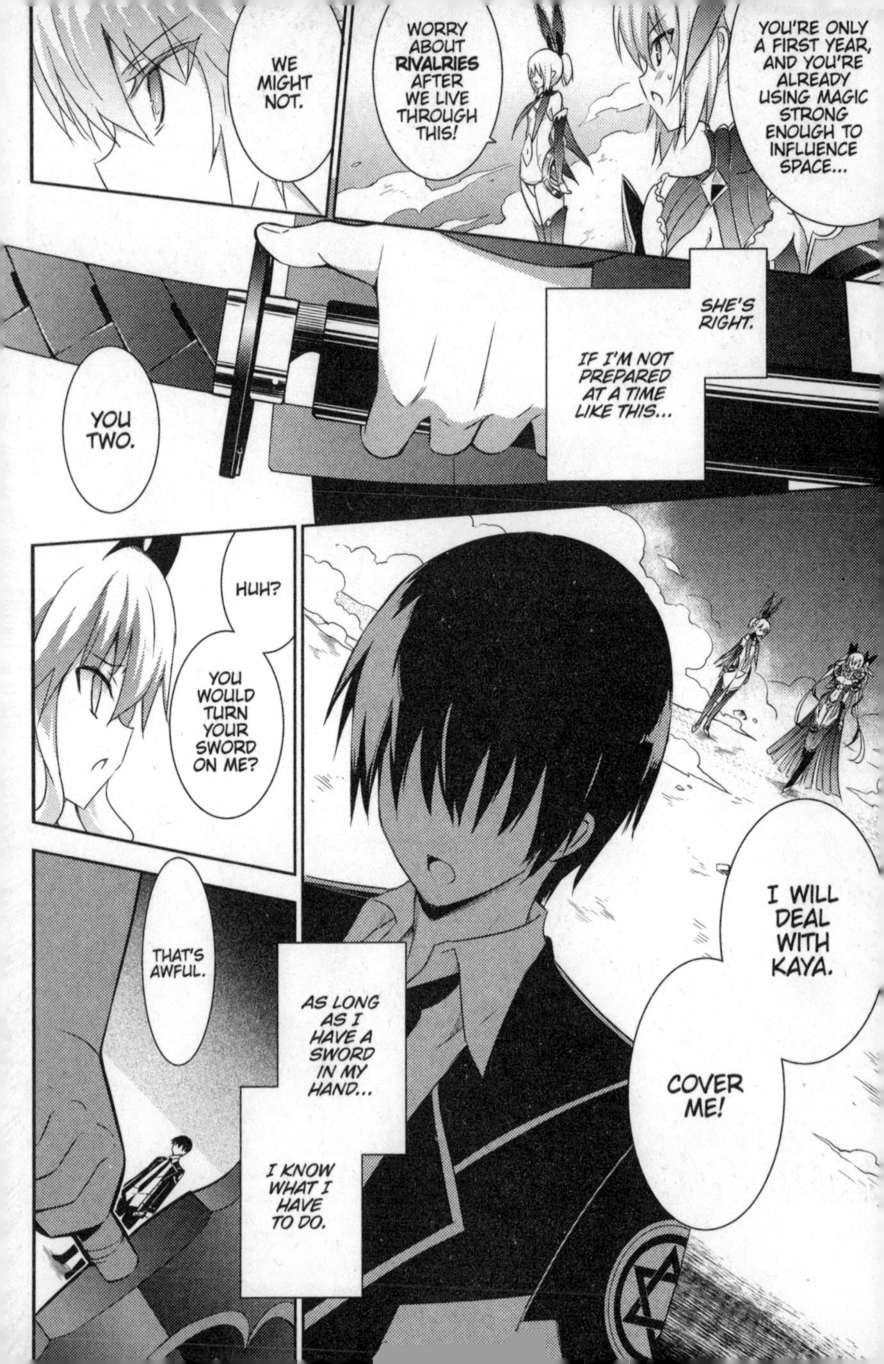
YOU'RE ONLY A FIRST YEAR, AND YOU'RE ALREADY USING MAGIC STRONG ENOUGH TO INFLUENCE SPACE...
WORRY ABOUT RIVALRIES AFTER WE LIVE THROUGH THIS!
WE MIGHT NOT.
SHE'S RIGHT.
IF I'M NOT PREPARED AT A TIME LIKE THIS...
YOU TWO.
I WILL DEAL WITH KAYA.
COVER ME!
HUH?
YOU WOULD TURN YOUR SWORD ON ME?
THAT'S AWFUL.
AS LONG AS I HAVE A SWORD IN MY HAND...
I KNOW WHAT I HAVE TO DO.

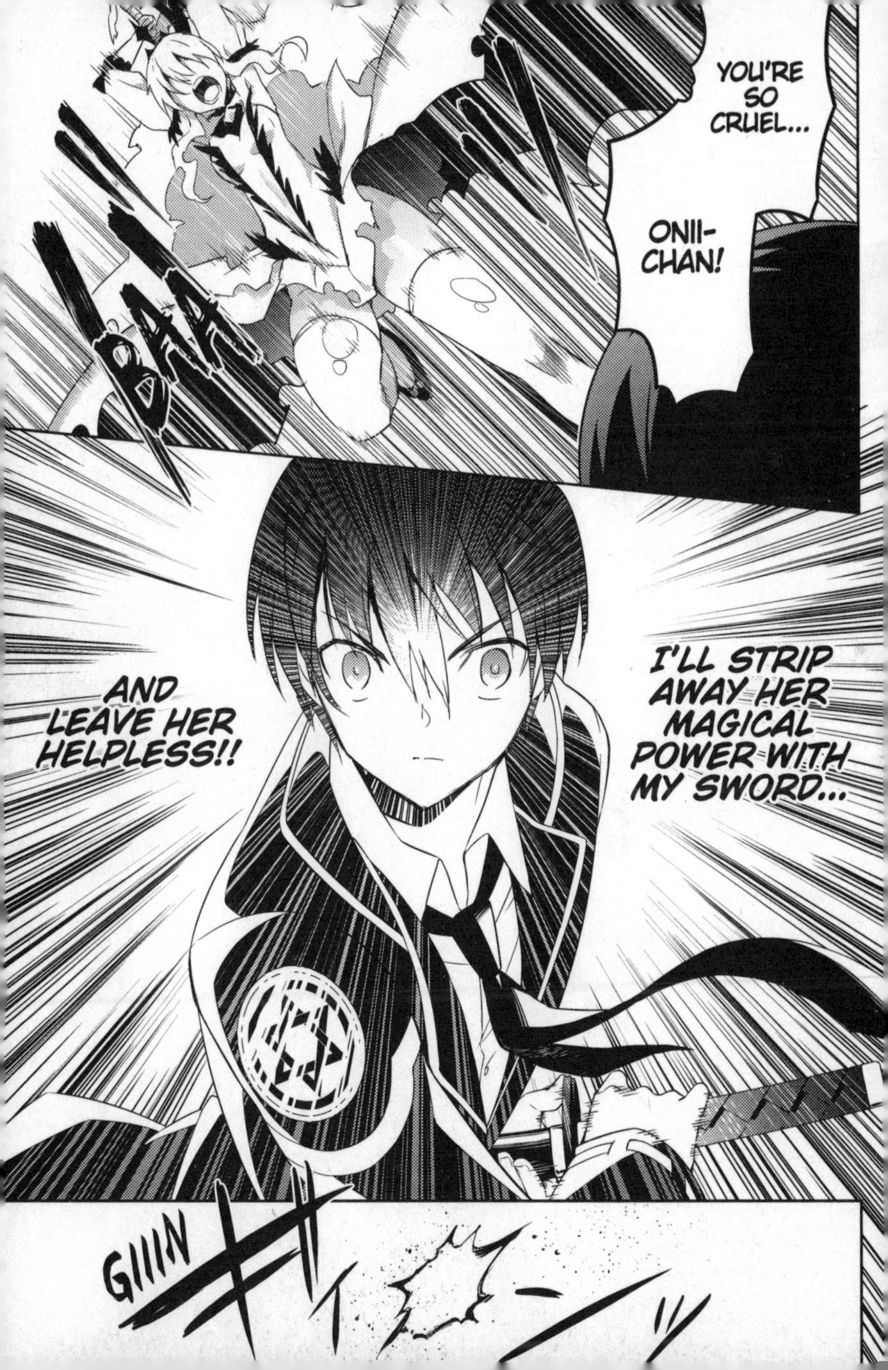
YOU'RE SO CRUEL...
ONII-CHAN!
I'LL STRIP AWAY HER MAGICAL POWER WITH MY SWORD...
AND LEAVE HER HELPLESS!!
GIIIN

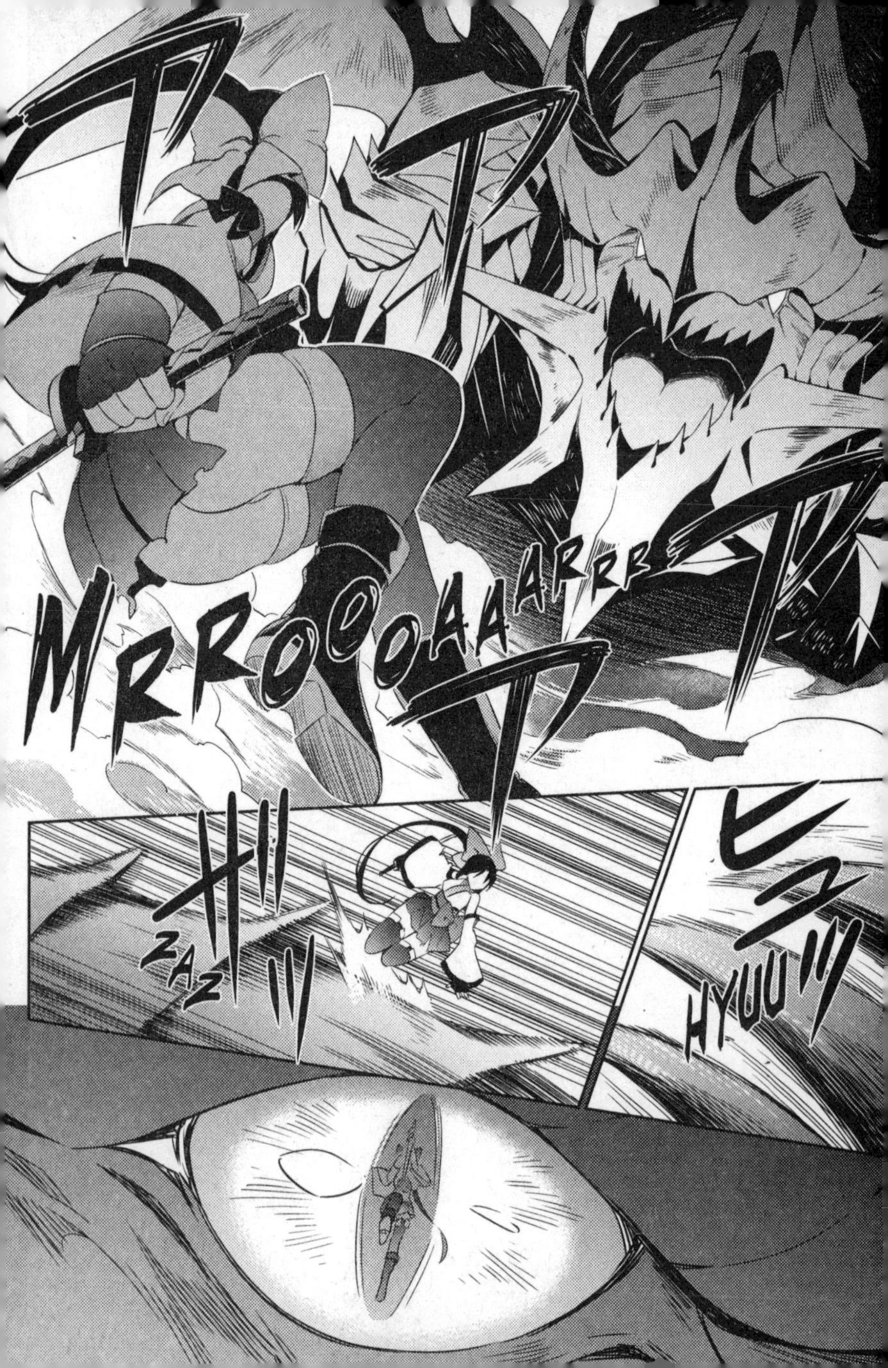
MRROOOOAAARRR
HYUU
ZAZ

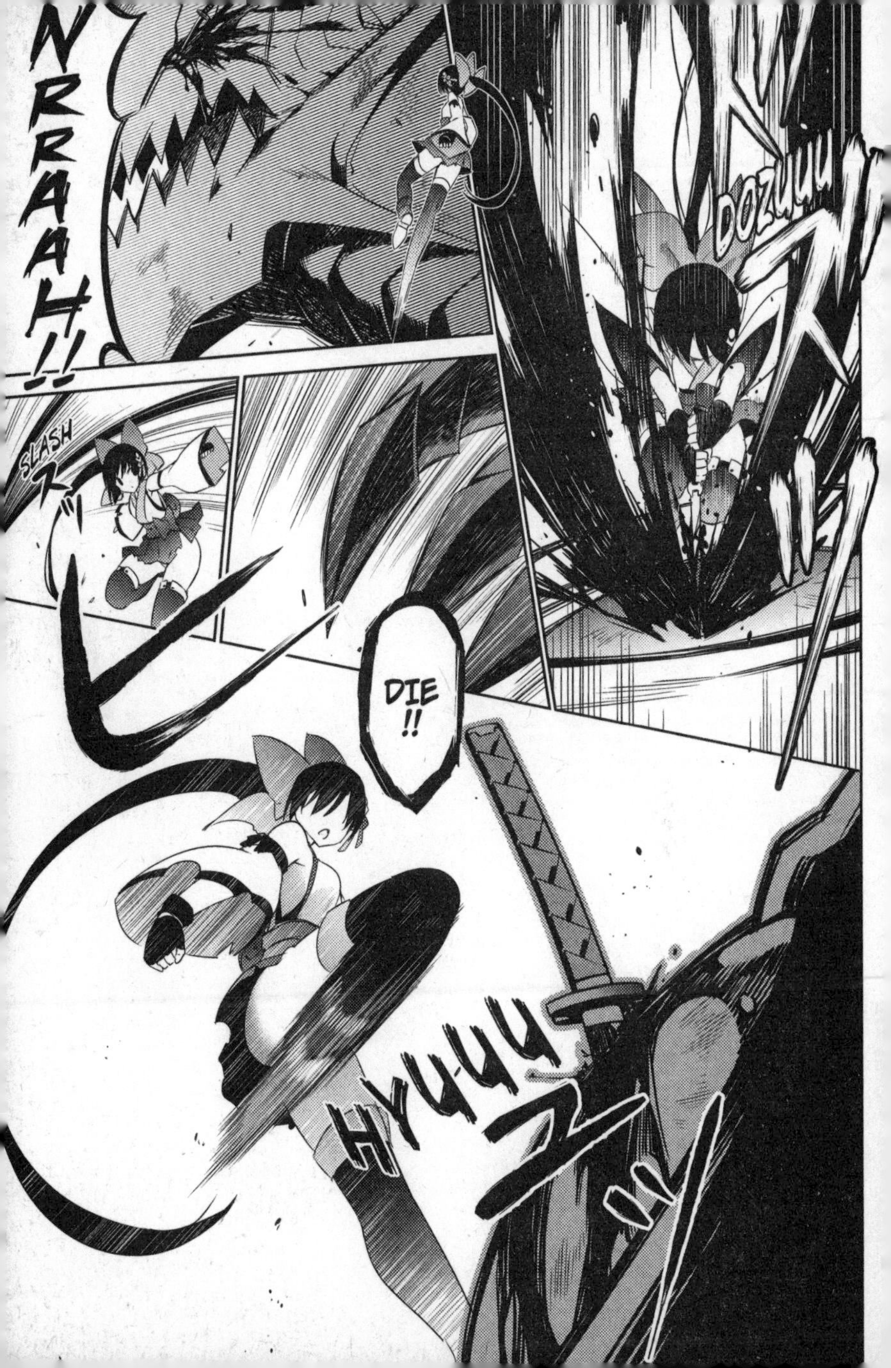
DOZUUU
NRRAAH!!
SLASH
DIE!!
HYUUU

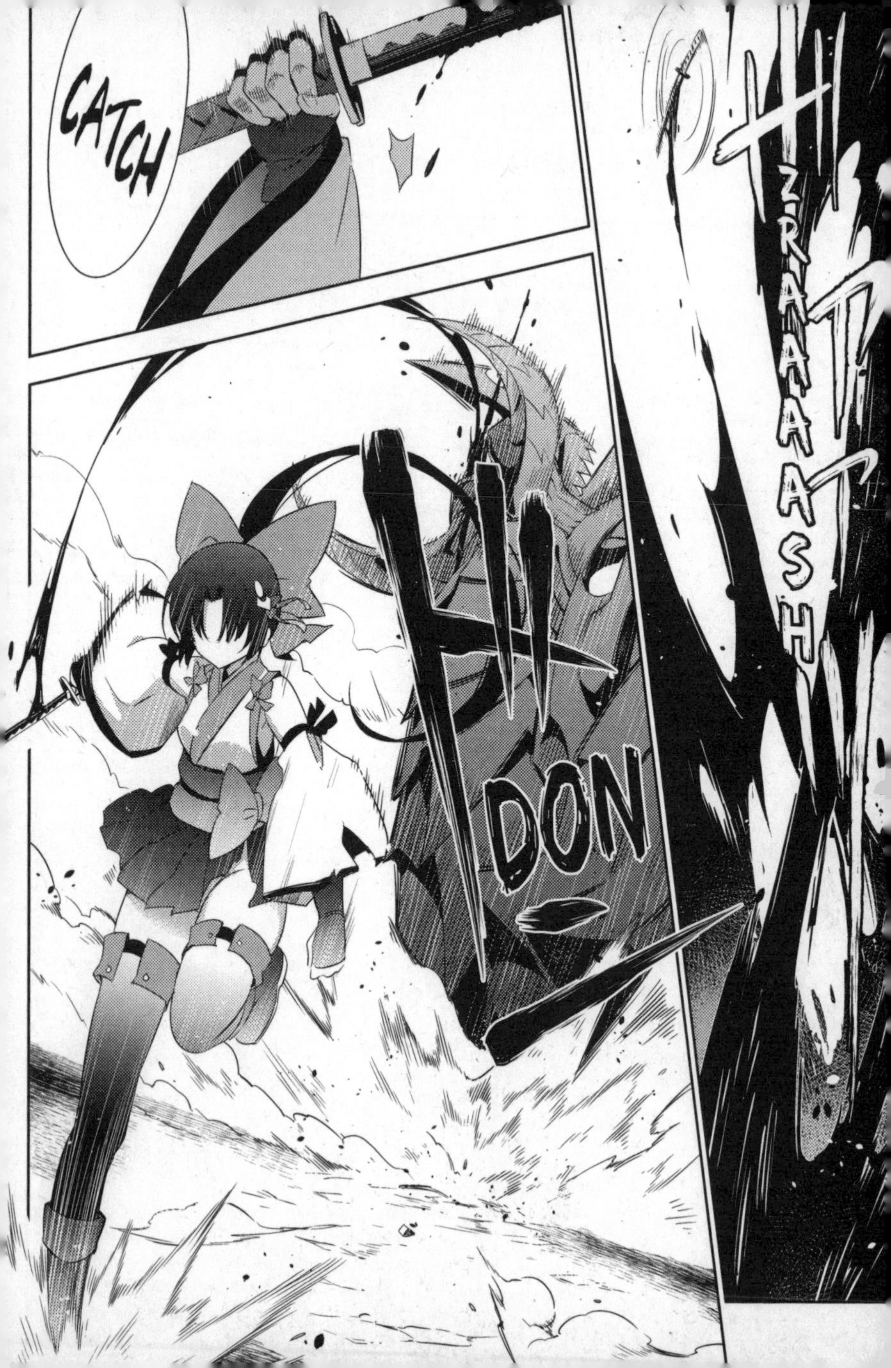
ZRAAAASH
CATCH
DON

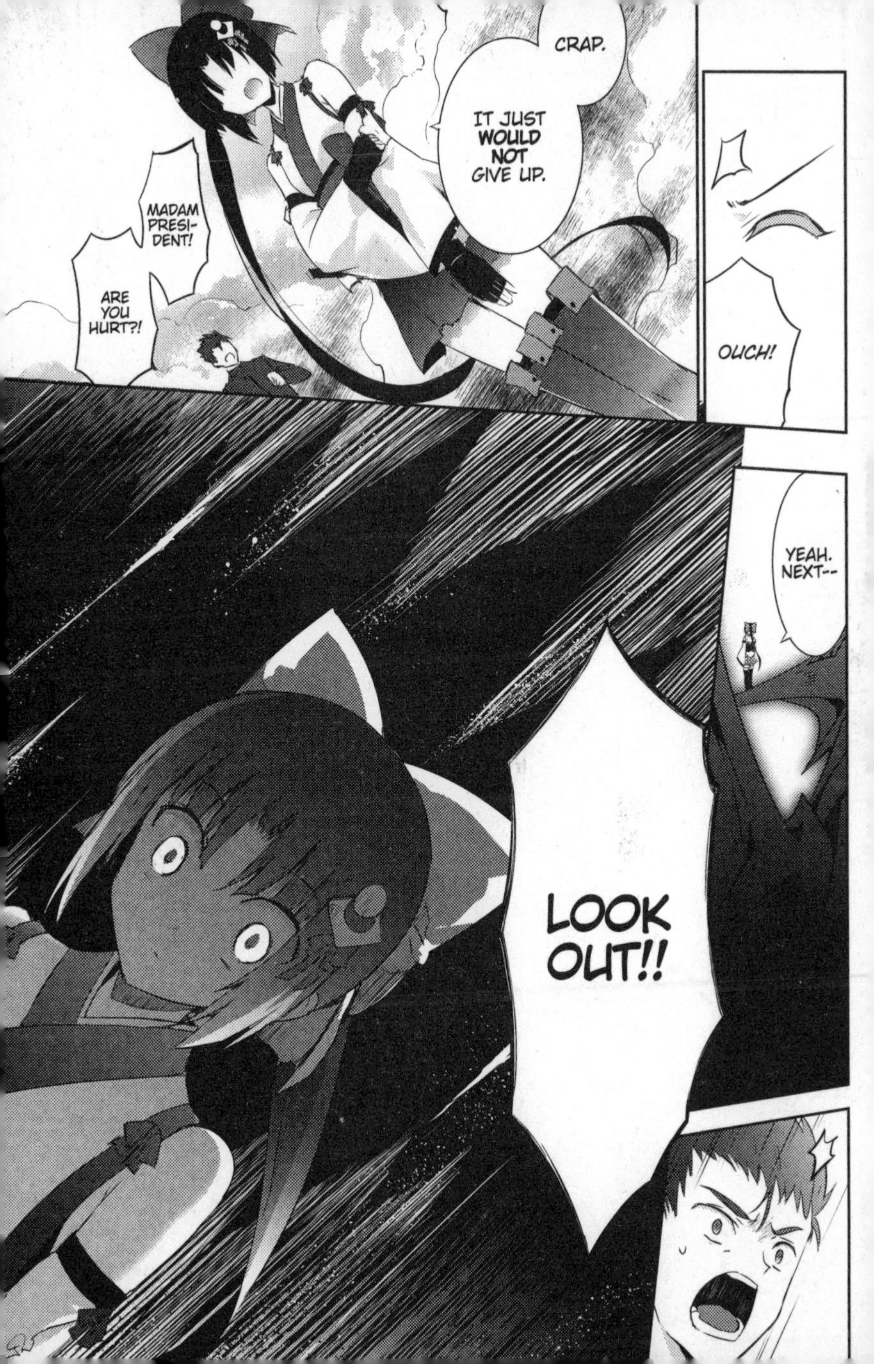
OUCH!
CRAP.
IT JUST WOULD NOT GIVE UP.
MADAM PRESIDENT!
ARE YOU HURT?!
YEAH. NEXT--
LOOK OUT!!

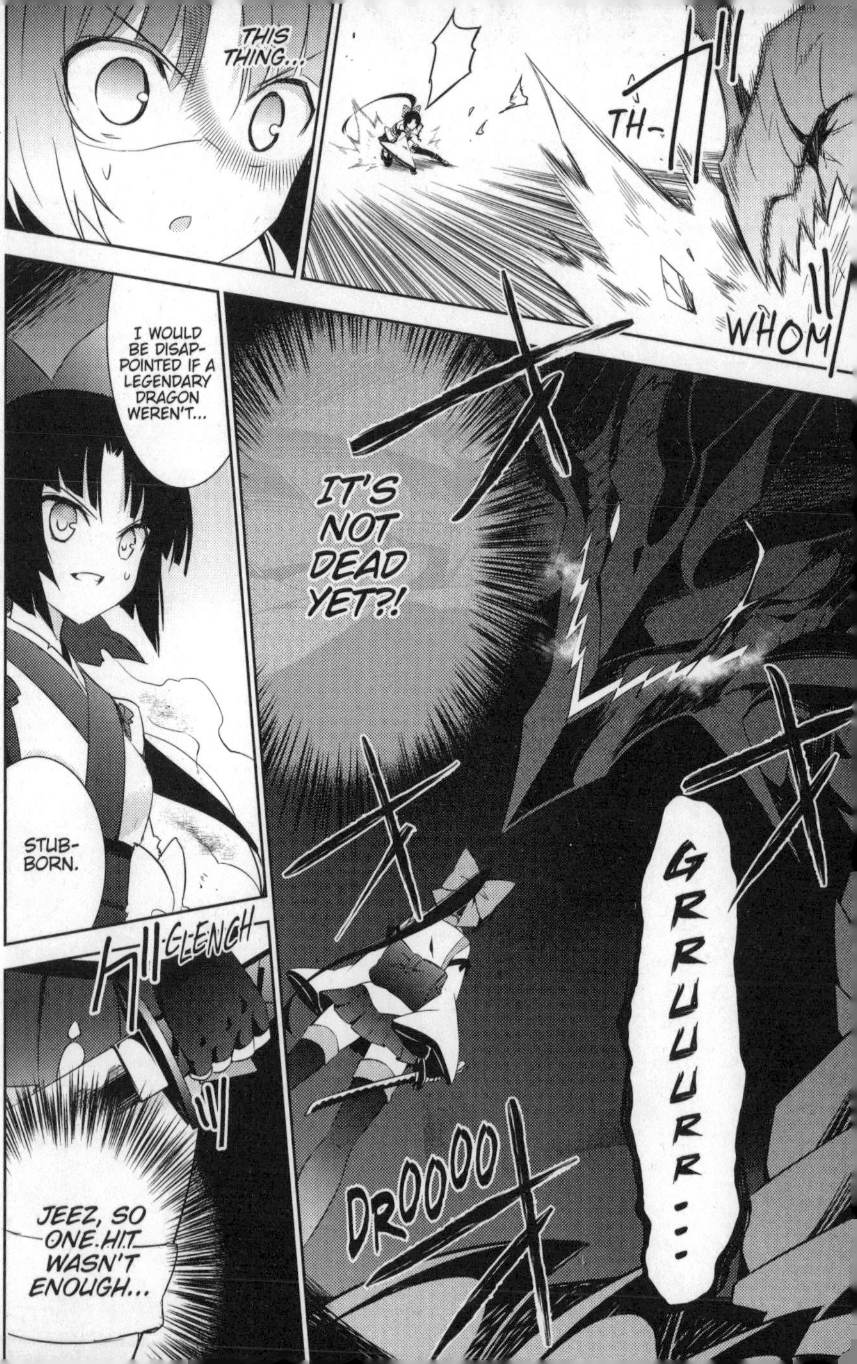
TH-
WHOM
THIS THING...
IT'S NOT DEAD YET?!
GRRUUURR...
DROOOO
I WOULD BE DISAPPOINTED IF A LEGENDARY DRAGON WEREN'T...
STUBBORN.
CLENCH
JEEZ, SO ONE HIT WASN'T ENOUGH...

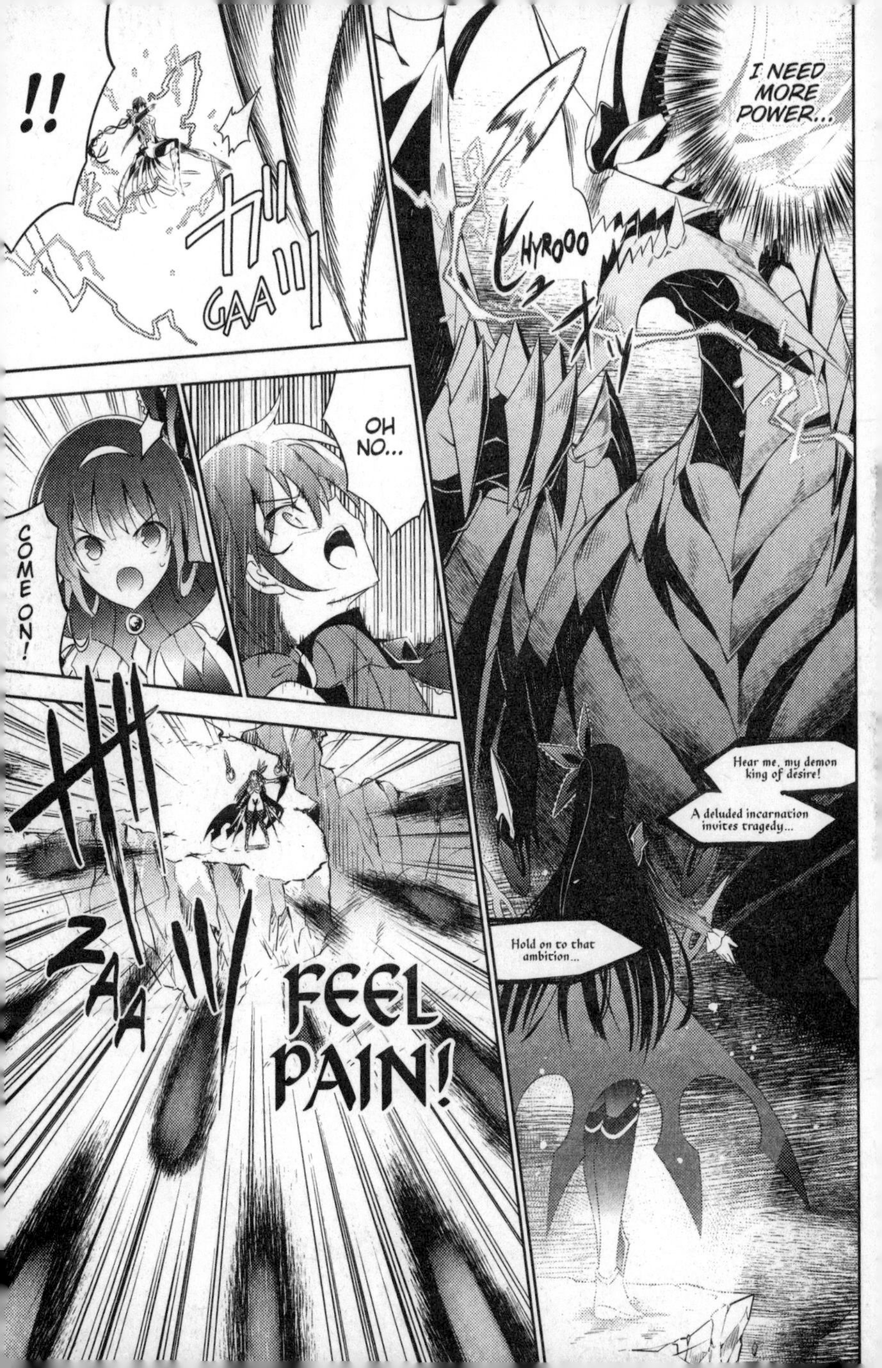
I NEED MORE POWER...
HYROOO
Hear me, my demon king of desire!
A deluded incarnation invites tragedy...
Hold on to that ambition...
!!
GAA
OH NO...
COME ON!
ZAA
FEEL PAIN!

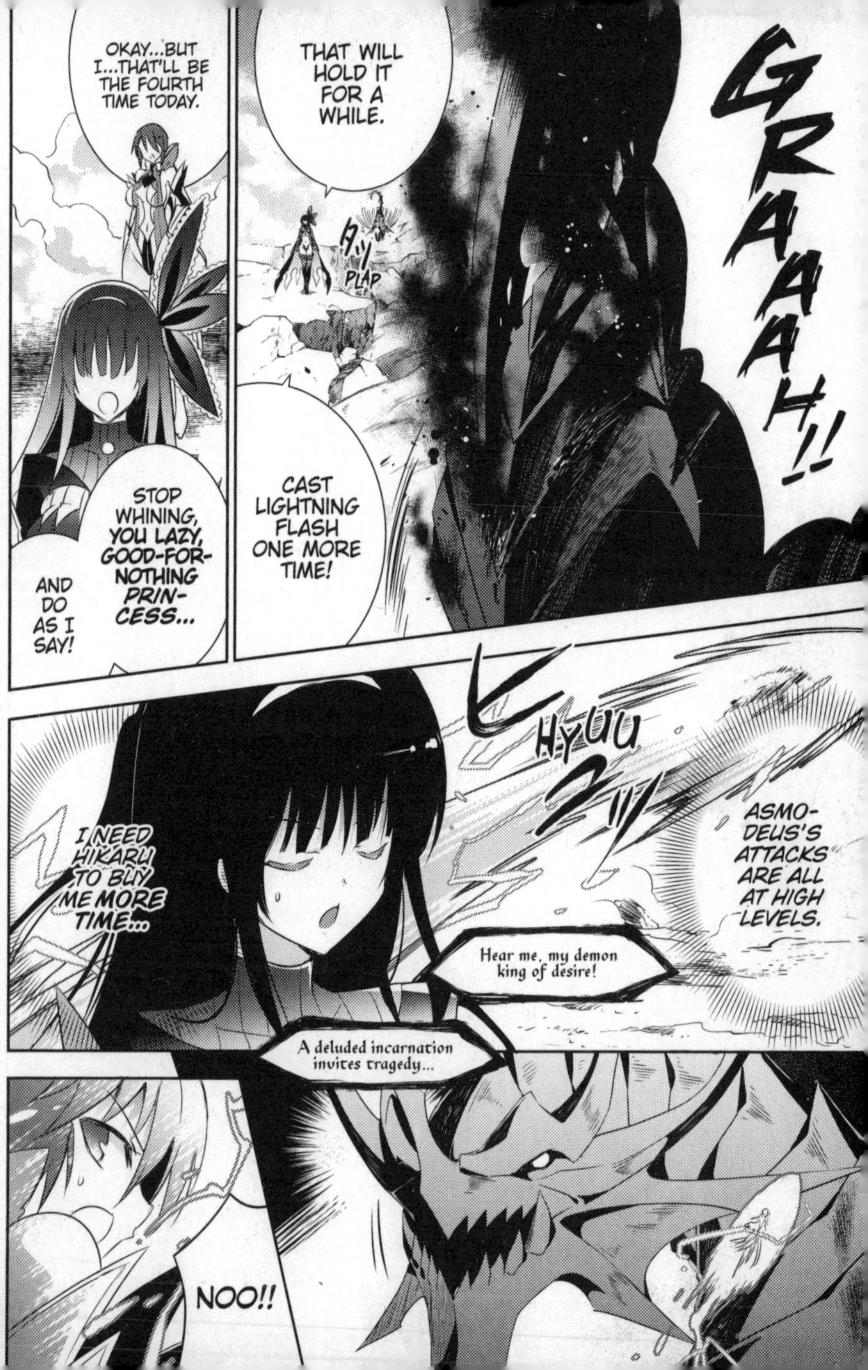
GRAAAH!!
THAT WILL HOLD IT FOR A WHILE.
PLAP
CAST LIGHTNING FLASH ONE MORE TIME!
OKAY...BUT I...THAT'LL BE THE FOURTH TIME TODAY.
STOP WHINING, YOU LAZY, GOOD-FOR-NOTHING PRIN-CESS...
AND DO AS I SAY!
HYUU
ASMO-DEUS'S ATTACKS ARE ALL AT HIGH LEVELS.
I NEED HIKARU TO BUY ME MORE TIME...
Hear me, my demon king of desire!
A deluded incarnation invites tragedy...
NOO!!

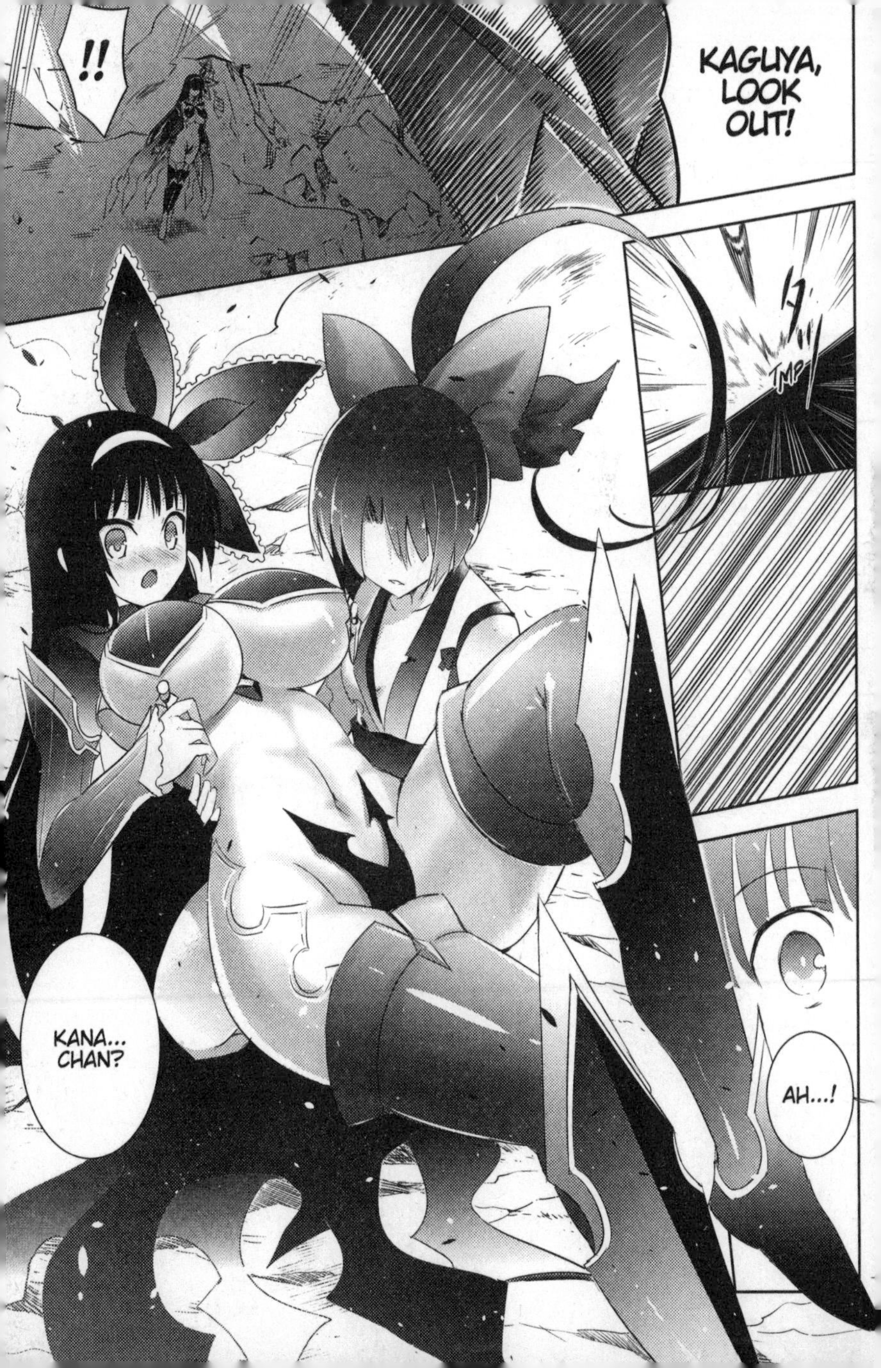
KAGUYA, LOOK OUT!
!!
TMP
AH...!
KANA... CHAN?

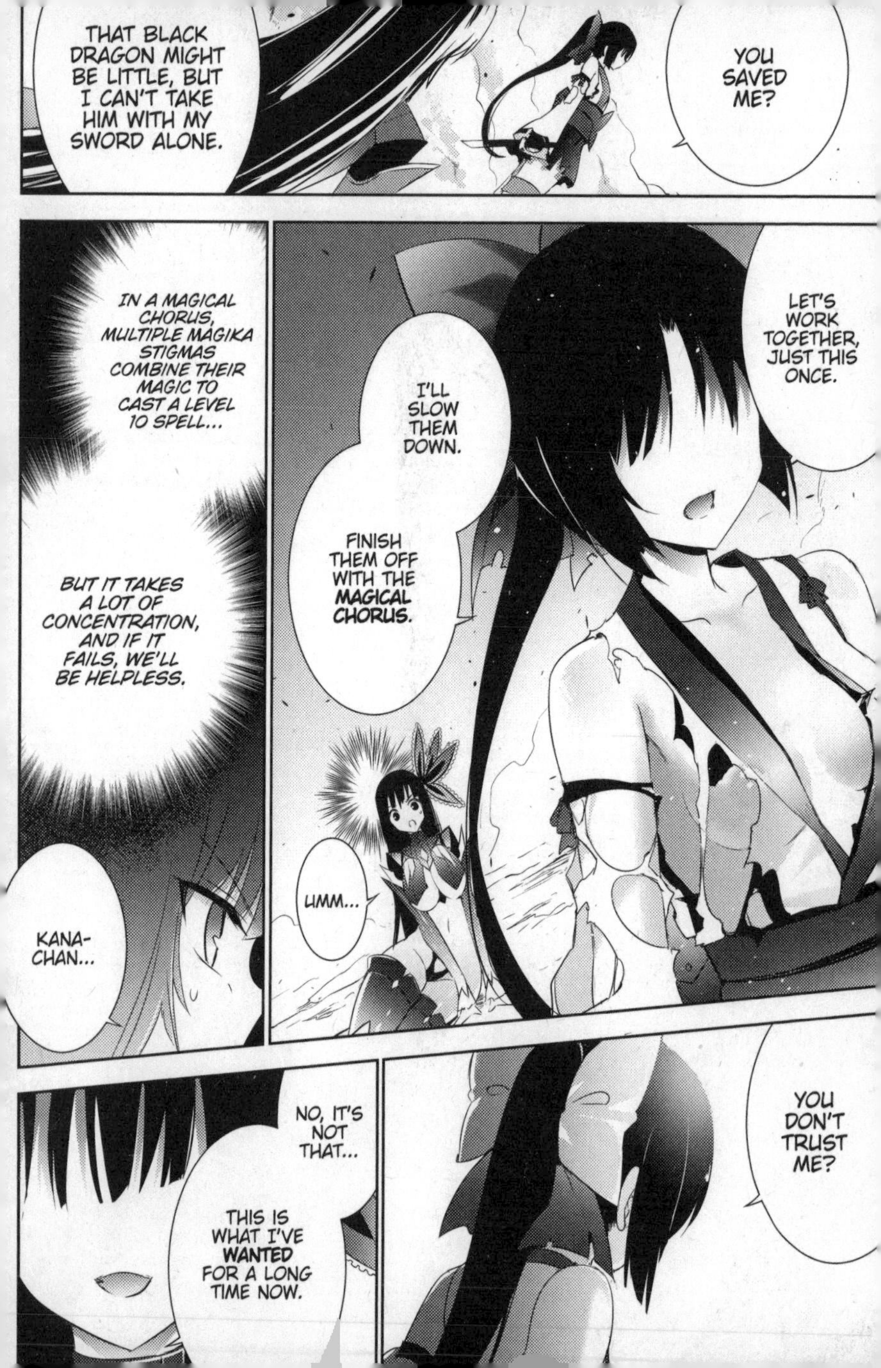
YOU SAVED ME?
THAT BLACK DRAGON MIGHT BE LITTLE, BUT I CAN'T TAKE HIM WITH MY SWORD ALONE.
LET'S WORK TOGETHER, JUST THIS ONCE.
I'LL SLOW THEM DOWN.
FINISH THEM OFF WITH THE **MAGICAL CHORUS.**
UMM...
IN A MAGICAL CHORUS, MULTIPLE MAGIKA STIGMAS COMBINE THEIR MAGIC TO CAST A LEVEL 10 SPELL...
BUT IT TAKES A LOT OF CONCENTRATION, AND IF IT FAILS, WE'LL BE HELPLESS.
KANA-CHAN...
YOU DON'T TRUST ME?
NO, IT'S NOT THAT...
THIS IS WHAT I'VE **WANTED** FOR A LONG TIME NOW.

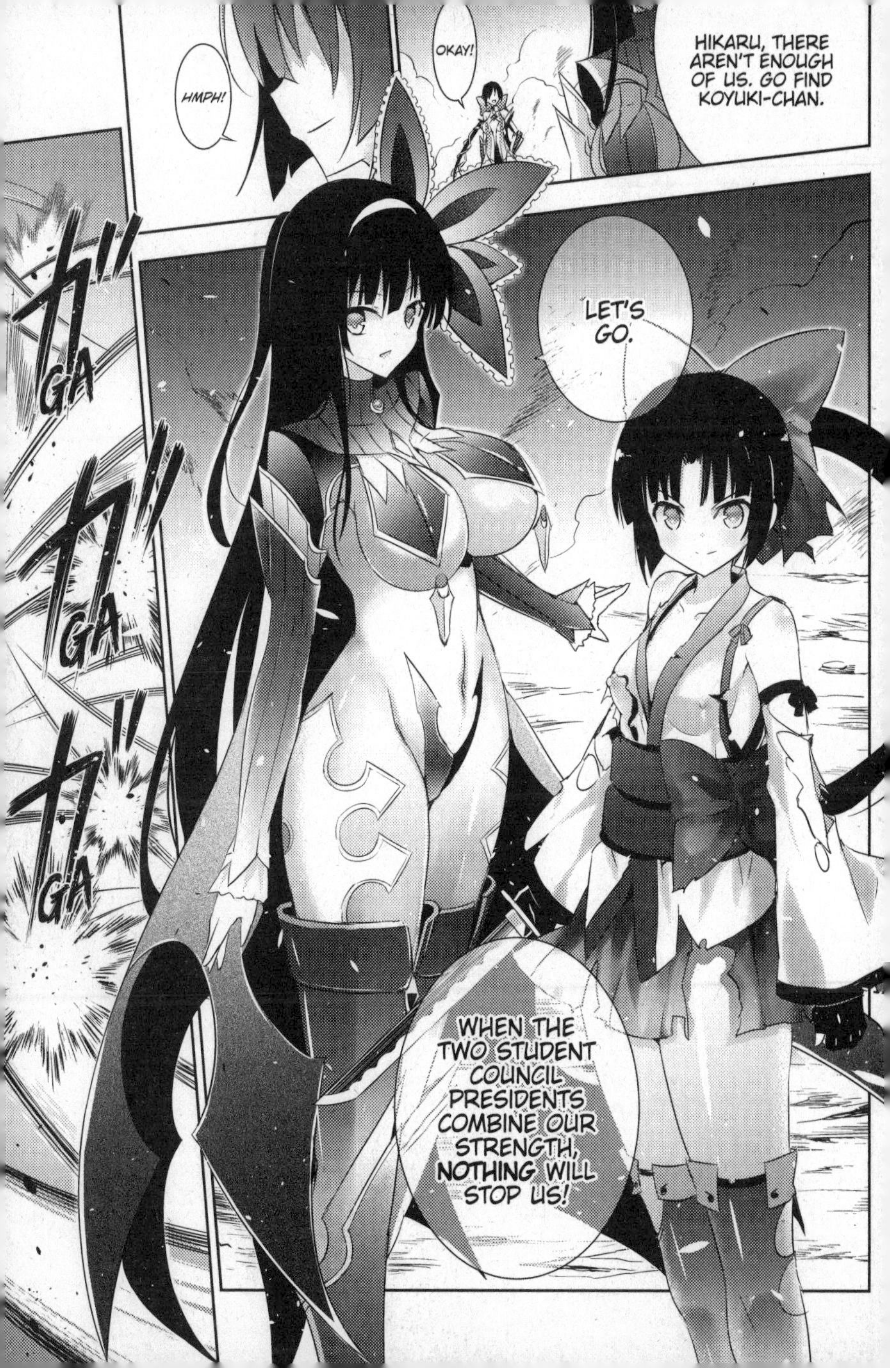
HIKARU, THERE AREN'T ENOUGH OF US. GO FIND KOYUKI-CHAN.
OKAY!
HMPH!
LET'S GO.
WHEN THE TWO STUDENT COUNCIL PRESIDENTS COMBINE OUR STRENGTH, NOTHING WILL STOP US!
ガ GA
ガ GA
ガ GA

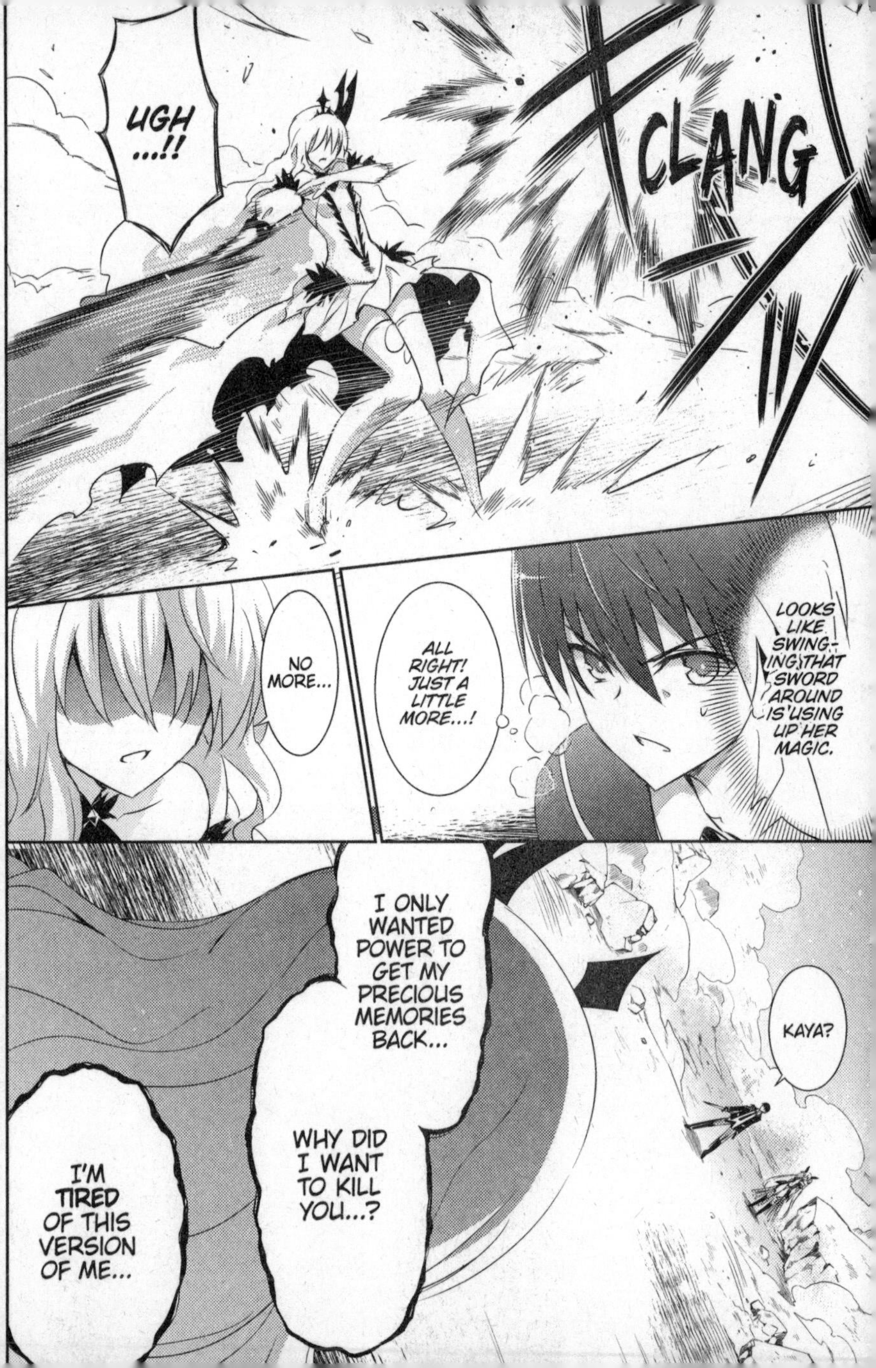
CLANG
UGH ...!!
LOOKS LIKE SWING-ING THAT SWORD AROUND IS USING UP HER MAGIC.
ALL RIGHT! JUST A LITTLE MORE...!
NO MORE...
KAYA?
I ONLY WANTED POWER TO GET MY PRECIOUS MEMORIES BACK...
WHY DID I WANT TO KILL YOU...?
I'M TIRED OF THIS VERSION OF ME...

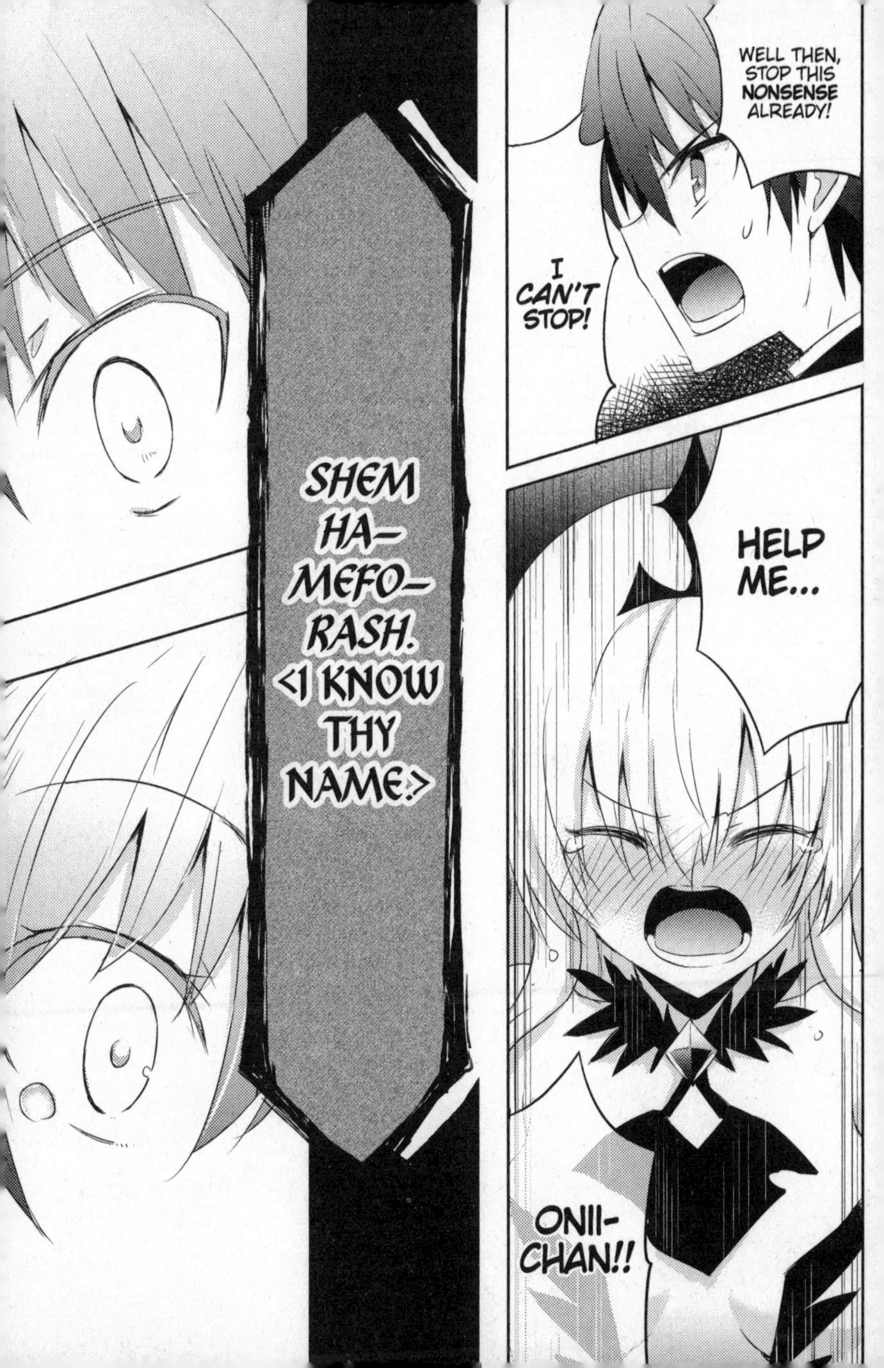
WELL THEN, STOP THIS NONSENSE ALREADY!
I CAN'T STOP!
HELP ME...
ONII-CHAN!!
SHEM HA-MEFO-RASH. <I KNOW THY NAME.>

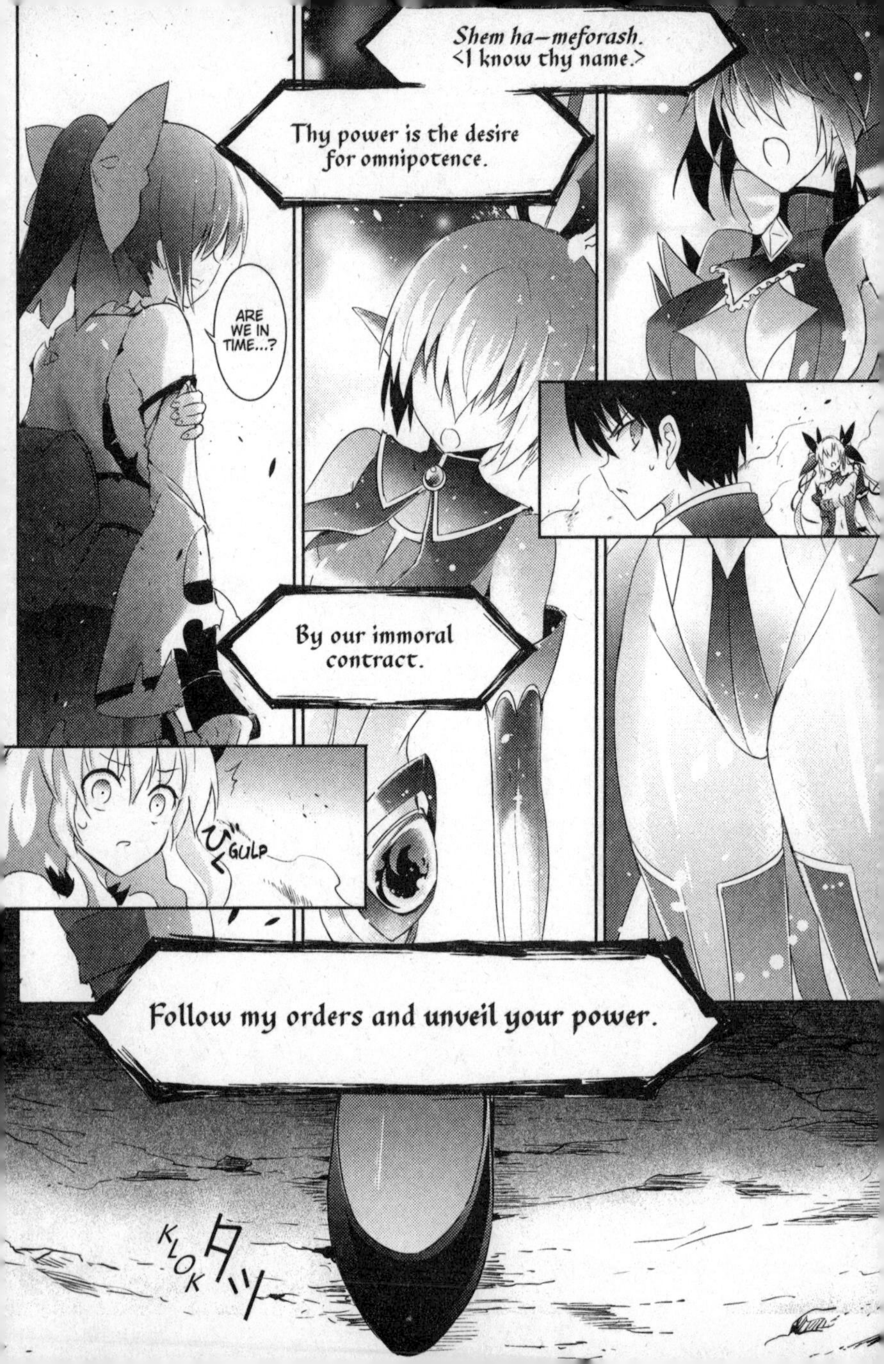
Shem ha-meforash.
<I know thy name.>
Thy power is the desire for omnipotence.
By our immoral contract.
ARE WE IN TIME...?
GULP
Follow my orders and unveil your power.
KLOK

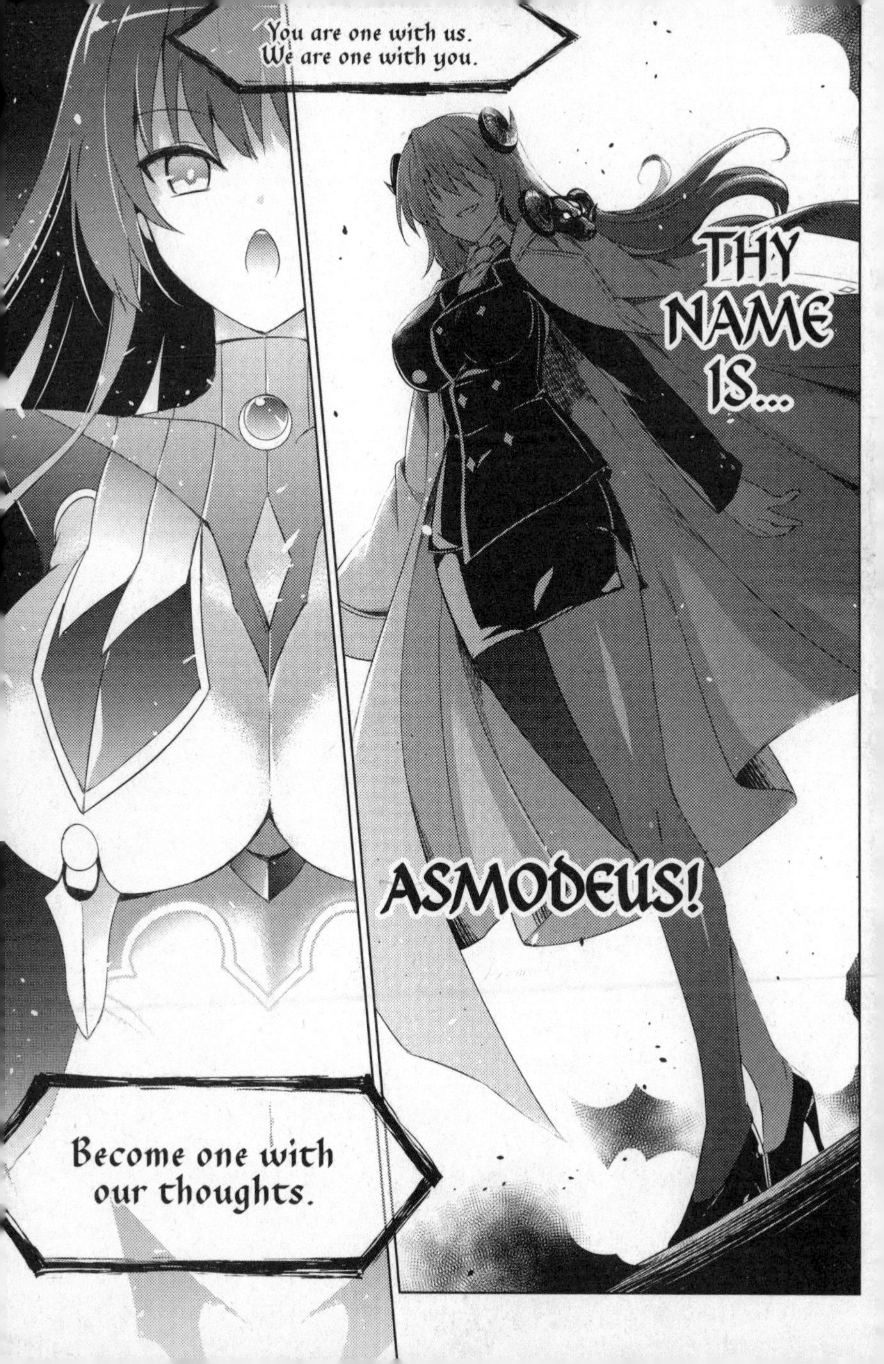
THY NAME IS...
ASMODEUS!
You are one with us. We are one with you.
Become one with our thoughts.

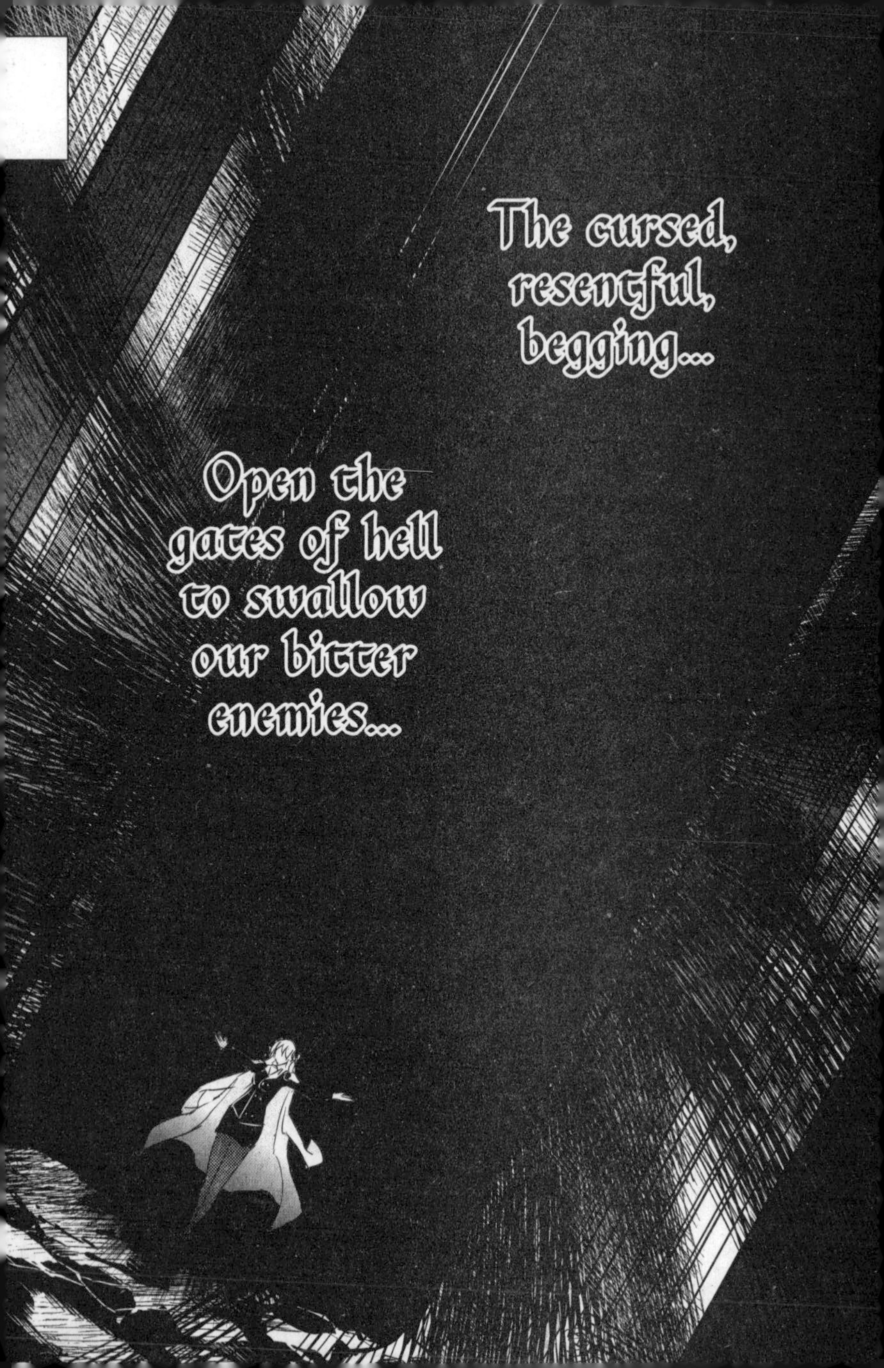
The cursed, resentful, begging...
Open the gates of hell to swallow our bitter enemies...

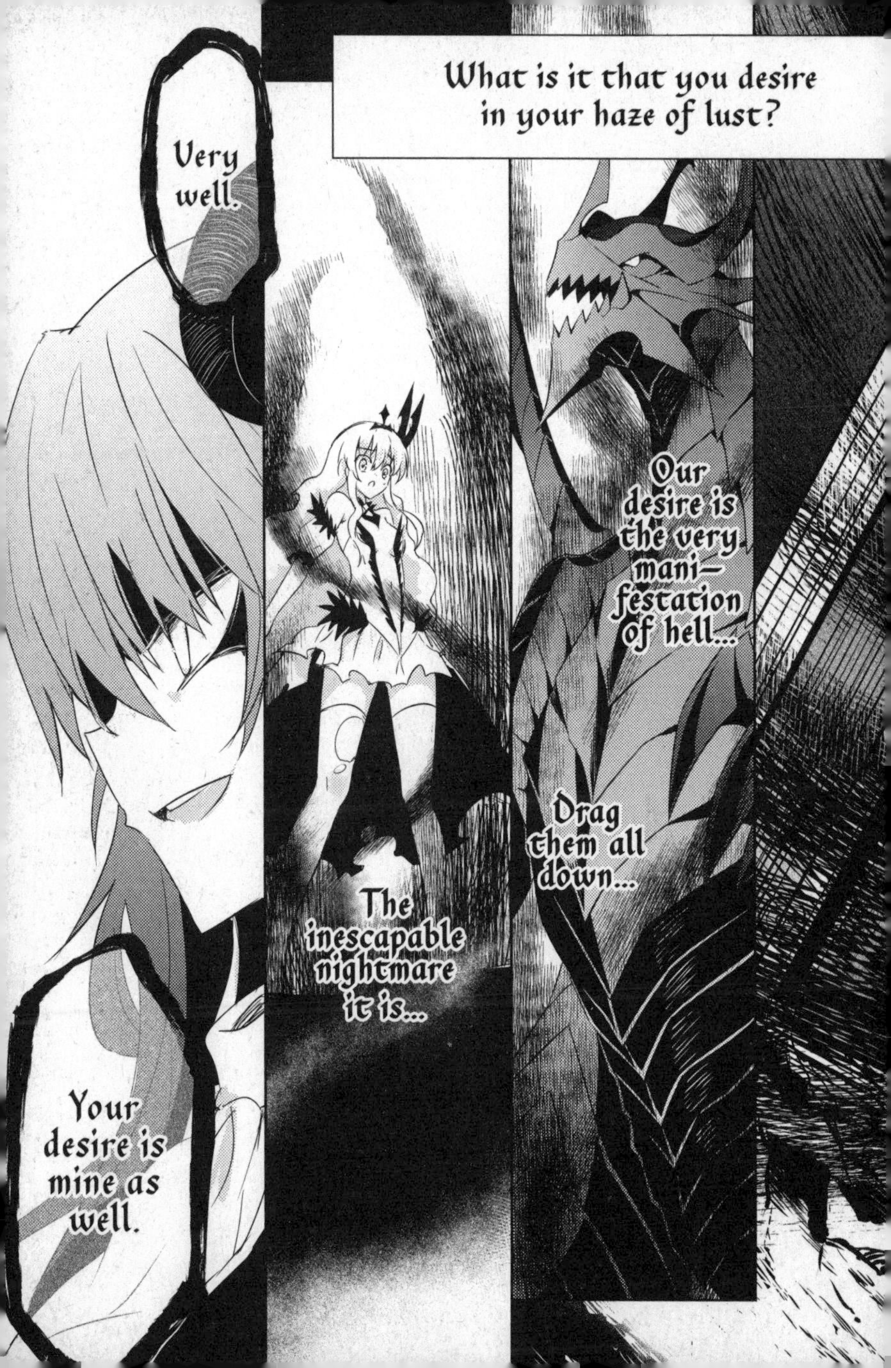
What is it that you desire in your haze of lust?
Our desire is the very mani-festation of hell...
Drag them all down...
The inescapable nightmare it is...
Very well.
Your desire is mine as well.

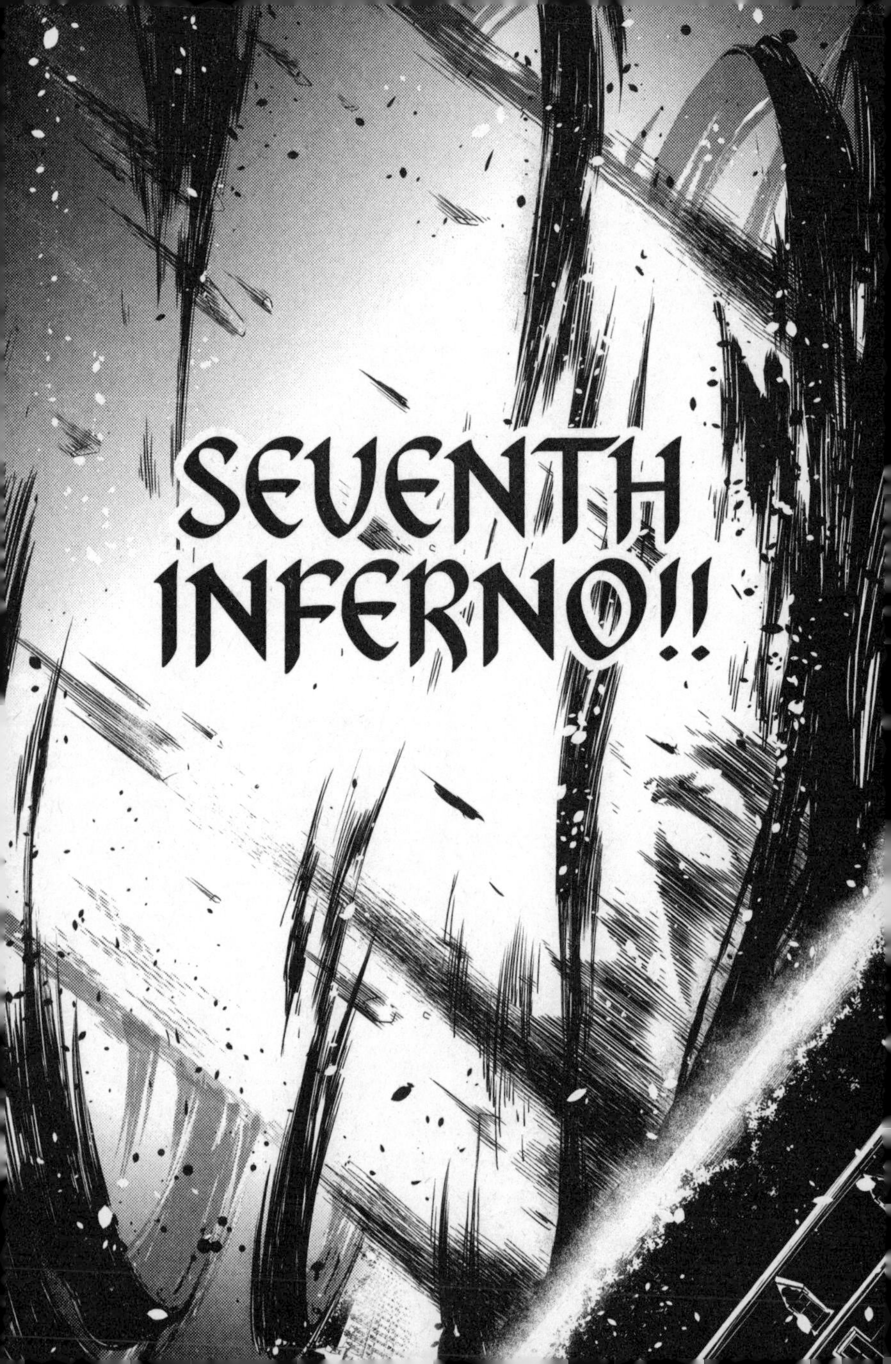
SEVENTH INFERNO!!

Magika
SWORDSMAN
AND SUMMONER

3

魔技科の剣士と召喚魔王

3

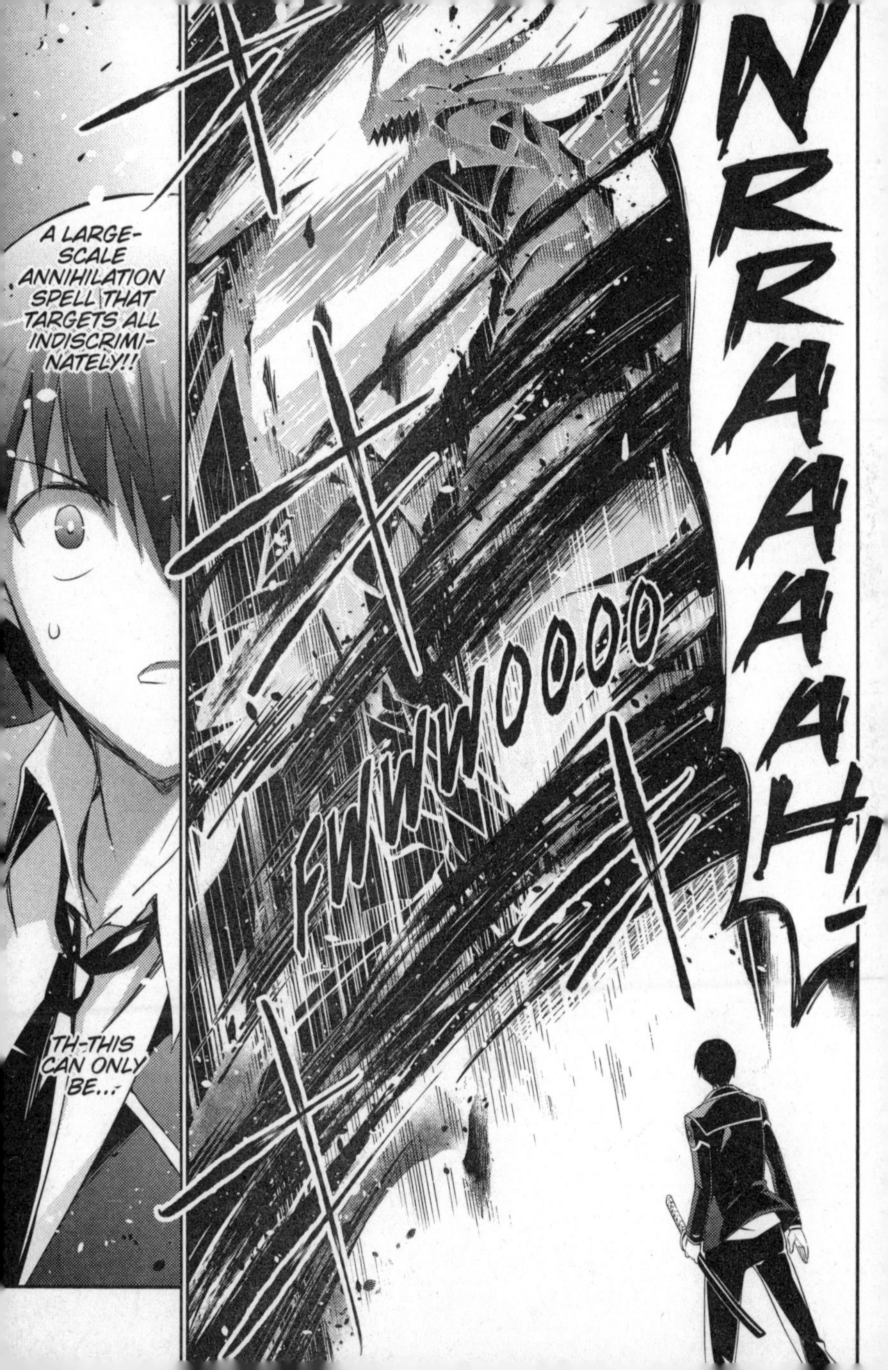
NRRAAAAH!!
FWWWOOOOO
A LARGE-SCALE ANNIHILATION SPELL THAT TARGETS ALL INDISCRIMINATELY!!
TH-THIS CAN ONLY BE...

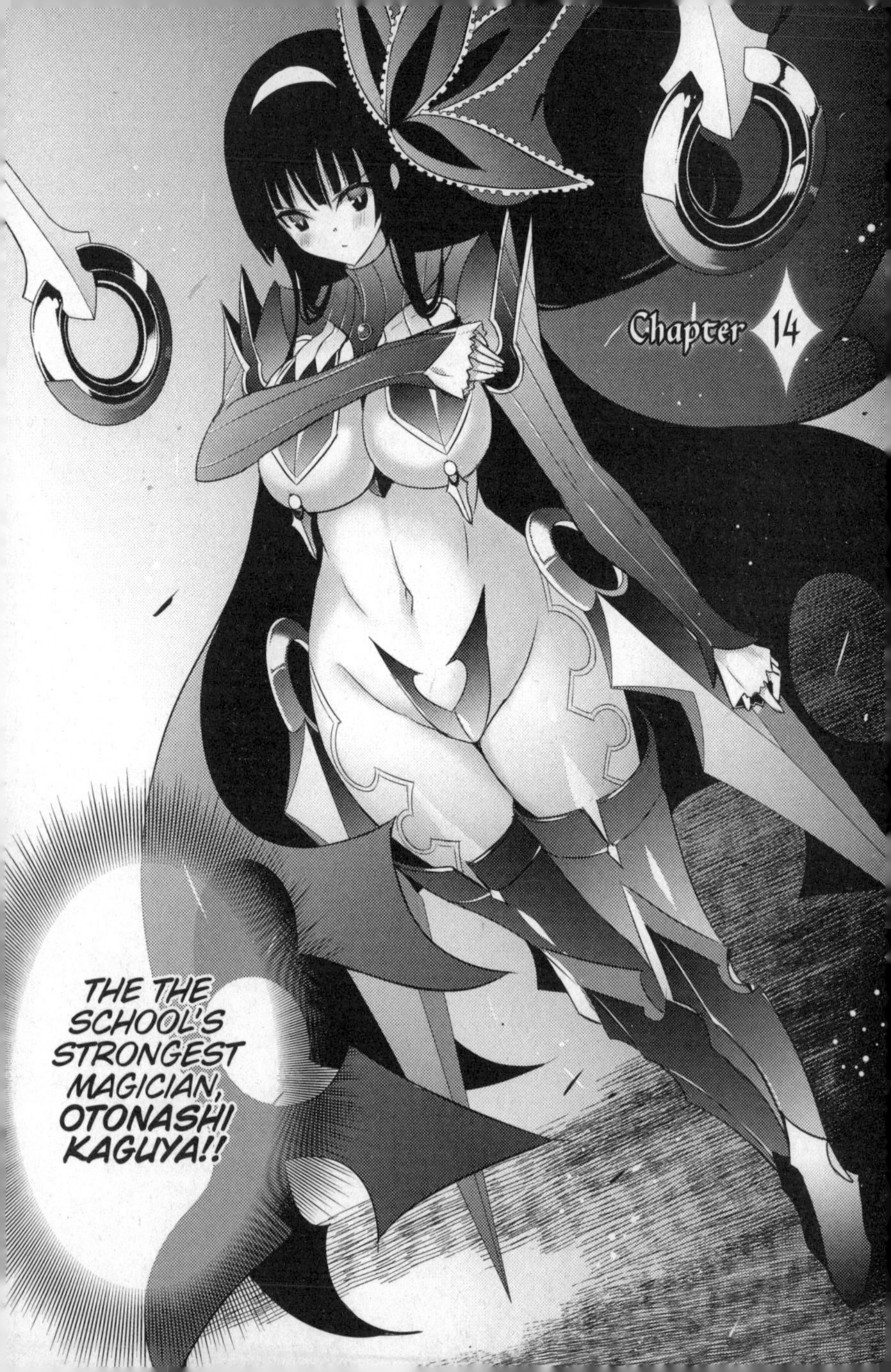
Chapter 14
THE THE SCHOOL'S STRONGEST MAGICIAN, OTONASHI KAGUYA!!

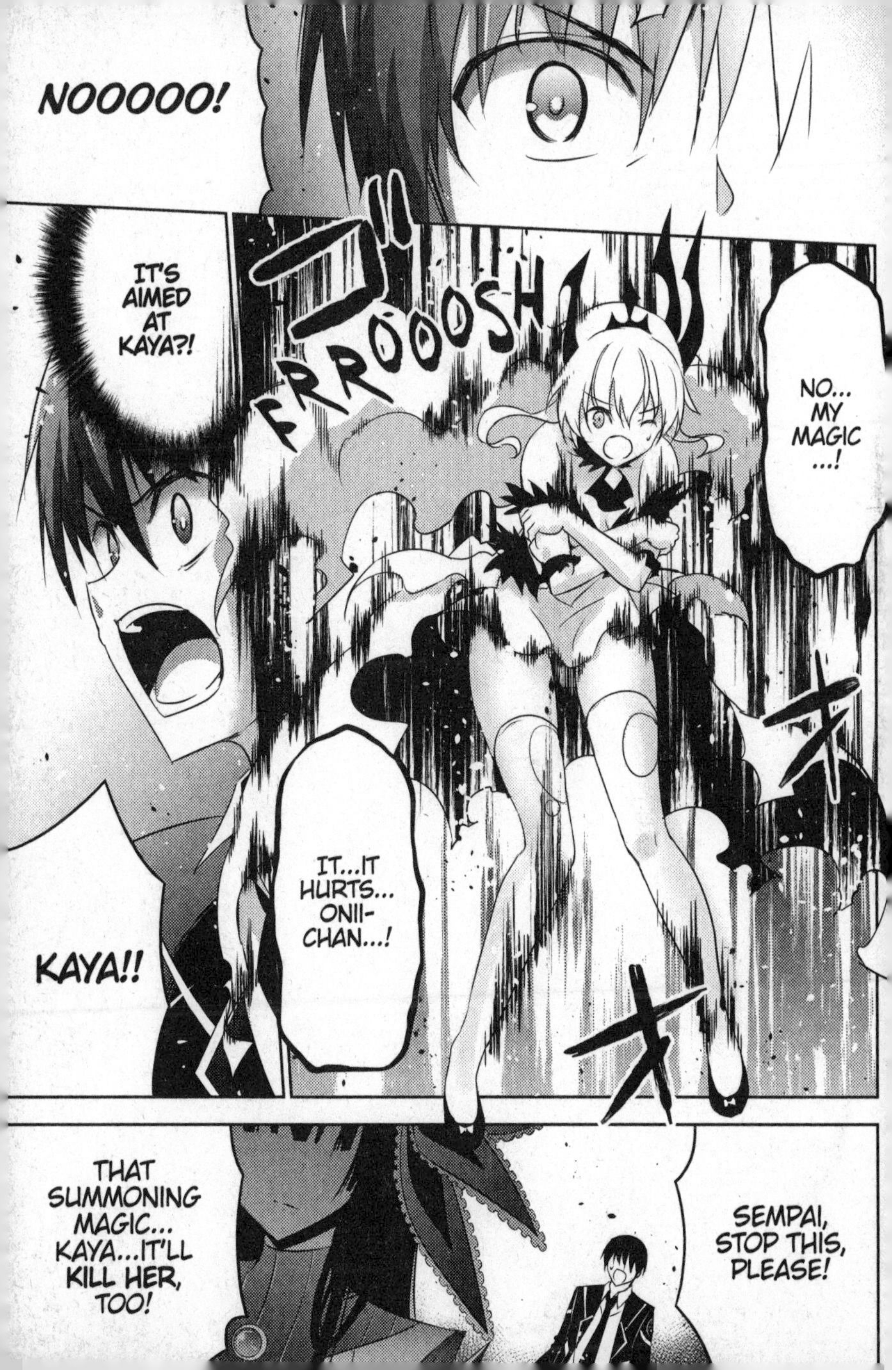
NOOOOO!
NO... MY MAGIC ...!
FRROOOSH
IT'S AIMED AT KAYA?!
IT...IT HURTS... ONII-CHAN...!
KAYA!!
SEMPAI, STOP THIS, PLEASE!
THAT SUMMONING MAGIC... KAYA...IT'LL KILL HER, TOO!

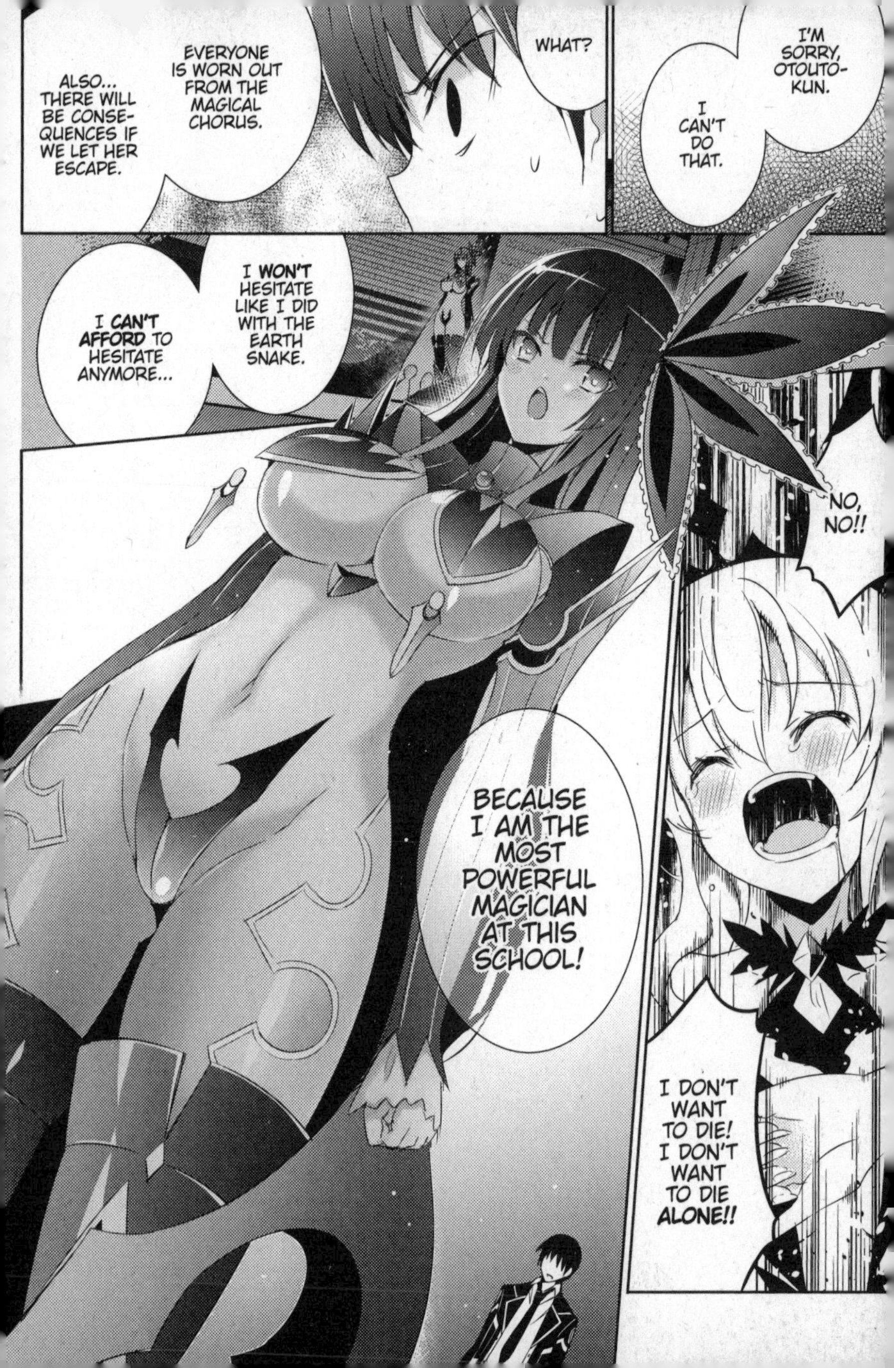
I'M SORRY, OTOUTO-KUN.
I CAN'T DO THAT.
WHAT?
EVERYONE IS WORN OUT FROM THE MAGICAL CHORUS.
ALSO... THERE WILL BE CONSE-QUENCES IF WE LET HER ESCAPE.
NO, NO!!
I DON'T WANT TO DIE! I DON'T WANT TO DIE **ALONE**!!
I **WON'T** HESITATE LIKE I DID WITH THE EARTH SNAKE.
I **CAN'T AFFORD** TO HESITATE ANYMORE...
BECAUSE I AM THE MOST POWERFUL MAGICIAN AT THIS SCHOOL!

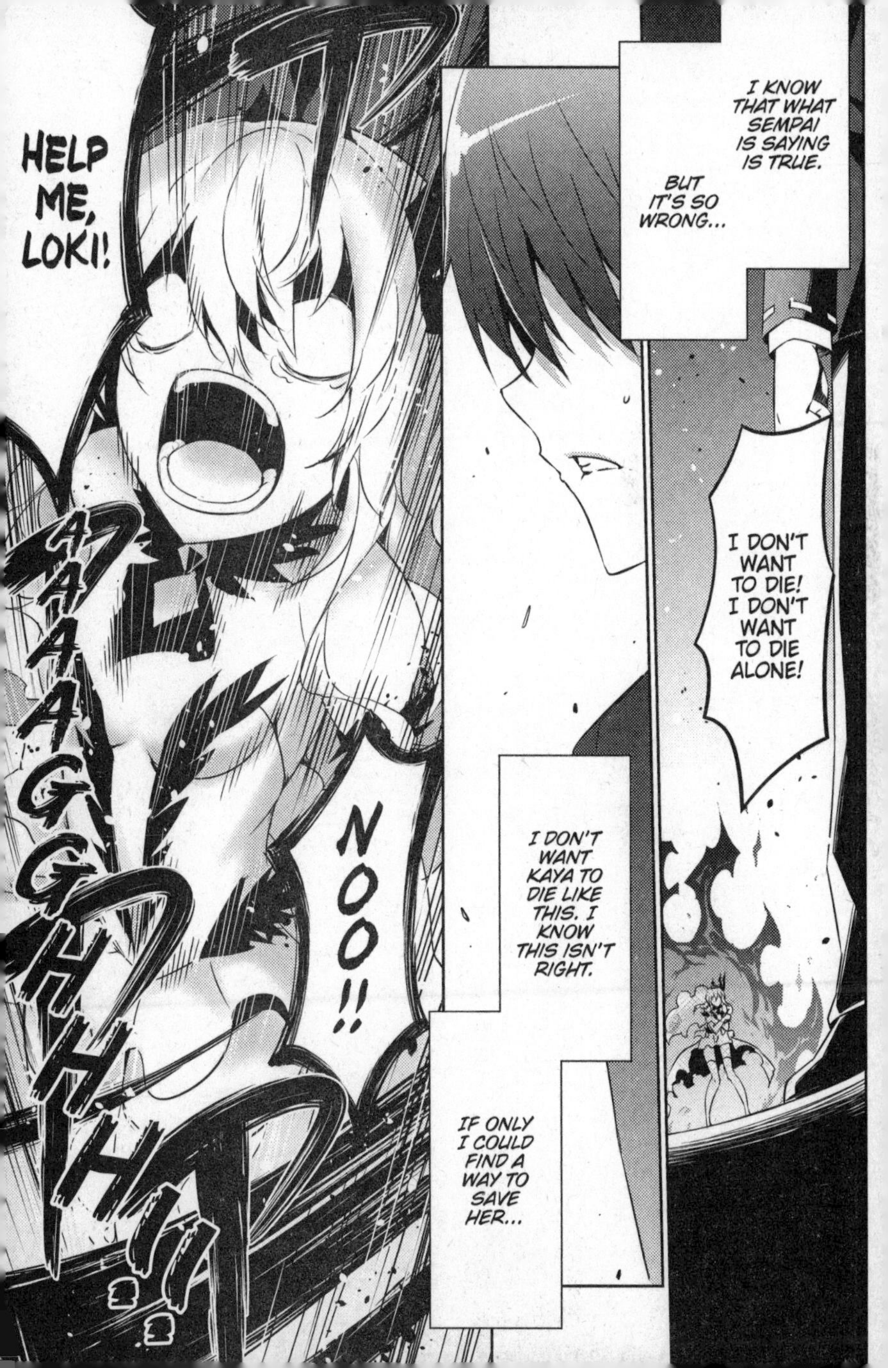
I KNOW THAT WHAT SEMPAI IS SAYING IS TRUE.
BUT IT'S SO WRONG...
I DON'T WANT TO DIE! I DON'T WANT TO DIE ALONE!
I DON'T WANT KAYA TO DIE LIKE THIS. I KNOW THIS ISN'T RIGHT.
IF ONLY I COULD FIND A WAY TO SAVE HER...
HELP ME, LOKI!
NOO!!
AAAAGGHHHH!!

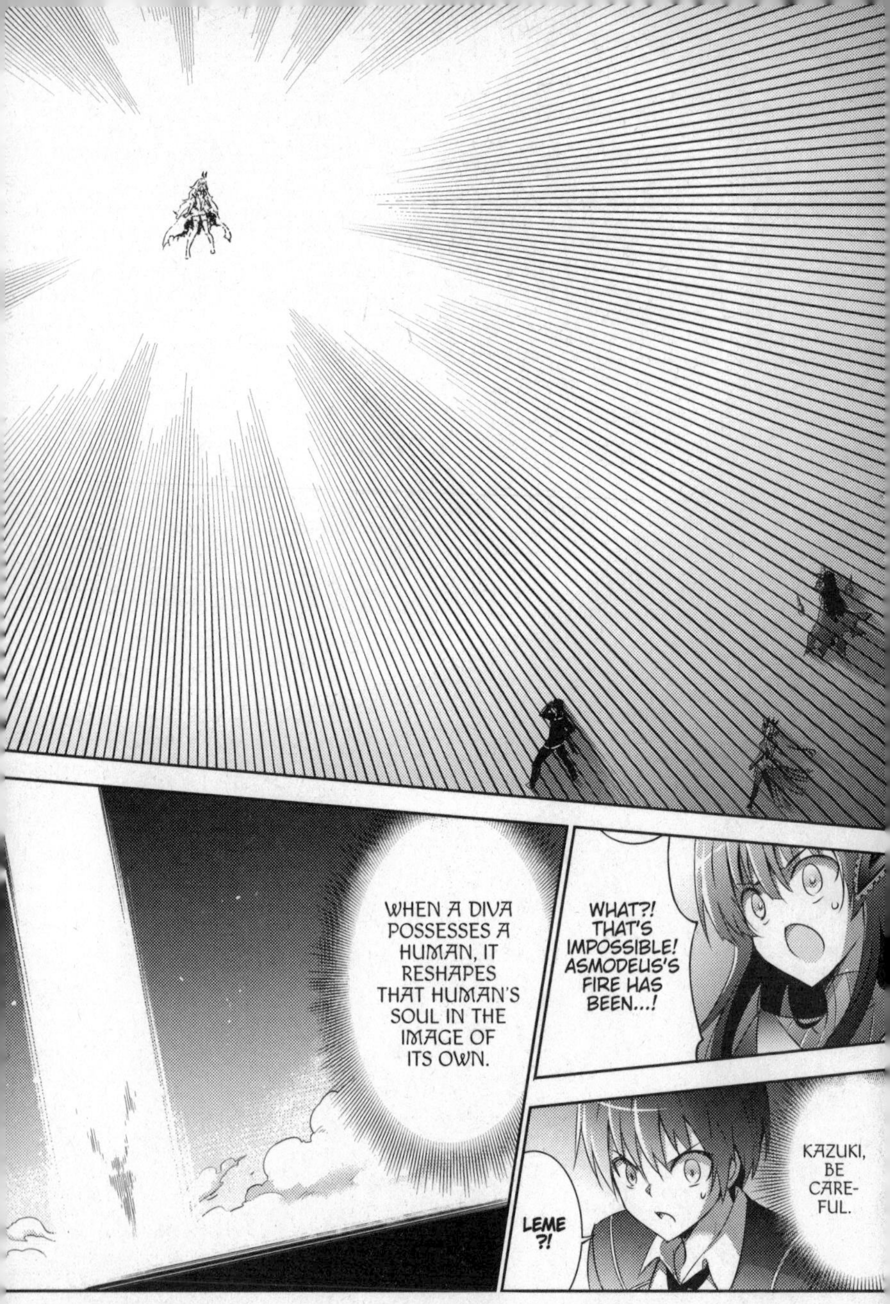
WHAT?! THAT'S IMPOSSIBLE! ASMODEUS'S FIRE HAS BEEN...!
KAZUKI, BE CARE-FUL.
LEME ?!
WHEN A DIVA POSSESSES A HUMAN, IT RESHAPES THAT HUMAN'S SOUL IN THE IMAGE OF ITS OWN.

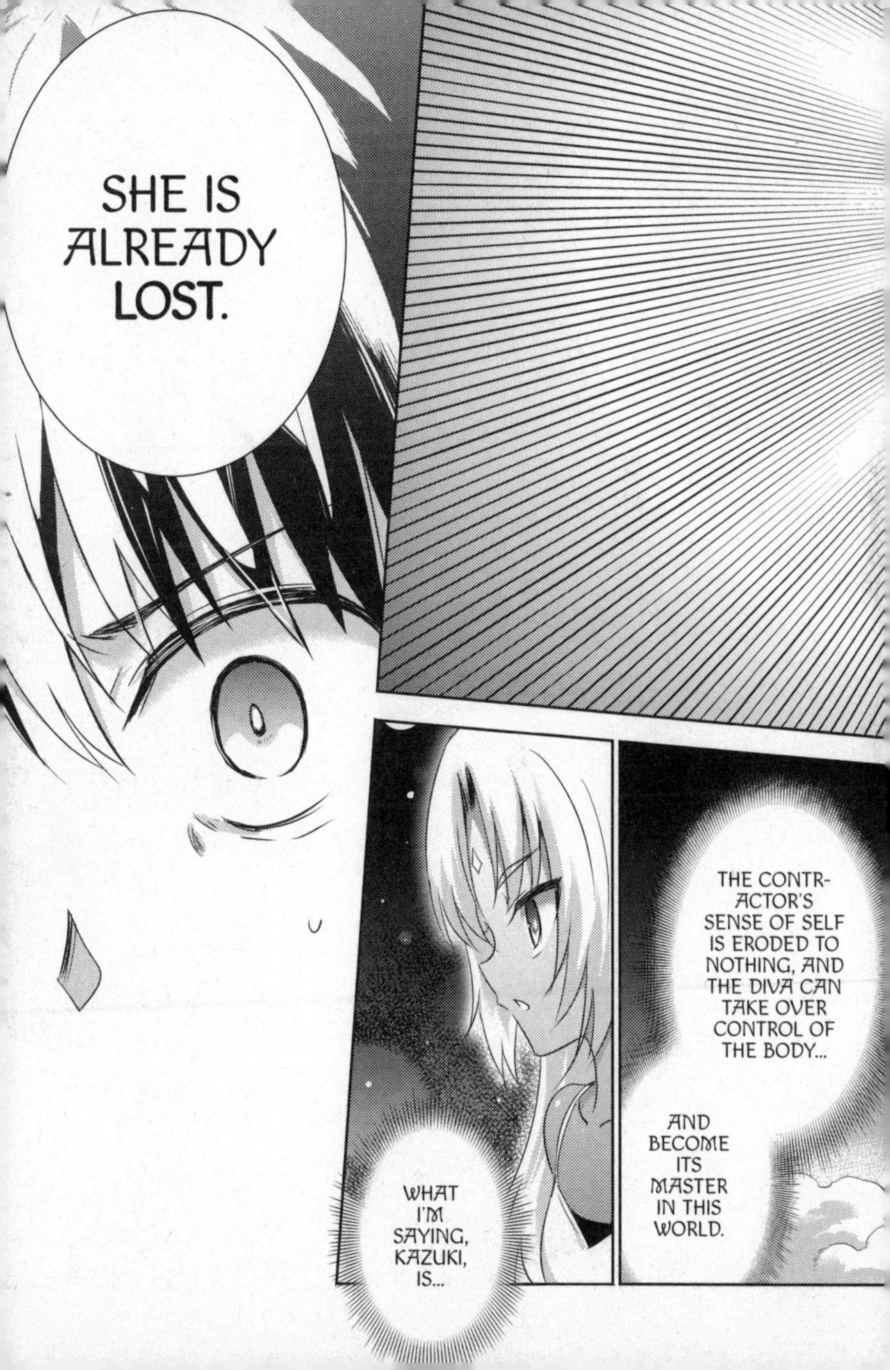
THE CONTR-ACTOR'S SENSE OF SELF IS ERODED TO NOTHING, AND THE DIVA CAN TAKE OVER CONTROL OF THE BODY...
AND BECOME ITS MASTER IN THIS WORLD.
WHAT I'M SAYING, KAZUKI, IS...
SHE IS ALREADY LOST.

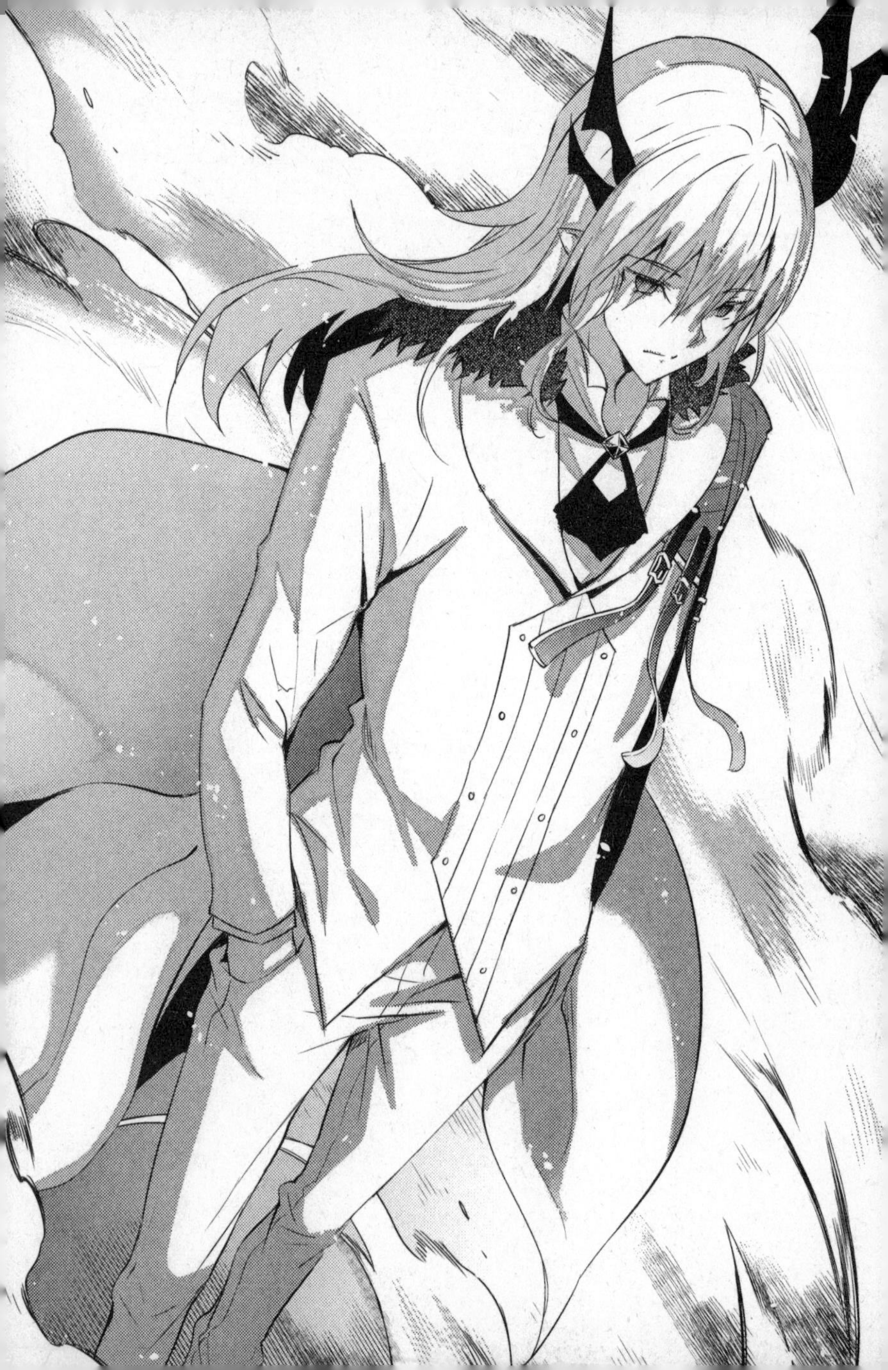

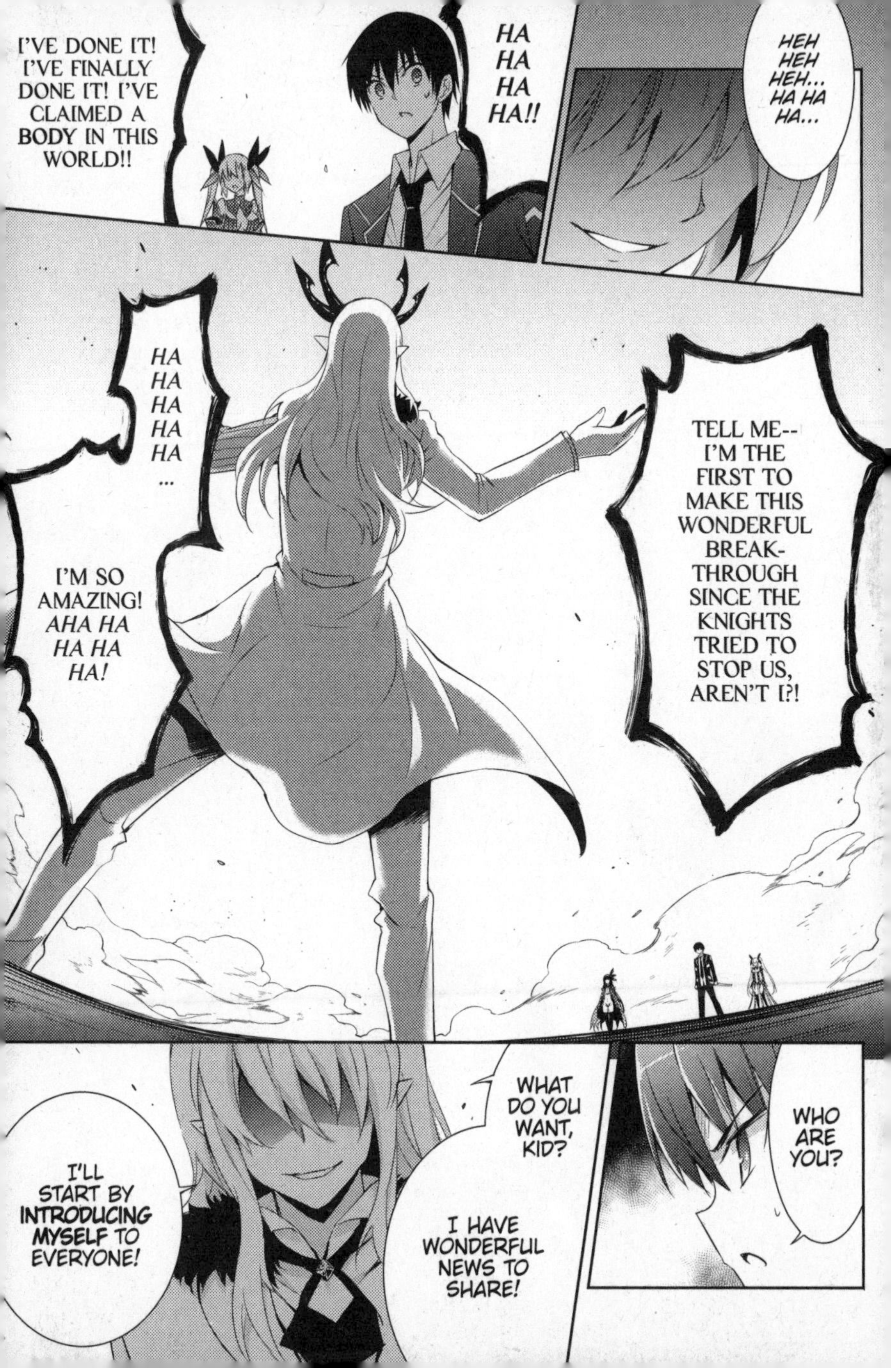

HEH HEH HEH... HA HA HA...
HA HA HA HA!!
I'VE DONE IT! I'VE FINALLY DONE IT! I'VE CLAIMED A BODY IN THIS WORLD!!
TELL ME-- I'M THE FIRST TO MAKE THIS WONDERFUL BREAK-THROUGH SINCE THE KNIGHTS TRIED TO STOP US, AREN'T I?!
HA HA HA HA HA ...
I'M SO AMAZING! AHA HA HA HA HA!
WHO ARE YOU?
WHAT DO YOU WANT, KID?
I HAVE WONDERFUL NEWS TO SHARE!
I'LL START BY INTRODUCING MYSELF TO EVERYONE!

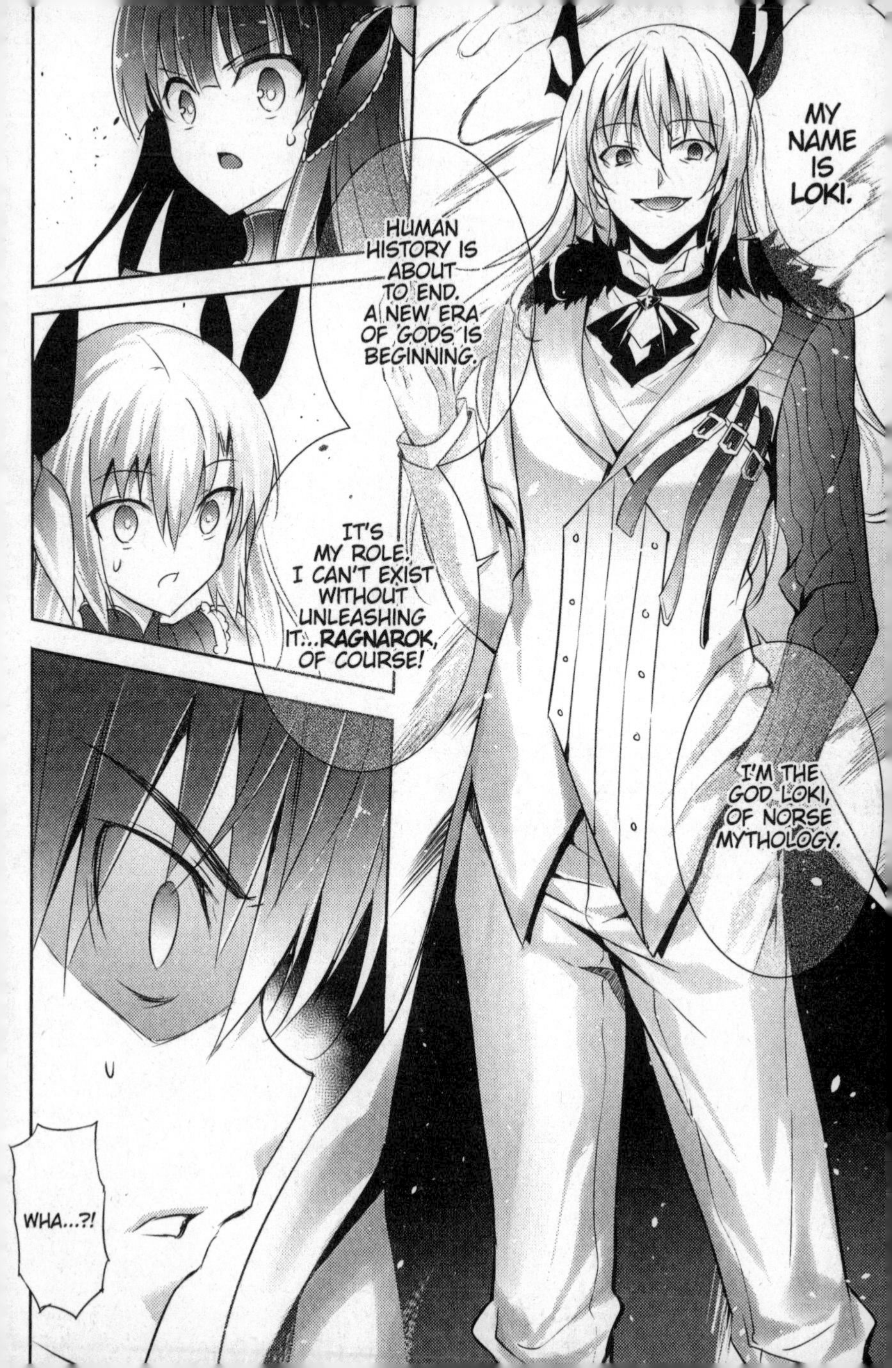
MY NAME IS LOKI.
HUMAN HISTORY IS ABOUT TO END. A NEW ERA OF GODS IS BEGINNING.
IT'S MY ROLE. I CAN'T EXIST WITHOUT UNLEASHING IT...RAGNAROK, OF COURSE!
I'M THE GOD LOKI, OF NORSE MYTHOLOGY.
WHA...?!

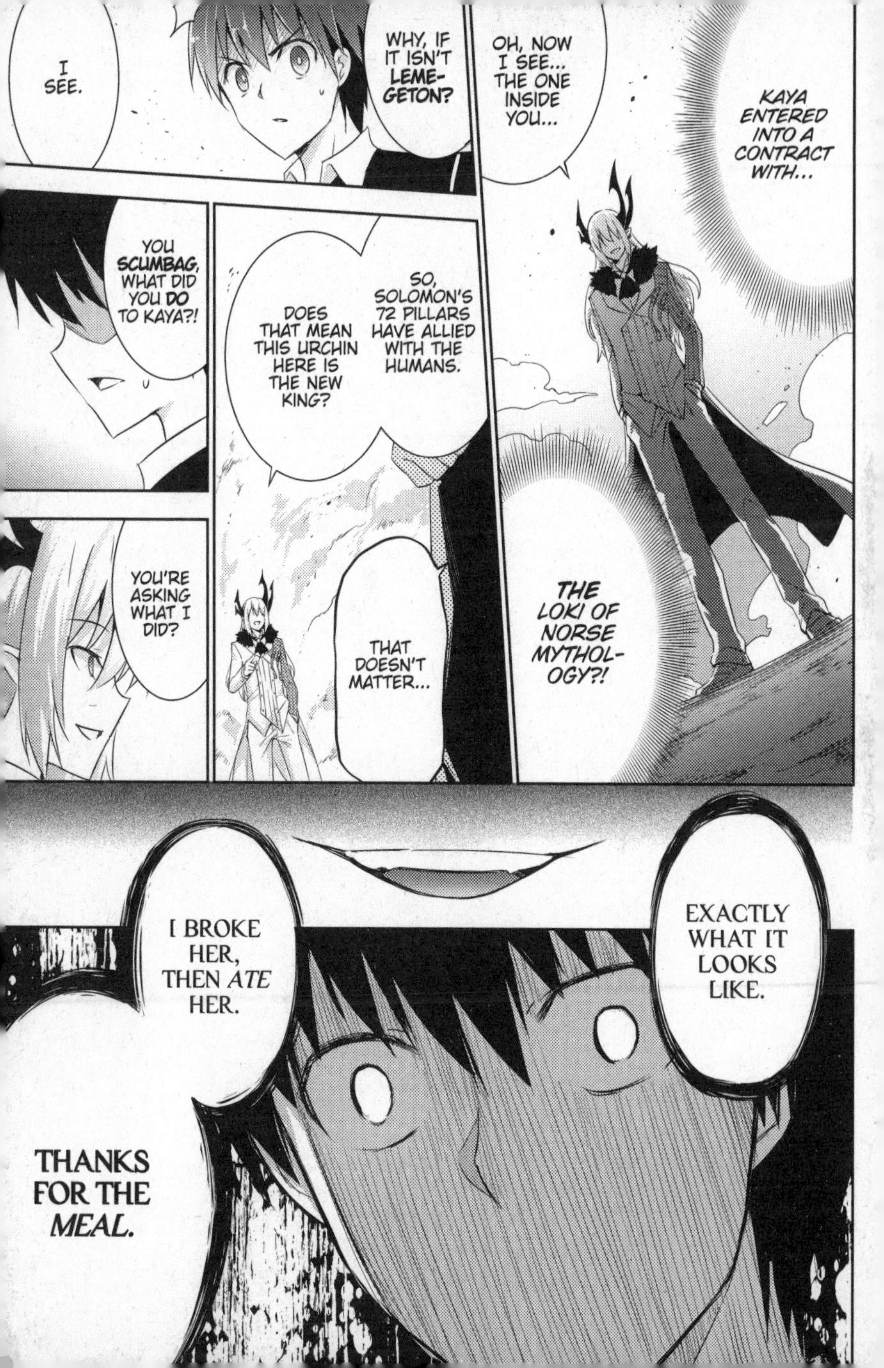
KAYA ENTERED INTO A CONTRACT WITH...
OH, NOW I SEE... THE ONE INSIDE YOU...
THE LOKI OF NORSE MYTHOLOGY?!
WHY, IF IT ISN'T LEMEGETON?
I SEE.
SO, SOLOMON'S 72 PILLARS HAVE ALLIED WITH THE HUMANS.
DOES THAT MEAN THIS URCHIN HERE IS THE NEW KING?
THAT DOESN'T MATTER...
YOU SCUMBAG, WHAT DID YOU DO TO KAYA?!
YOU'RE ASKING WHAT I DID?
EXACTLY WHAT IT LOOKS LIKE.
I BROKE HER, THEN ATE HER.
THANKS FOR THE MEAL.

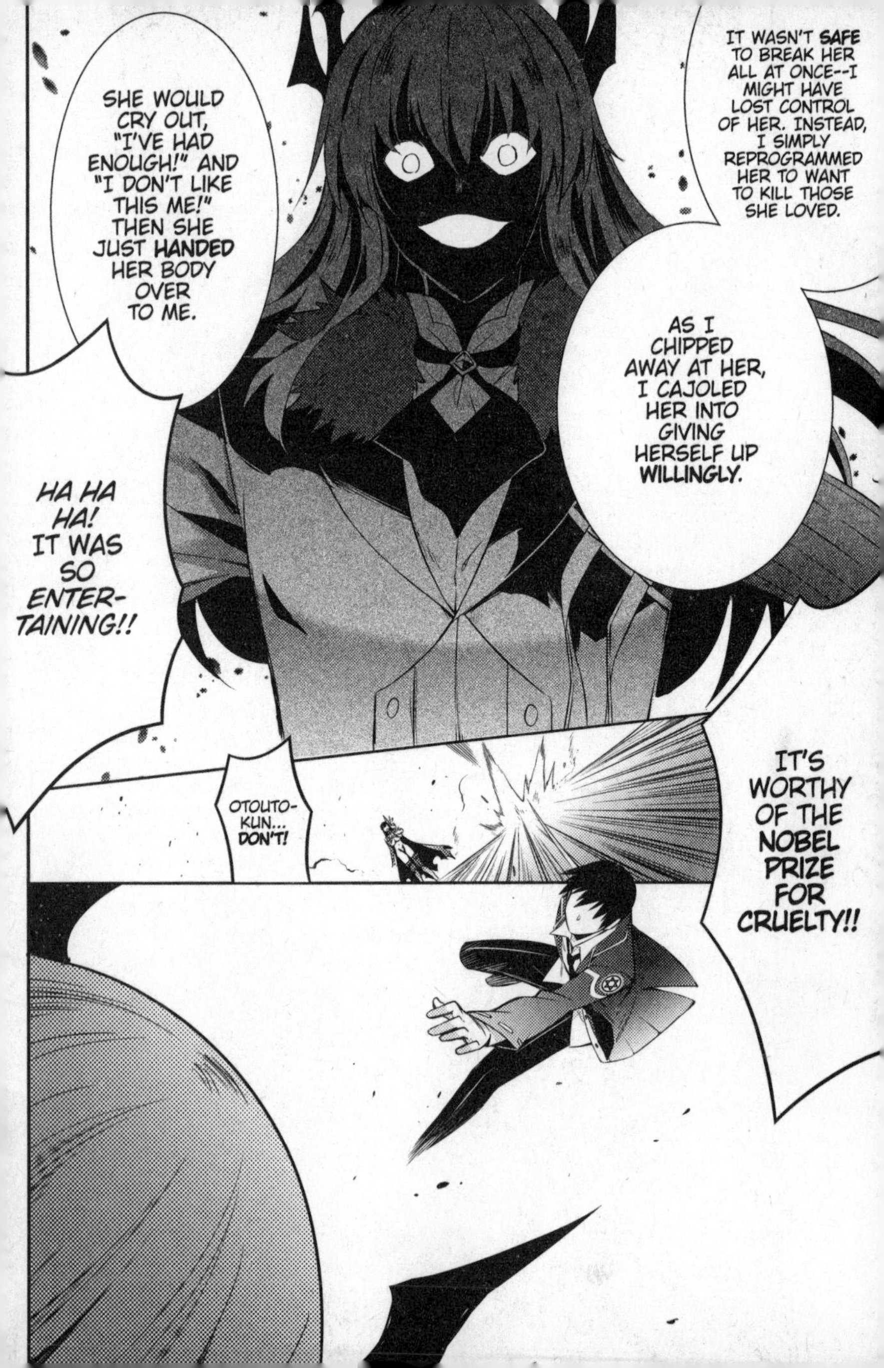
IT WASN'T SAFE TO BREAK HER ALL AT ONCE--I MIGHT HAVE LOST CONTROL OF HER. INSTEAD, I SIMPLY REPROGRAMMED HER TO WANT TO KILL THOSE SHE LOVED.
AS I CHIPPED AWAY AT HER, I CAJOLED HER INTO GIVING HERSELF UP WILLINGLY.
SHE WOULD CRY OUT, "I'VE HAD ENOUGH!" AND "I DON'T LIKE THIS ME!" THEN SHE JUST HANDED HER BODY OVER TO ME.
HA HA HA! IT WAS SO ENTER-TAINING!!
IT'S WORTHY OF THE NOBEL PRIZE FOR CRUELTY!!
OTOUTO-KUN... DON'T!

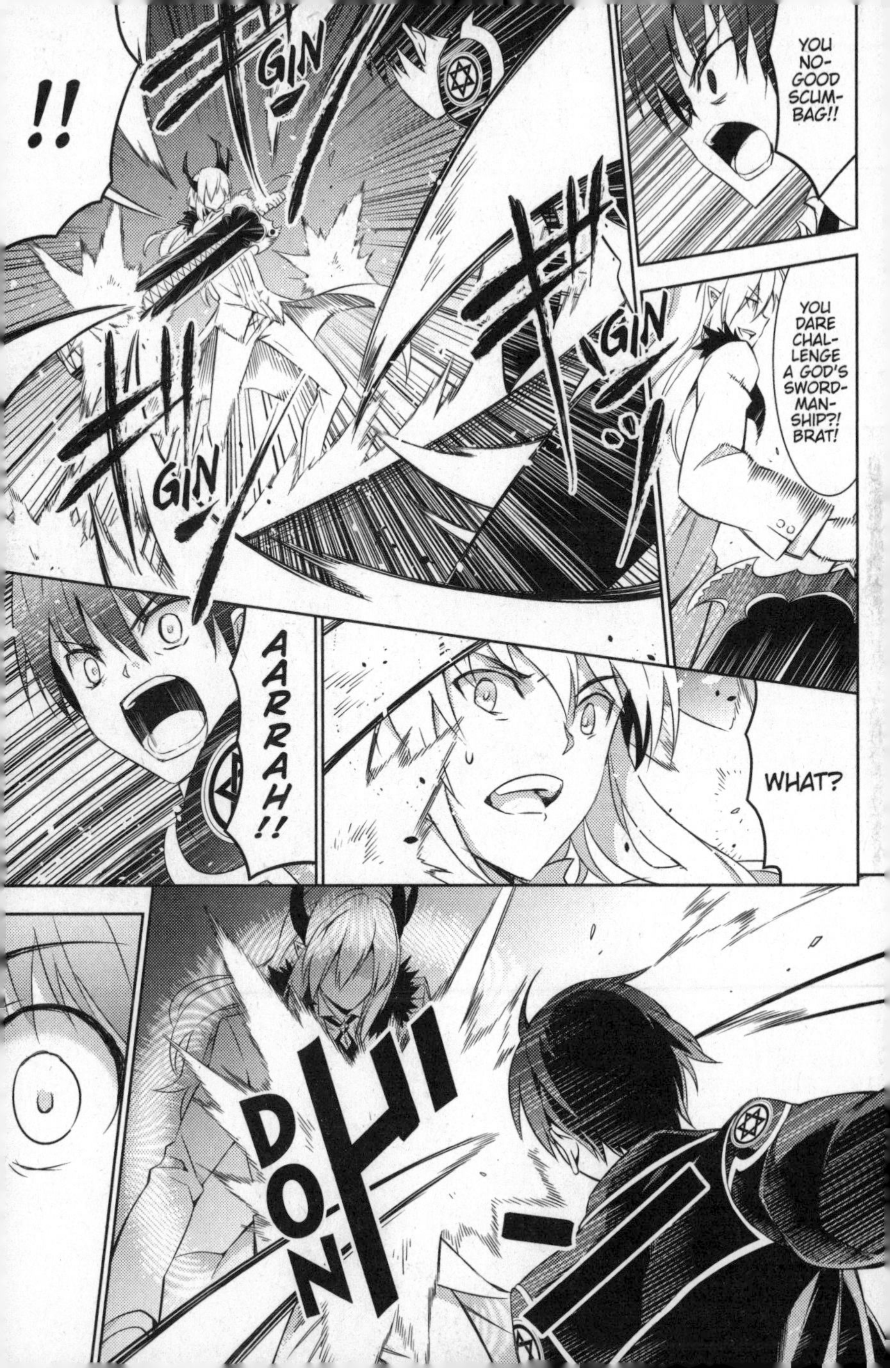
YOU NO-GOOD SCUMBAG!!
!!
GIN
GIN
GIN
YOU DARE CHALLENGE A GOD'S SWORDMANSHIP?! BRAT!
WHAT?
AARRAH!!
DON-

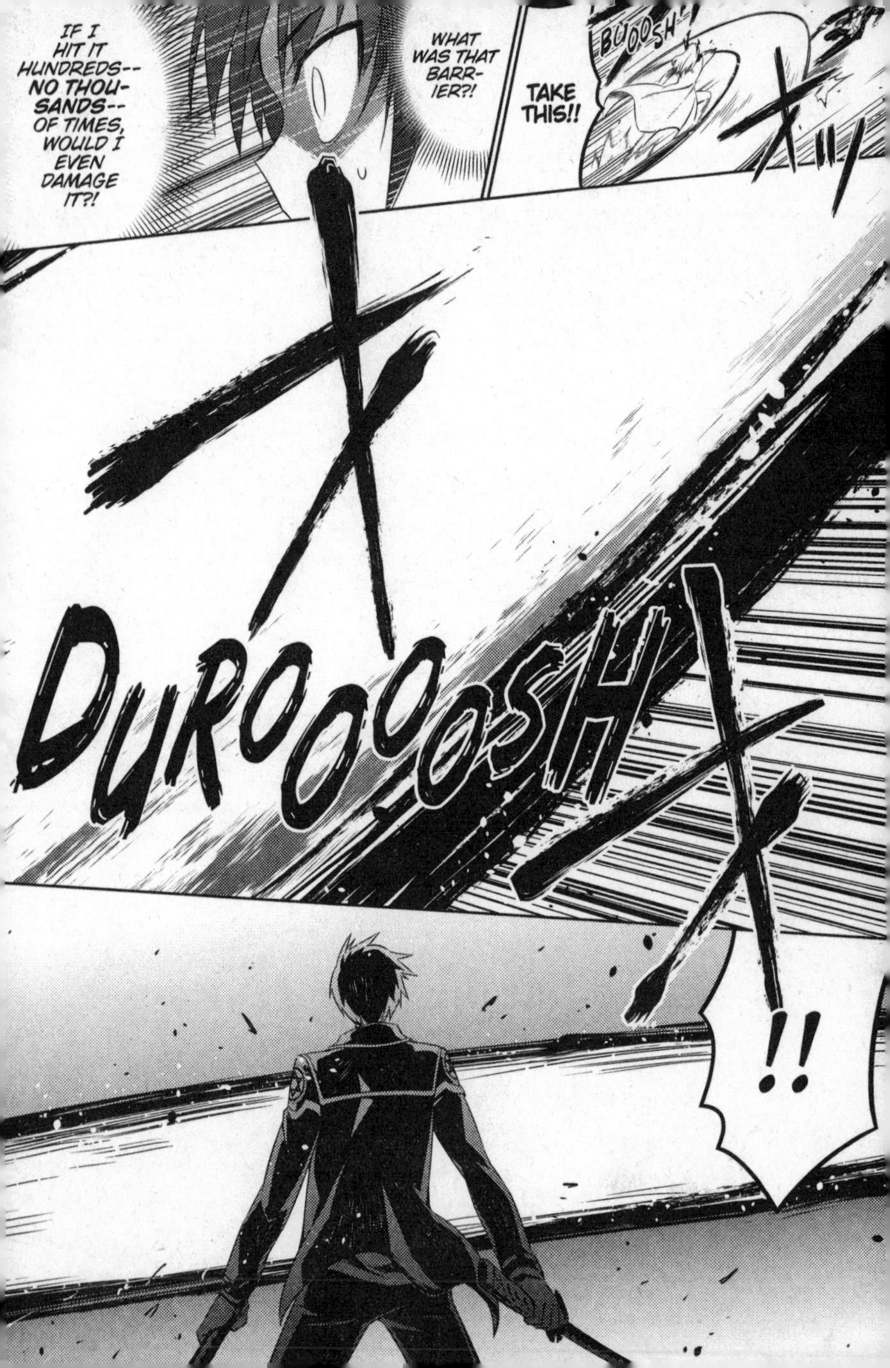
BUOOSH
TAKE THIS!!
WHAT WAS THAT BARRIER?!
IF I HIT IT HUNDREDS-- NO THOUSANDS-- OF TIMES, WOULD I EVEN DAMAGE IT?!
DUROOOOSH
!!

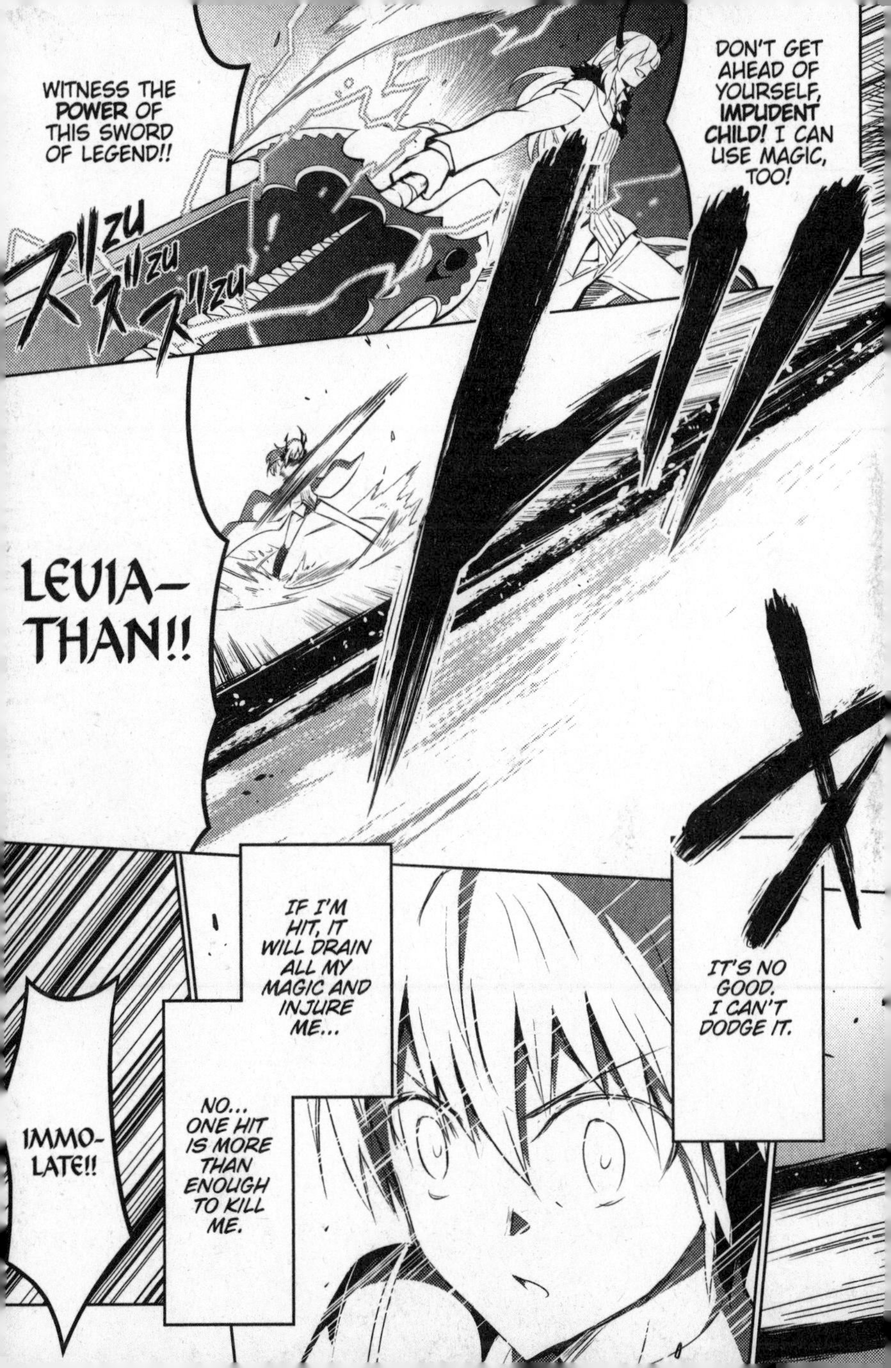

DON'T GET AHEAD OF YOURSELF, IMPUDENT CHILD! I CAN USE MAGIC, TOO!
WITNESS THE POWER OF THIS SWORD OF LEGEND!!
ズZU ズZU ズZU
LEVIA-THAN!!
IT'S NO GOOD. I CAN'T DODGE IT.
IF I'M HIT, IT WILL DRAIN ALL MY MAGIC AND INJURE ME...
NO... ONE HIT IS MORE THAN ENOUGH TO KILL ME.
IMMO-LATE!!

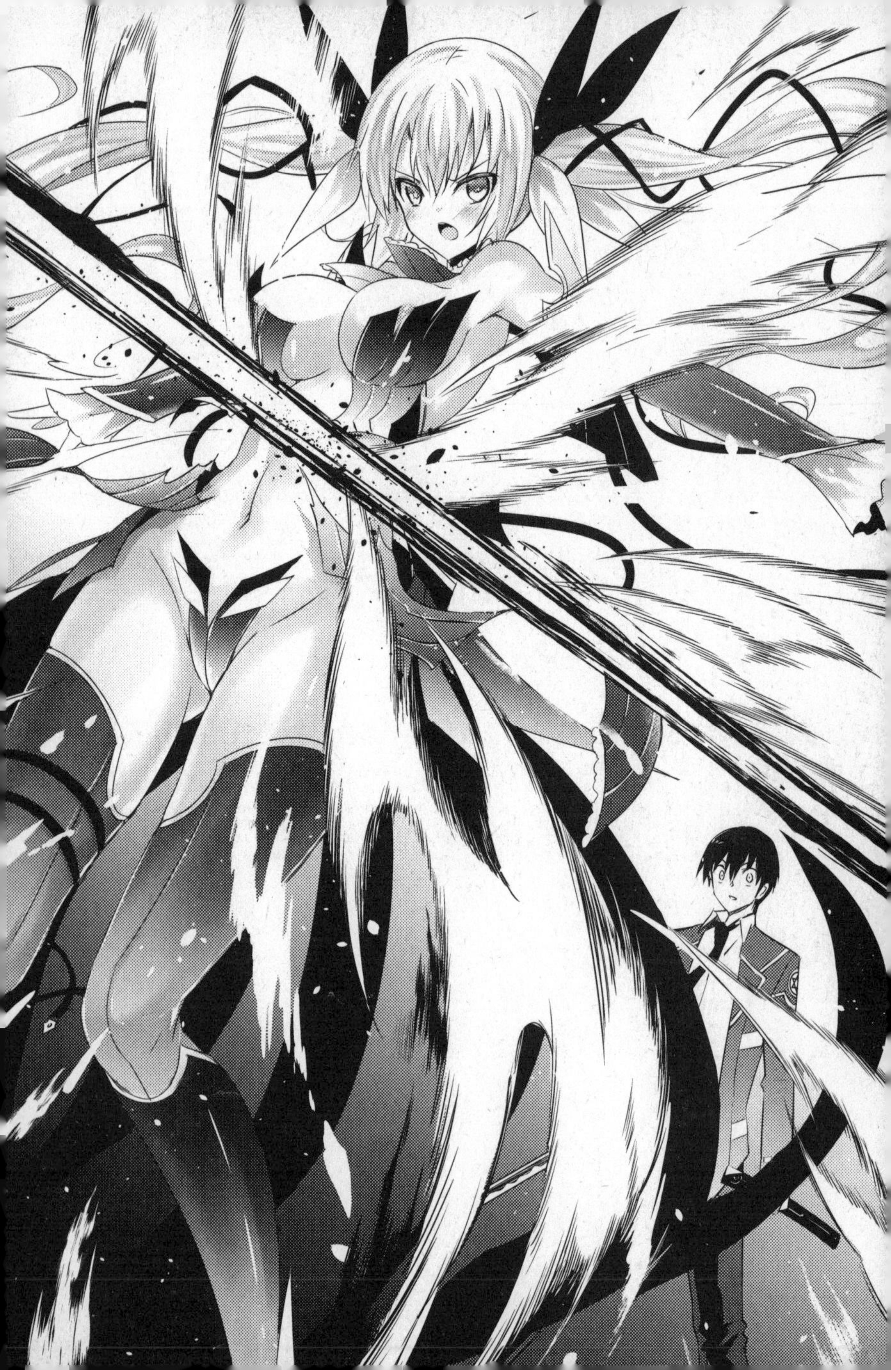

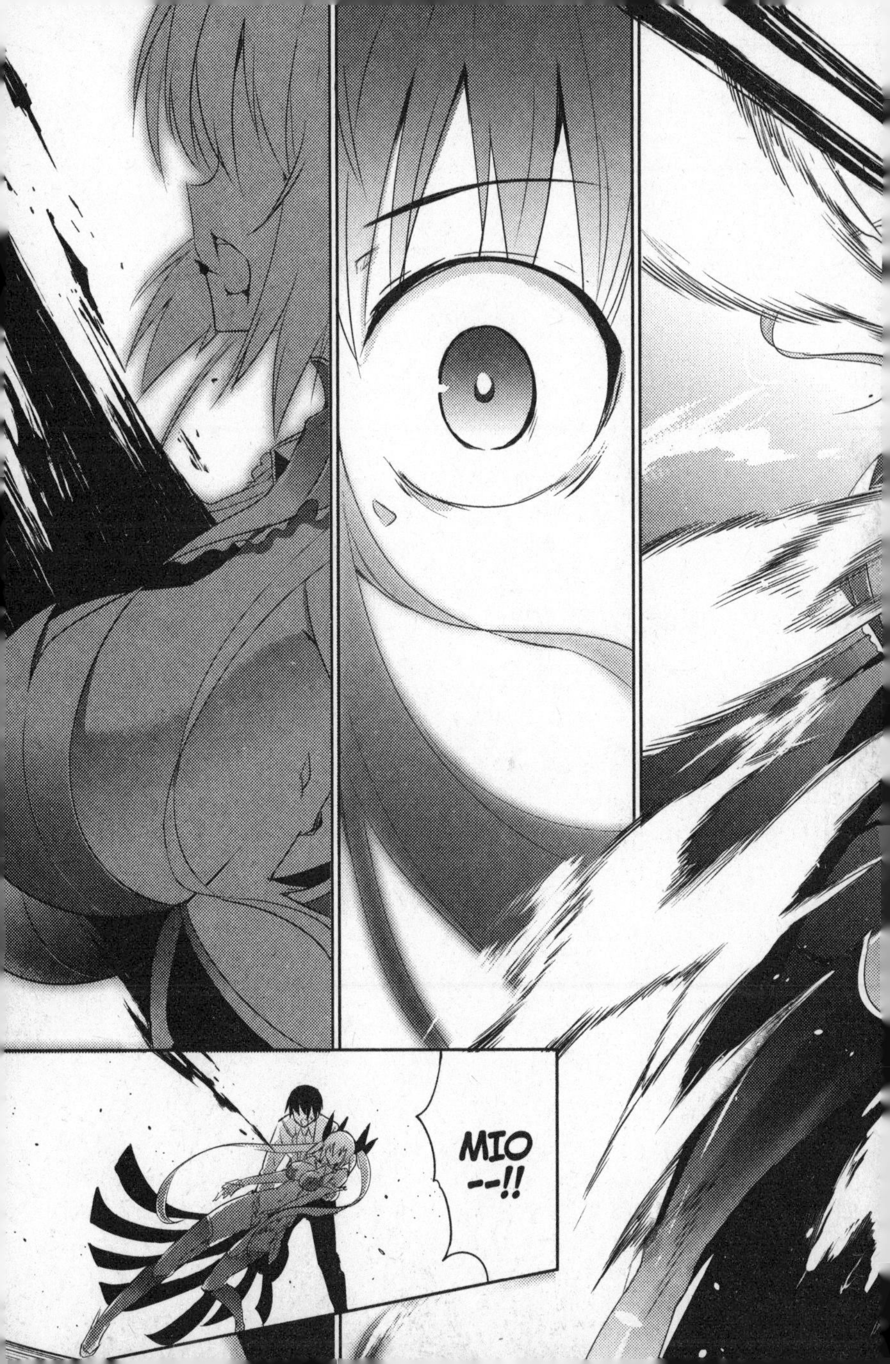
MIO
--!!

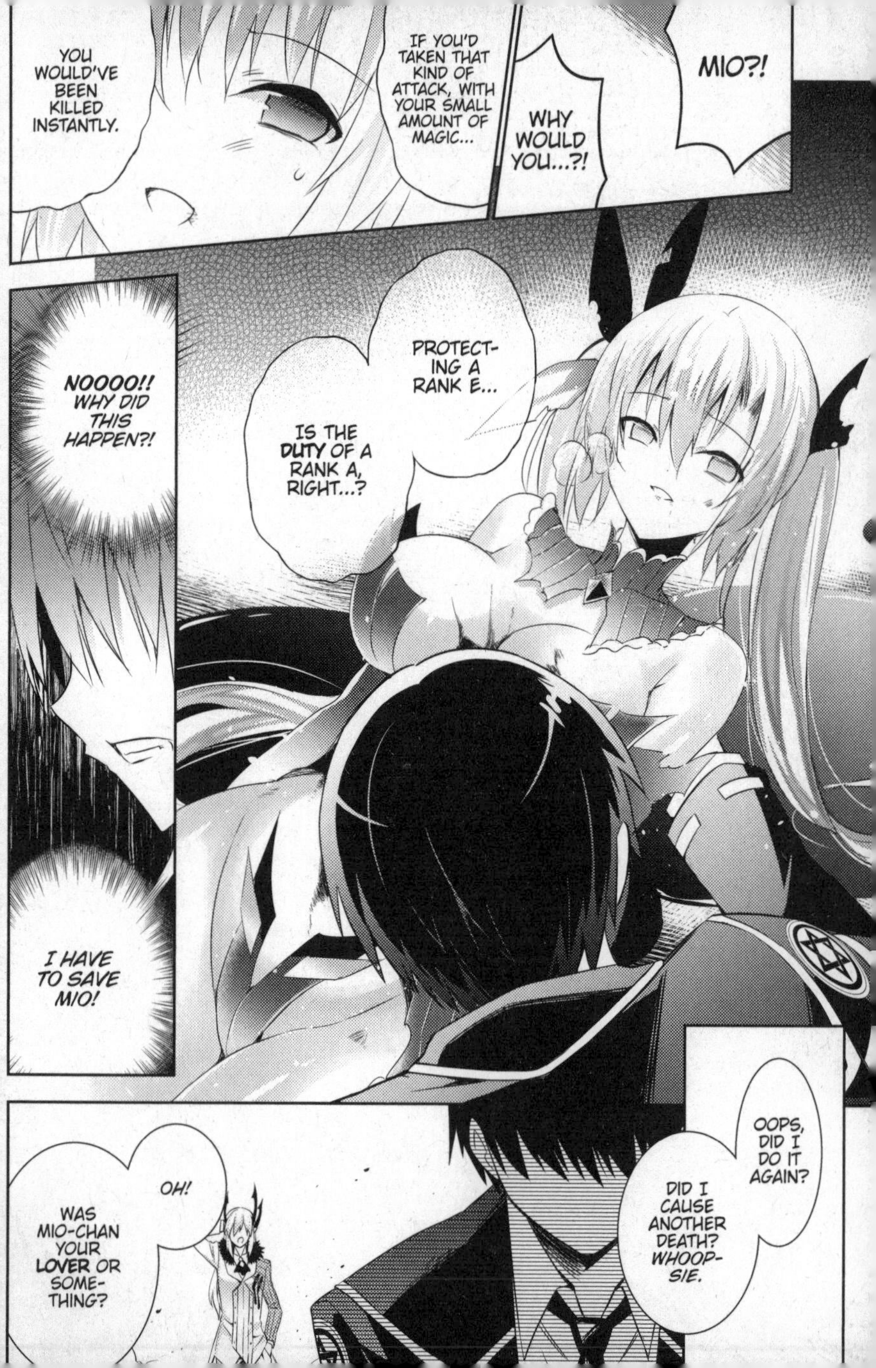
MIO?!
WHY WOULD YOU...?!
IF YOU'D TAKEN THAT KIND OF ATTACK, WITH YOUR SMALL AMOUNT OF MAGIC...
YOU WOULD'VE BEEN KILLED INSTANTLY.
PROTECTING A RANK E...
IS THE DUTY OF A RANK A, RIGHT...?
NOOOO!! WHY DID THIS HAPPEN?!
I HAVE TO SAVE MIO!
OOPS, DID I DO IT AGAIN?
DID I CAUSE ANOTHER DEATH? WHOOPSIE.
OH!
WAS MIO-CHAN YOUR LOVER OR SOMETHING?

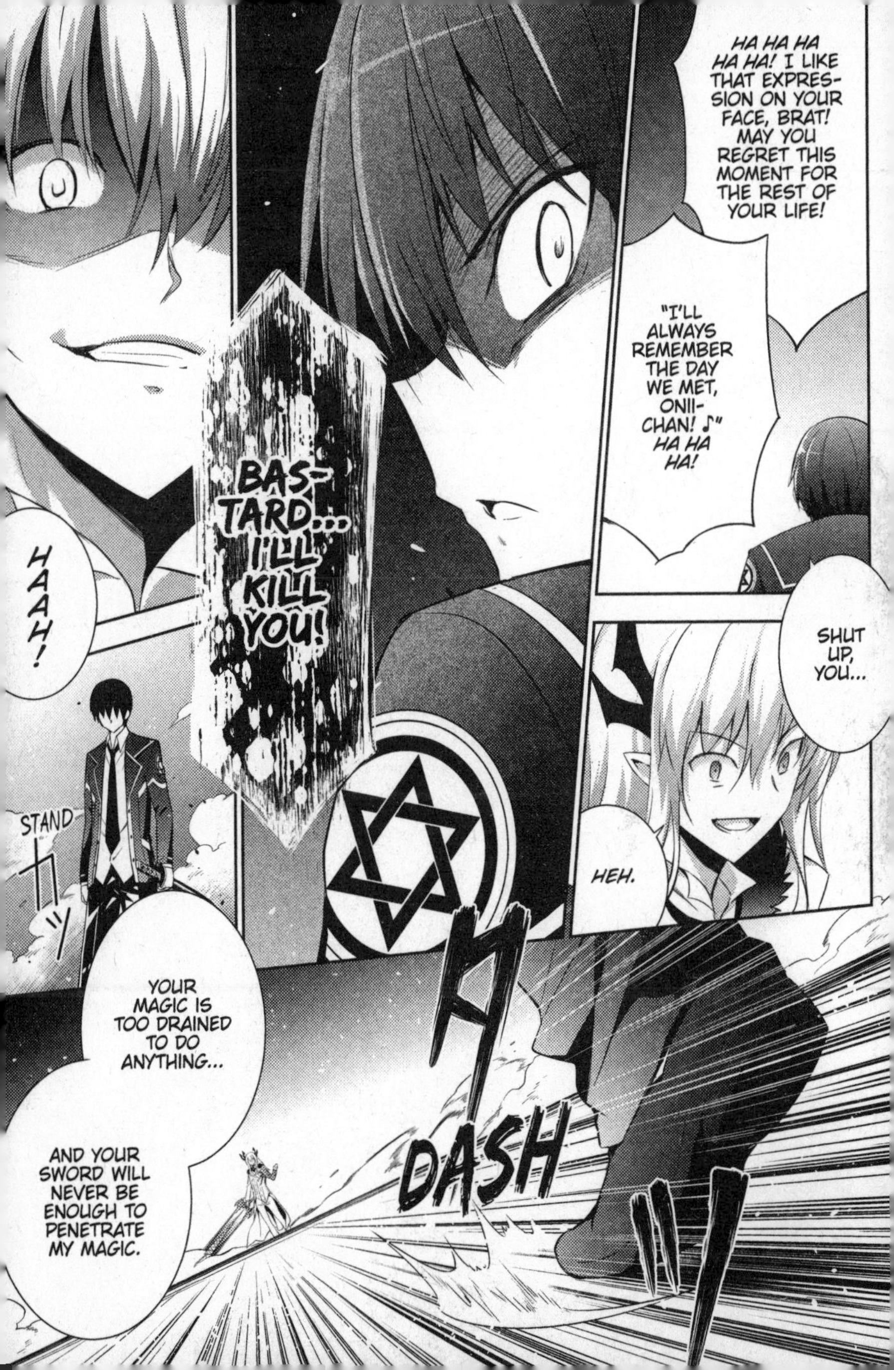

HA HA HA HA HA! I LIKE THAT EXPRESSION ON YOUR FACE, BRAT! MAY YOU REGRET THIS MOMENT FOR THE REST OF YOUR LIFE!
"I'LL ALWAYS REMEMBER THE DAY WE MET, ONII-CHAN! ♪" HA HA HA!
SHUT UP, YOU...
HEH.
BASTARD... I'LL KILL YOU!
HAAAH!
DASH
YOUR MAGIC IS TOO DRAINED TO DO ANYTHING...
AND YOUR SWORD WILL NEVER BE ENOUGH TO PENETRATE MY MAGIC.
STAND

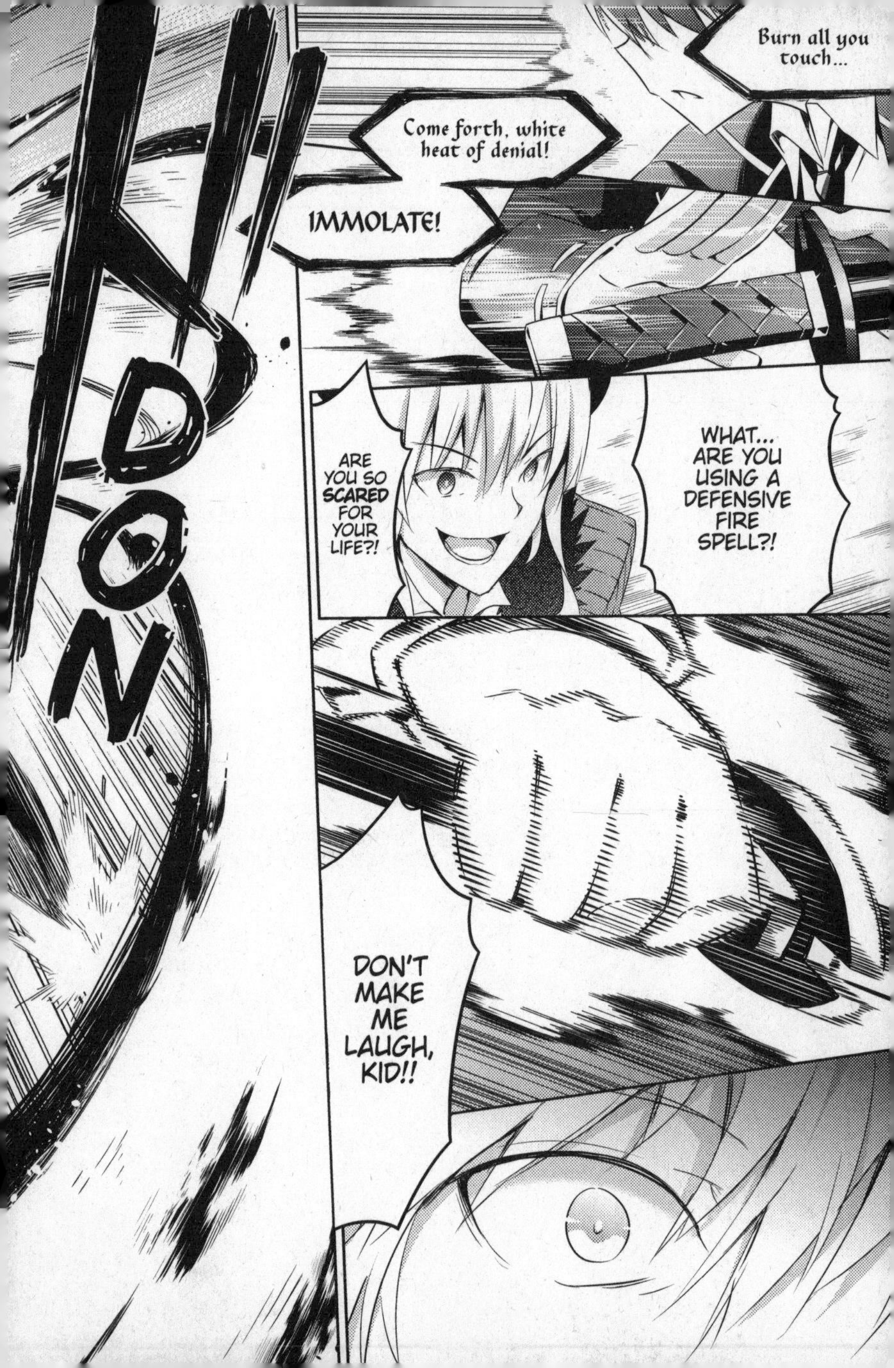
Burn all you touch...
Come forth, white heat of denial!
IMMOLATE!
WHAT... ARE YOU USING A DEFENSIVE FIRE SPELL?!
ARE YOU SO SCARED FOR YOUR LIFE?!
DON'T MAKE ME LAUGH, KID!!
DON

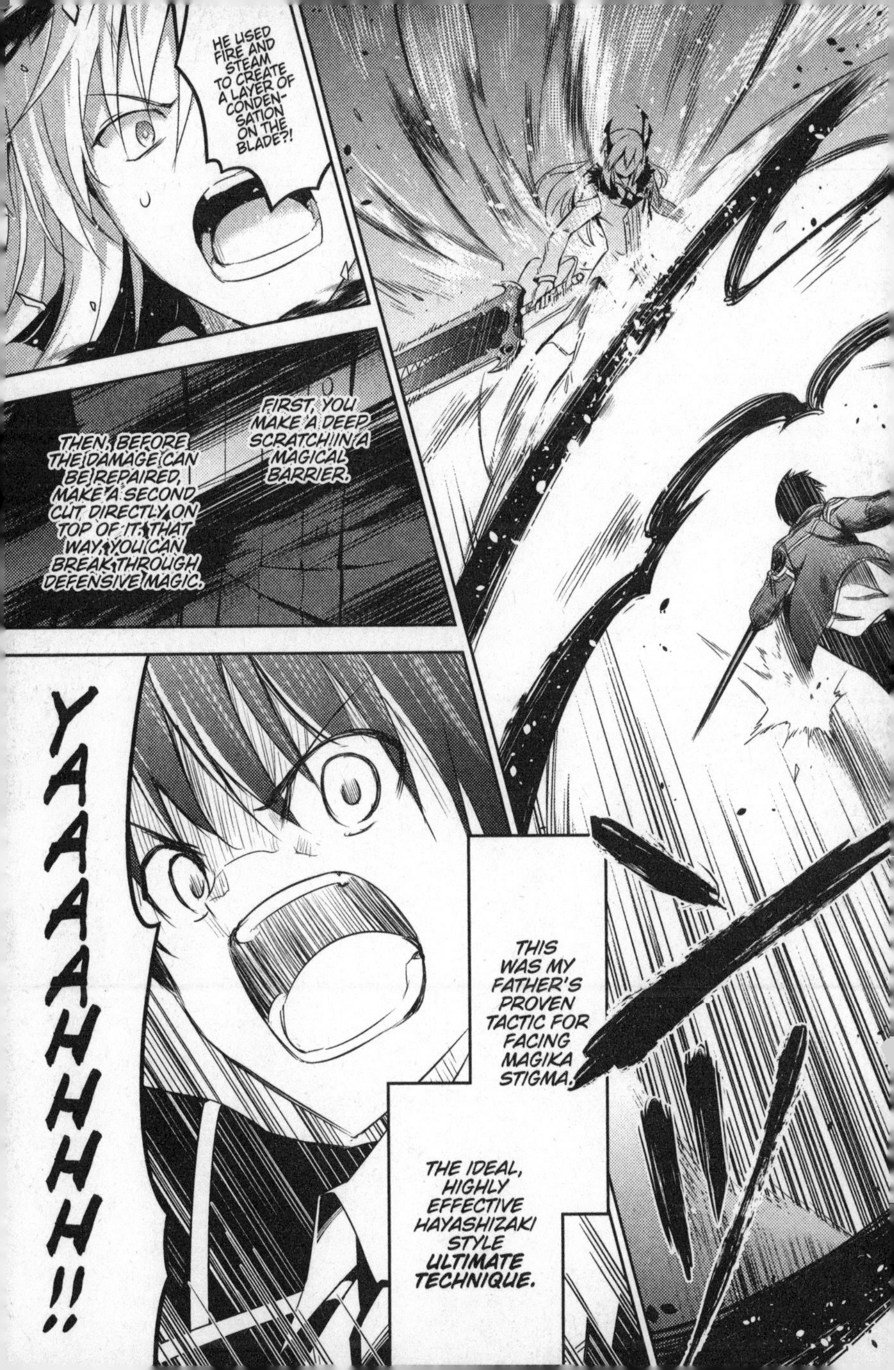

HE USED FIRE AND STEAM TO CREATE A LAYER OF CONDEN-SATION ON THE BLADE?!
FIRST, YOU MAKE A DEEP SCRATCH IN A MAGICAL BARRIER.
THEN, BEFORE THE DAMAGE CAN BE REPAIRED, MAKE A SECOND CUT DIRECTLY ON TOP OF IT. THAT WAY, YOU CAN BREAK THROUGH DEFENSIVE MAGIC.
YAAAAAHHHHH!!
THIS WAS MY FATHER'S PROVEN TACTIC FOR FACING MAGIKA STIGMA.
THE IDEAL, HIGHLY EFFECTIVE HAYASHIZAKI STYLE ULTIMATE TECHNIQUE.

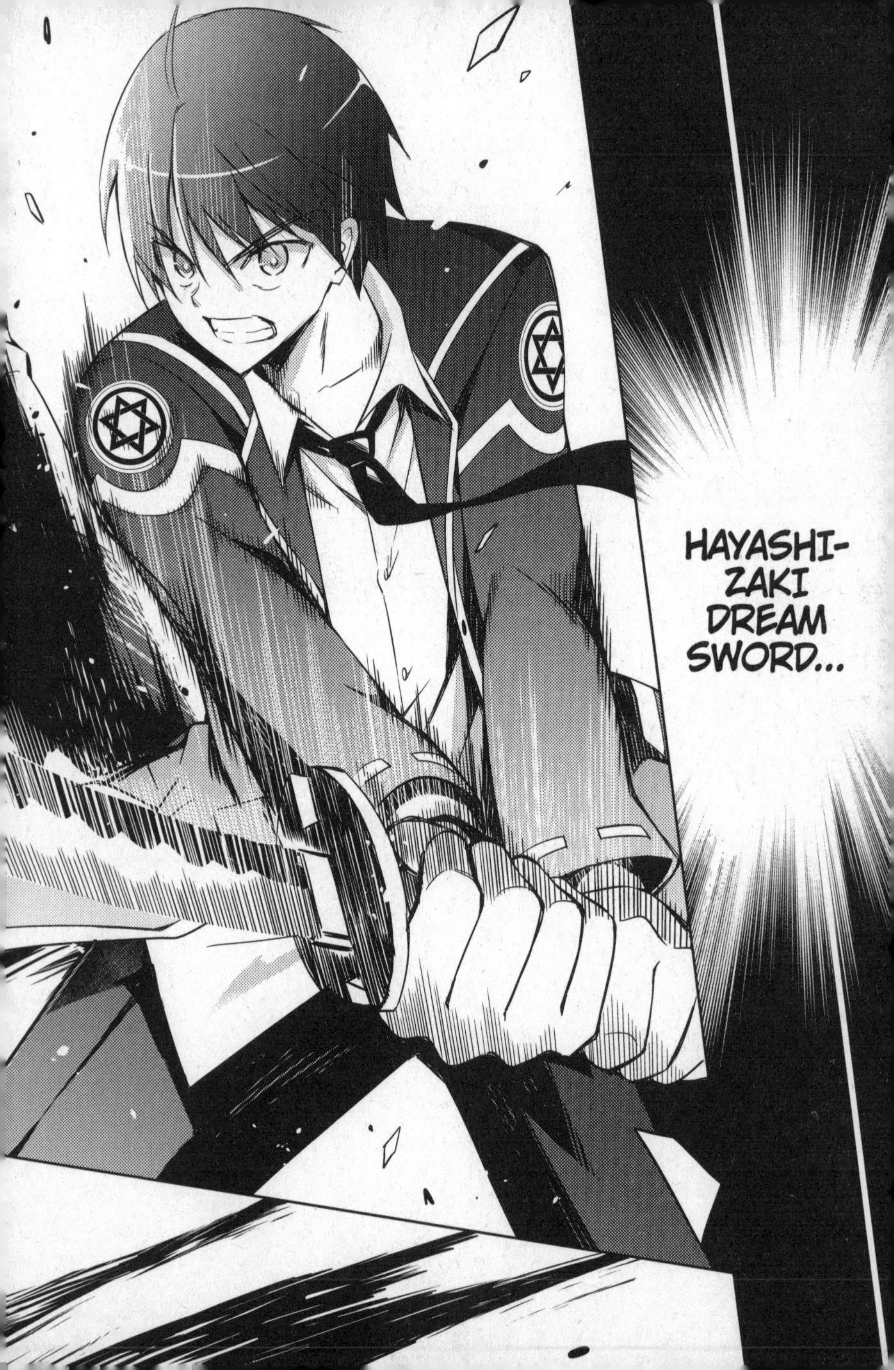
HAYASHI-
ZAKI
DREAM
SWORD...

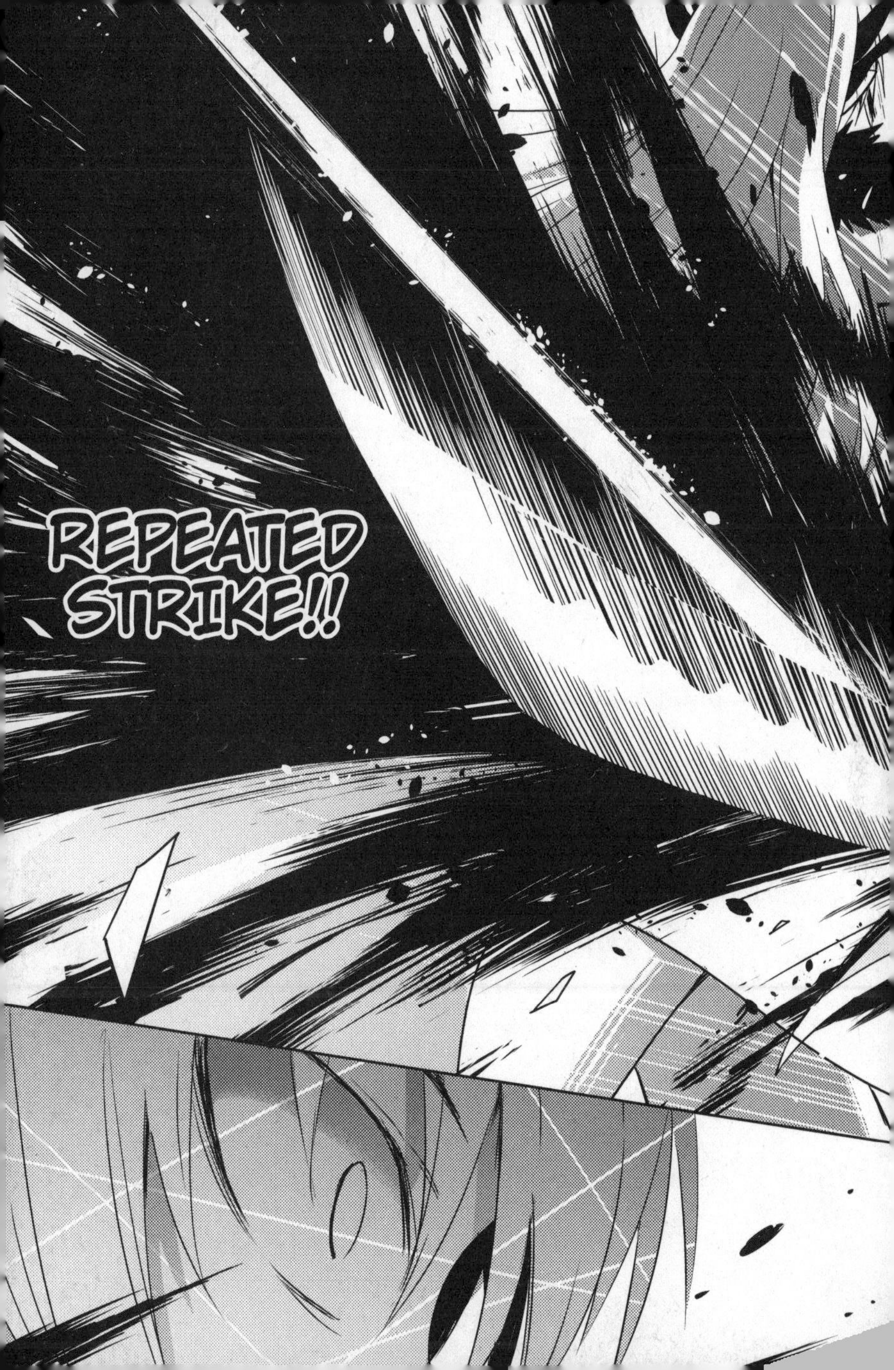
REPEATED STRIKE!!

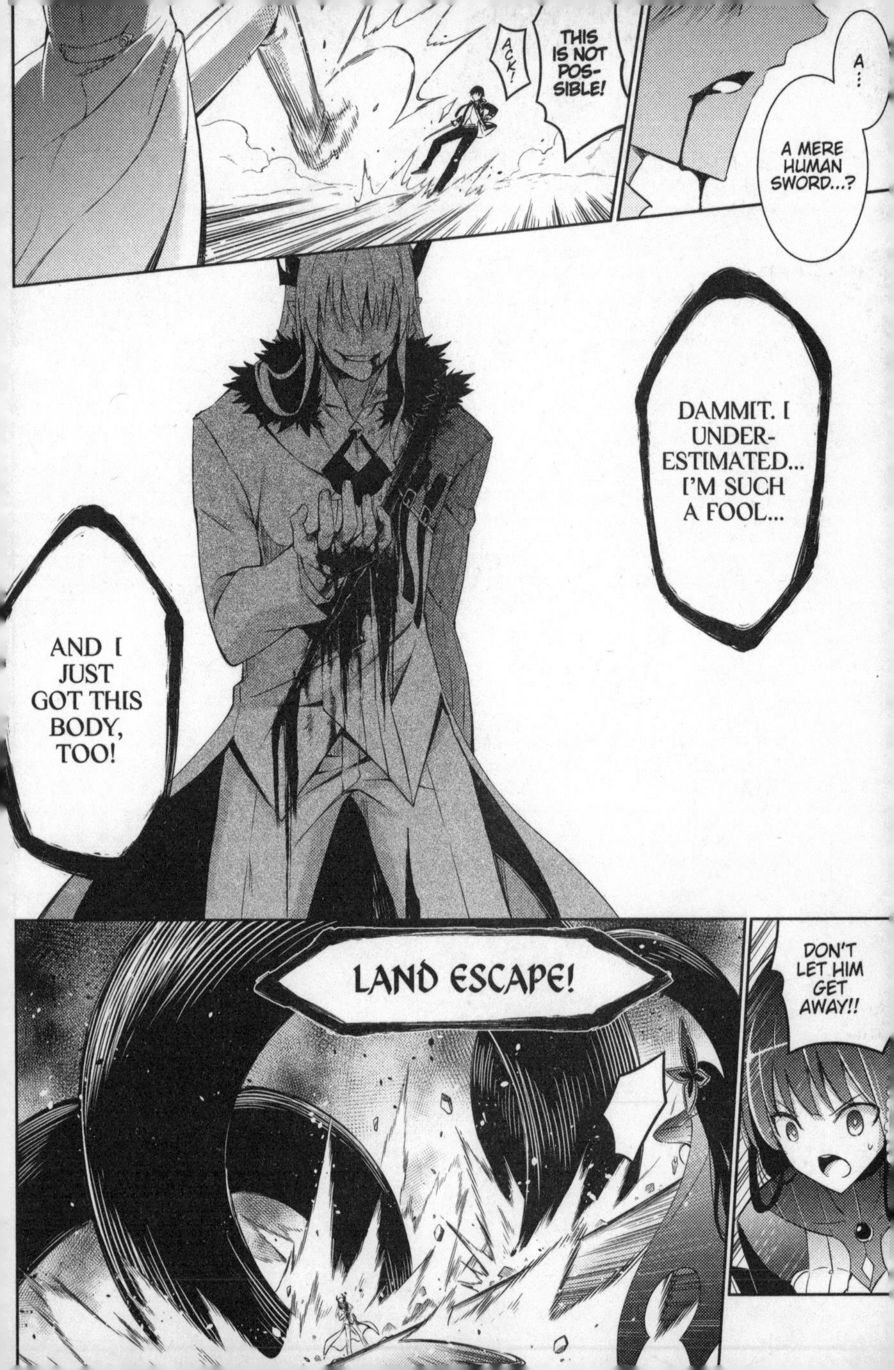
A...
A MERE HUMAN SWORD...?
THIS IS NOT POS-SIBLE!
ACK!
DAMMIT. I UNDER-ESTIMATED... I'M SUCH A FOOL...
AND I JUST GOT THIS BODY, TOO!
DON'T LET HIM GET AWAY!!
LAND ESCAPE!

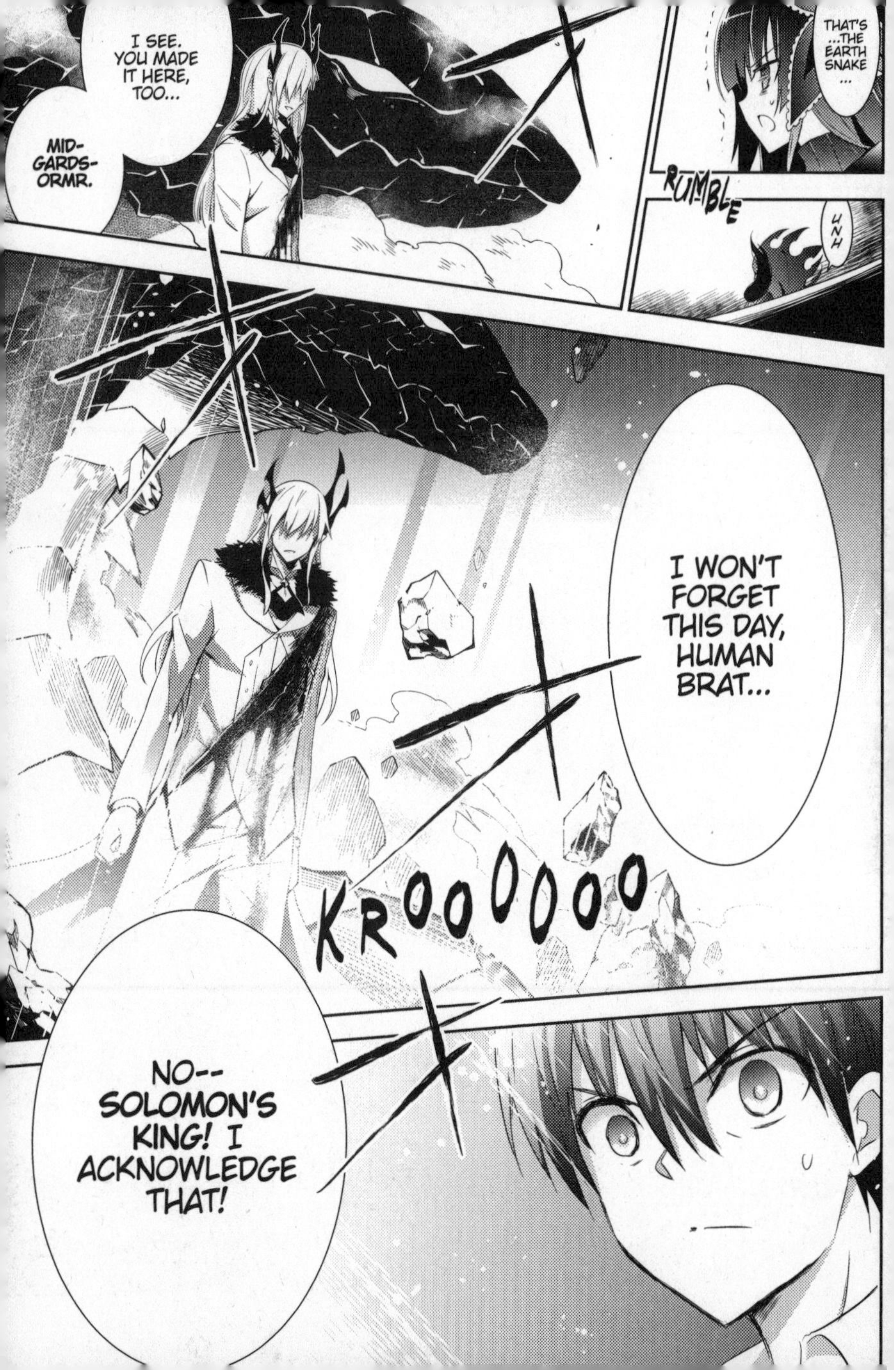
THAT'S ...THE EARTH SNAKE ...
RUMBLE
UNH
I SEE. YOU MADE IT HERE, TOO...
MID-GARDS-ORMR.
I WON'T FORGET THIS DAY, HUMAN BRAT...
KROOOOOO
NO-- SOLOMON'S KING! I ACKNOWLEDGE THAT!

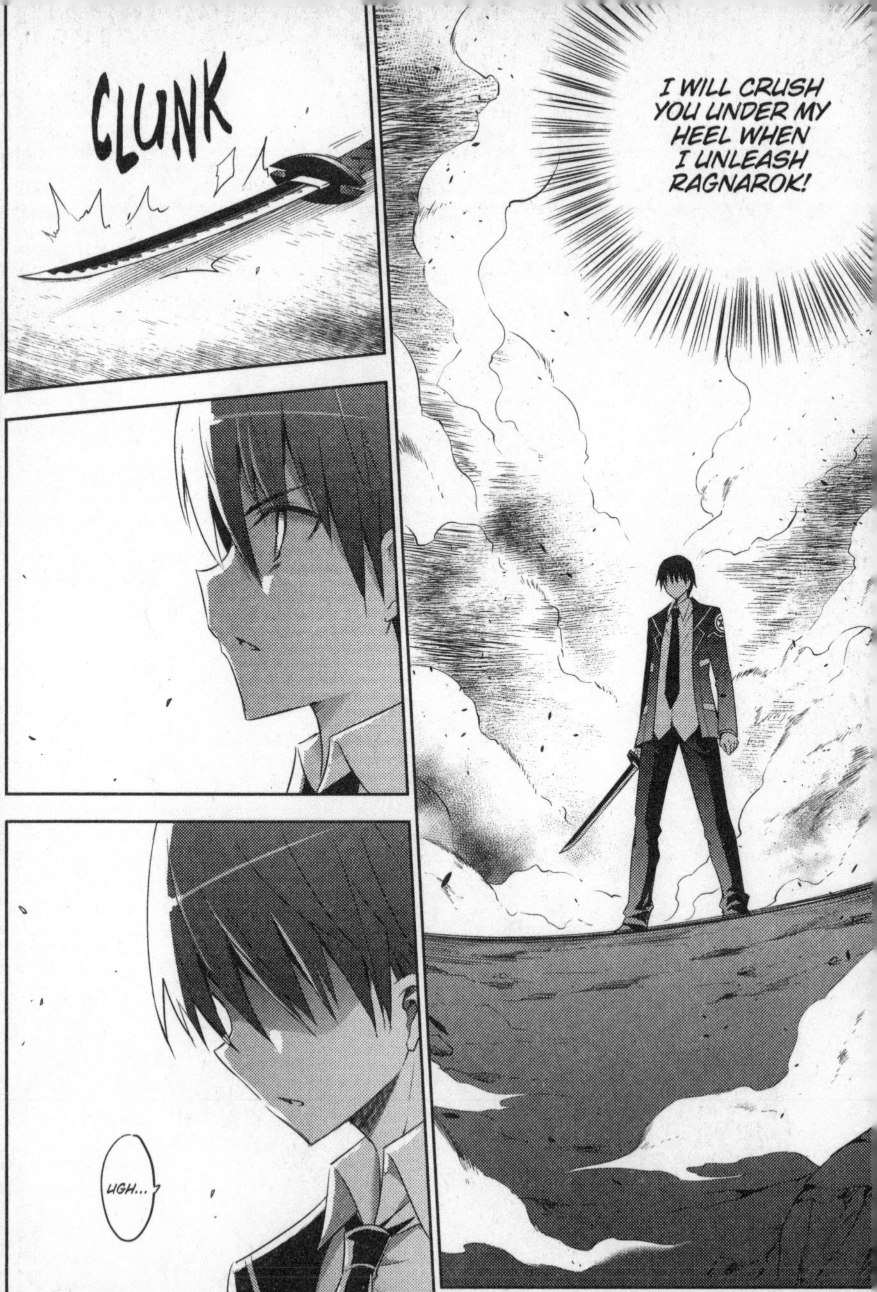
I WILL CRUSH YOU UNDER MY HEEL WHEN I UNLEASH RAGNAROK!
CLUNK
UGH...

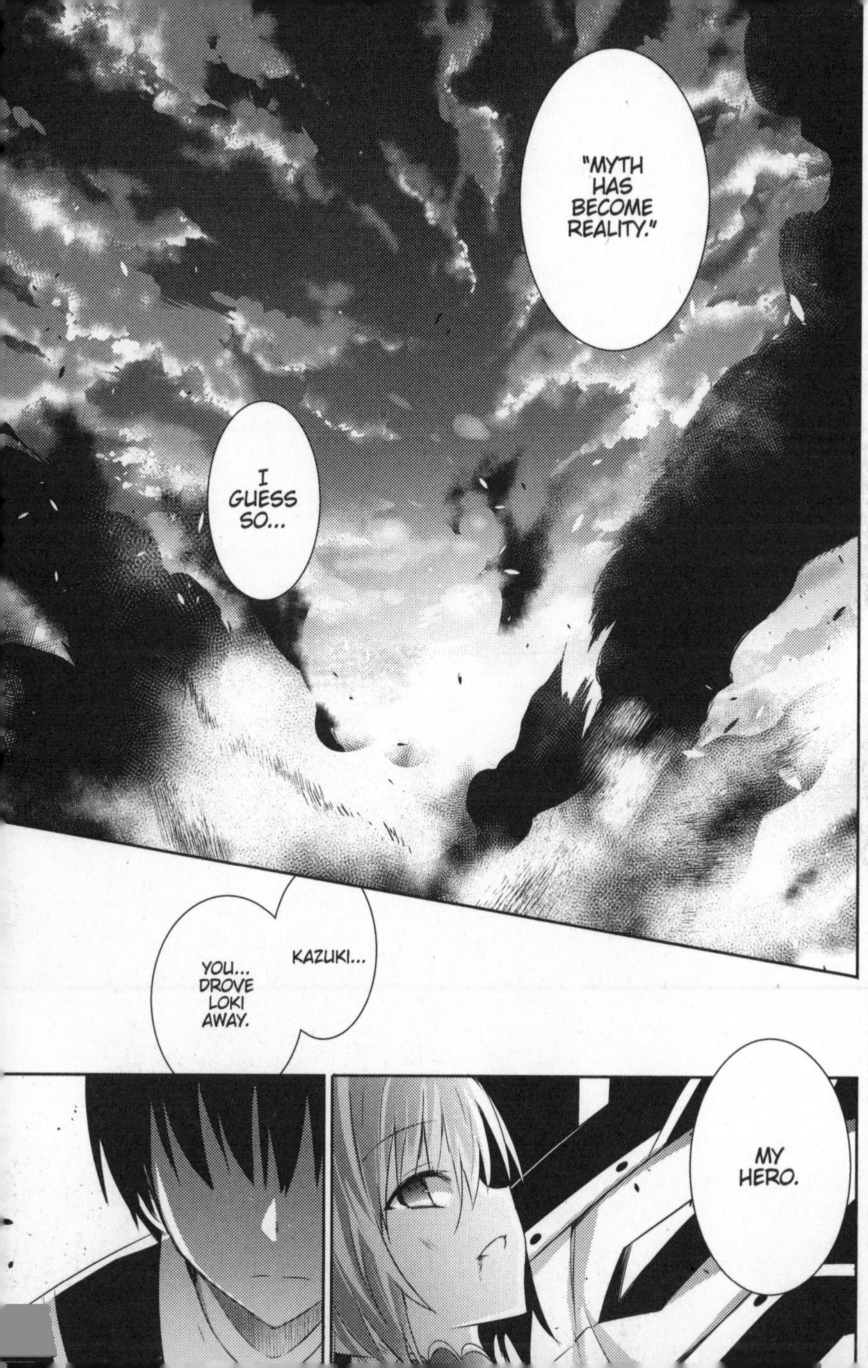
"MYTH HAS BECOME REALITY."
I GUESS SO...
KAZUKI...
YOU... DROVE LOKI AWAY.
MY HERO.

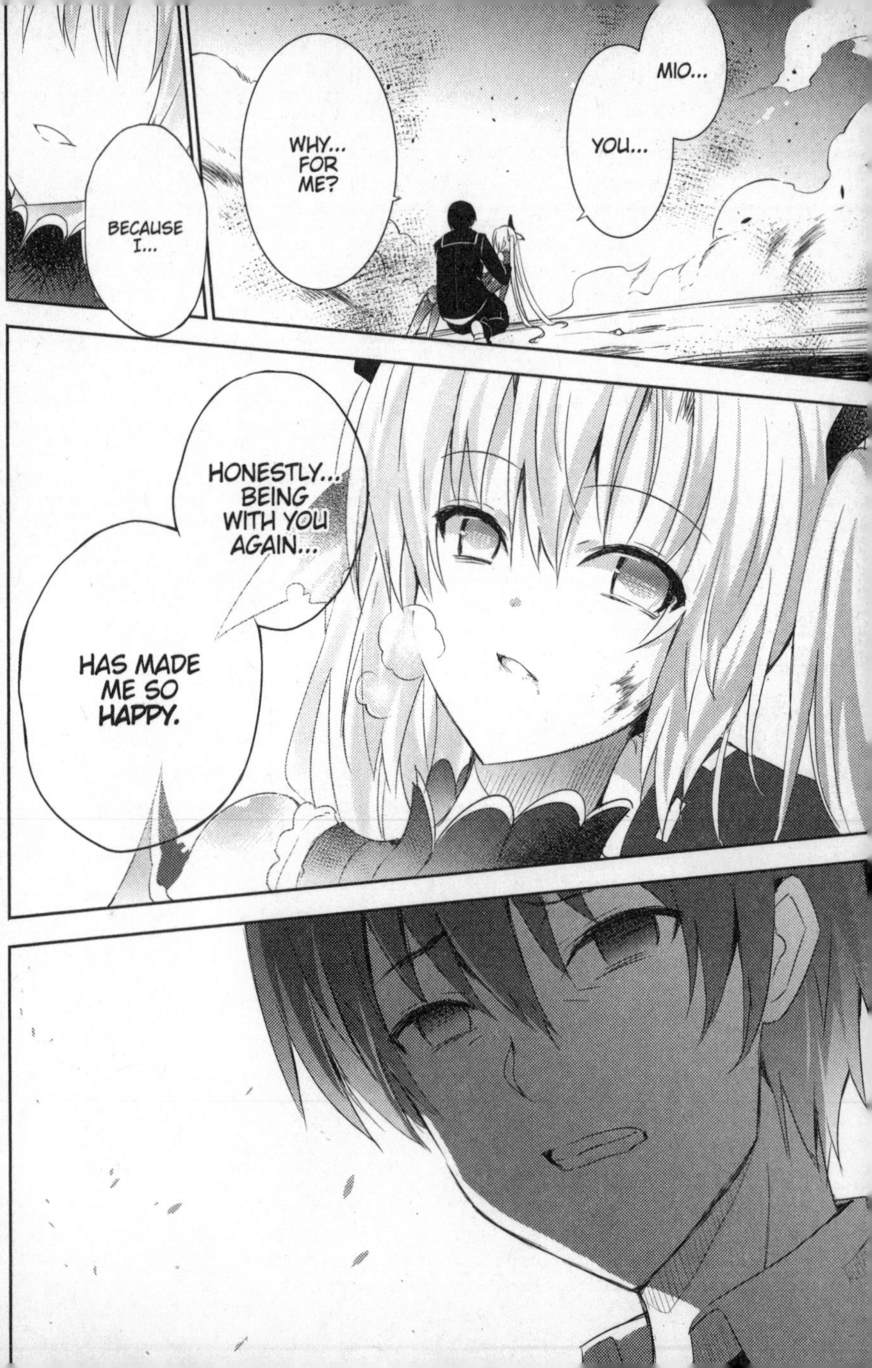
MIO... YOU...
WHY... FOR ME?
BECAUSE I...
HONESTLY... BEING WITH YOU AGAIN...
HAS MADE ME SO HAPPY.

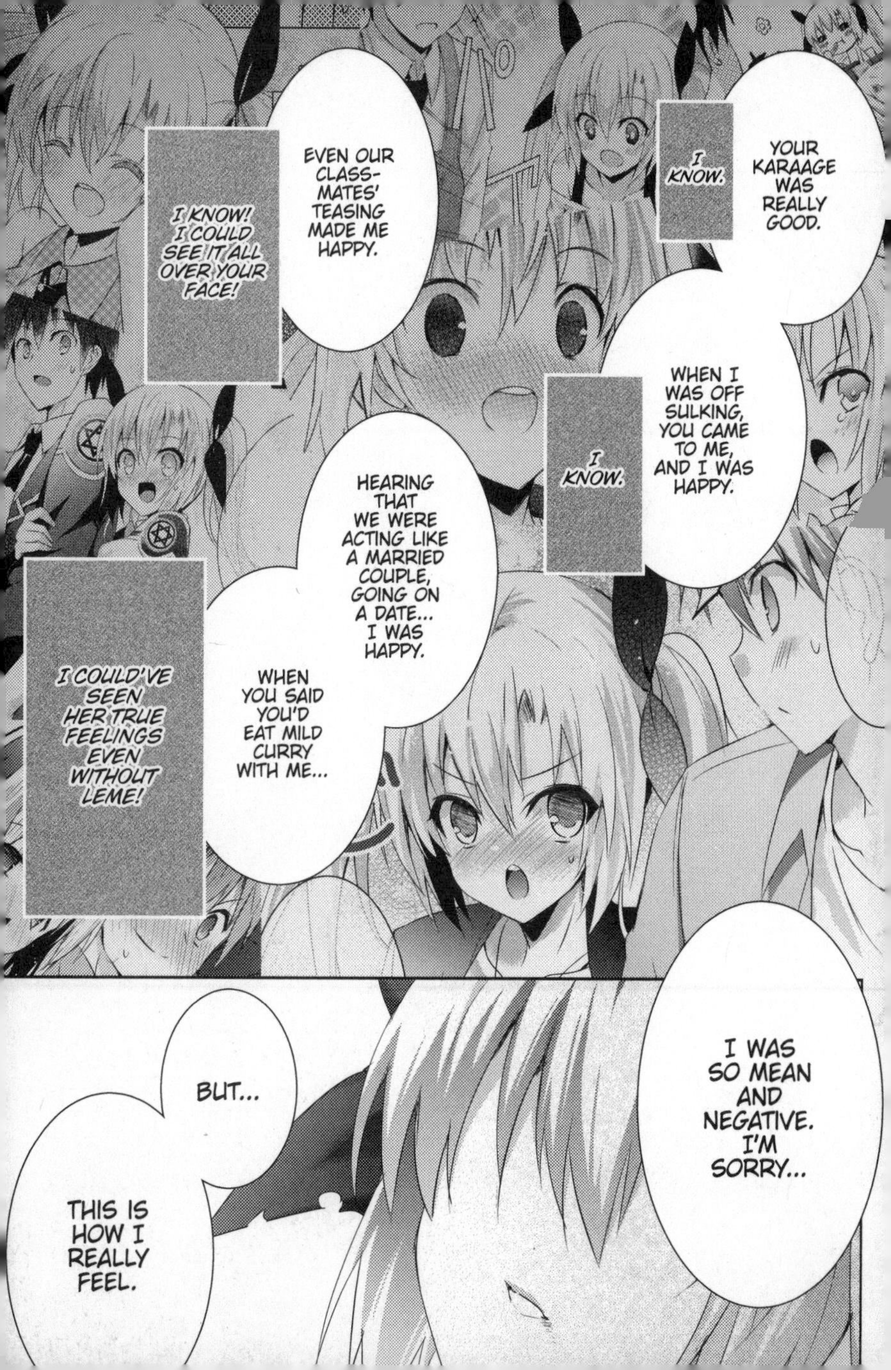
YOUR KARAAGE WAS REALLY GOOD.
I KNOW.
EVEN OUR CLASS-MATES' TEASING MADE ME HAPPY.
I KNOW! I COULD SEE IT ALL OVER YOUR FACE!
WHEN I WAS OFF SULKING, YOU CAME TO ME, AND I WAS HAPPY.
I KNOW.
HEARING THAT WE WERE ACTING LIKE A MARRIED COUPLE, GOING ON A DATE... I WAS HAPPY.
WHEN YOU SAID YOU'D EAT MILD CURRY WITH ME...
I COULD'VE SEEN HER TRUE FEELINGS EVEN WITHOUT LEME!
I WAS SO MEAN AND NEGATIVE. I'M SORRY...
BUT...
THIS IS HOW I REALLY FEEL.

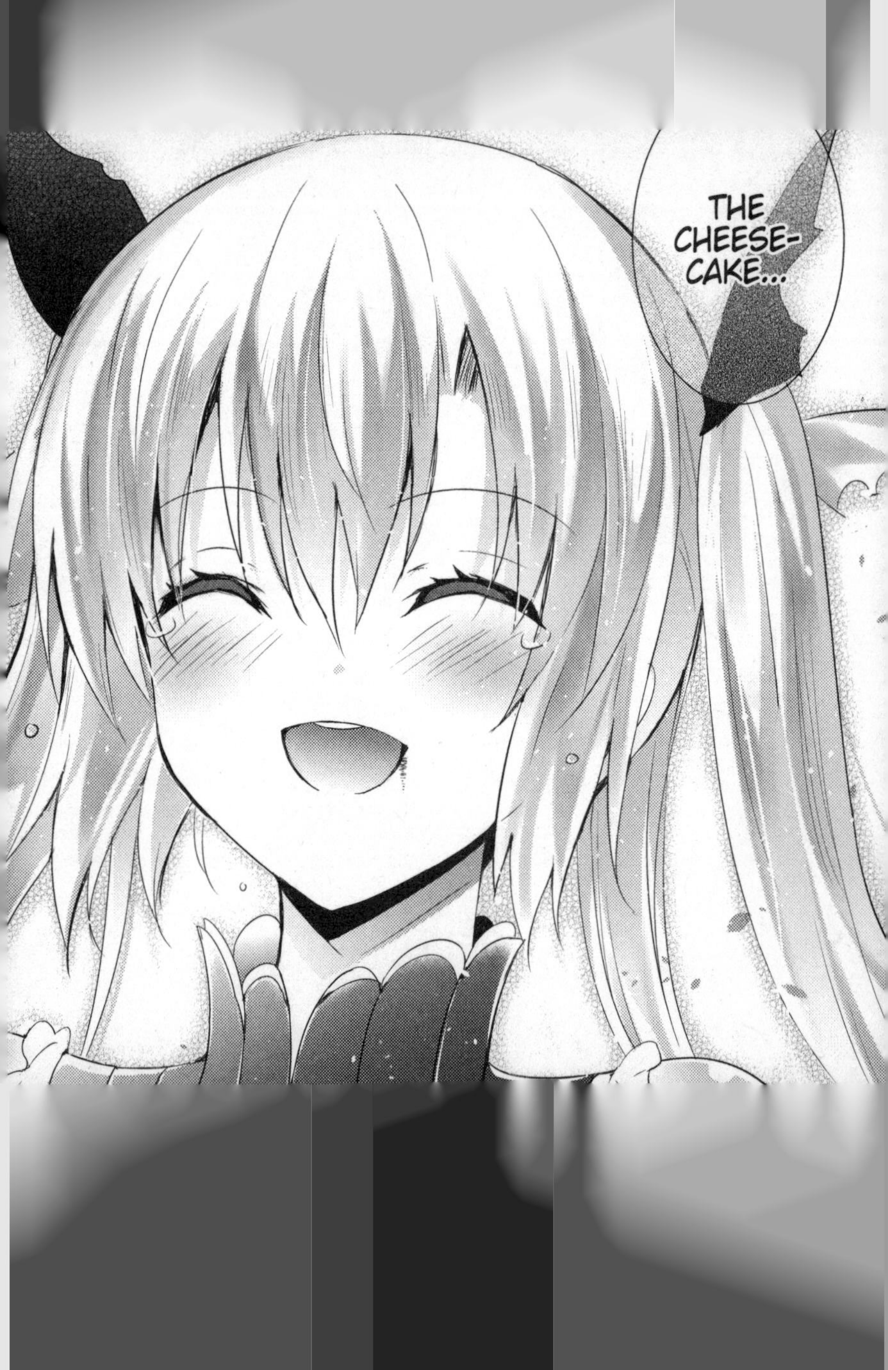
THE CHEESE-CAKE...

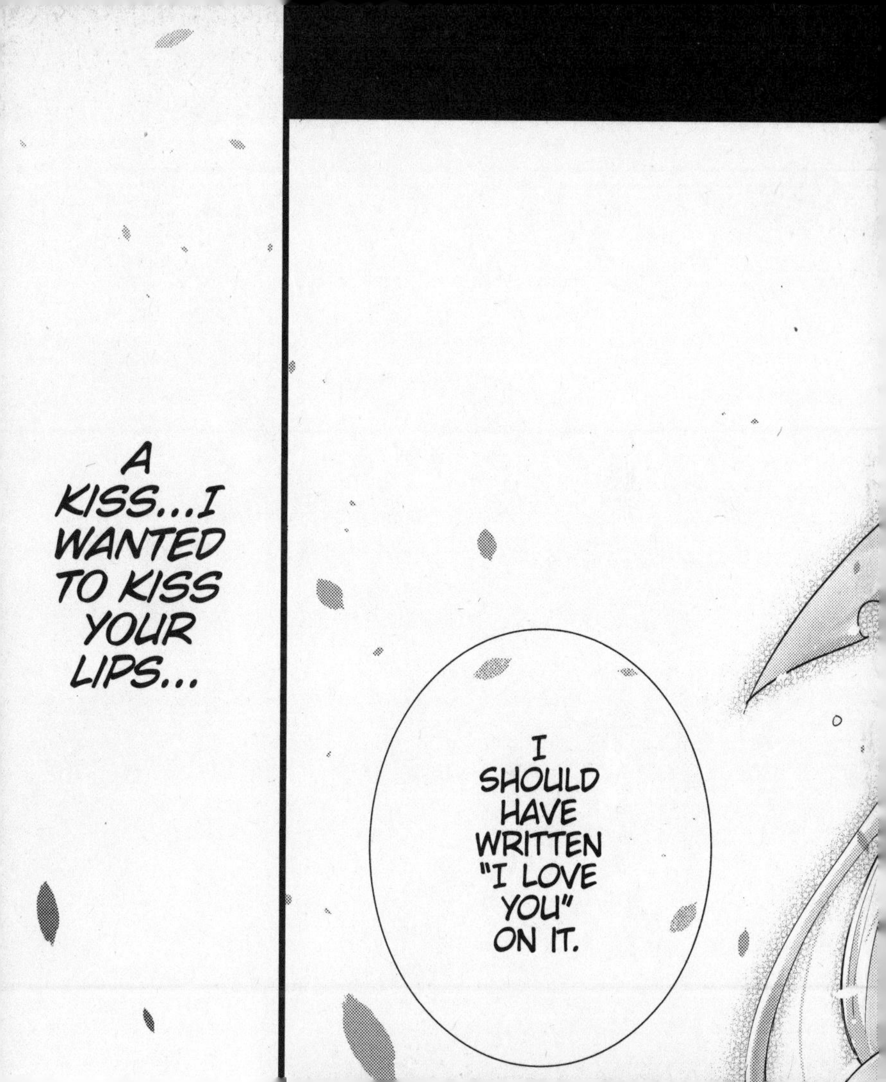
I SHOULD HAVE WRITTEN "I LOVE YOU" ON IT.
A KISS...I WANTED TO KISS YOUR LIPS...

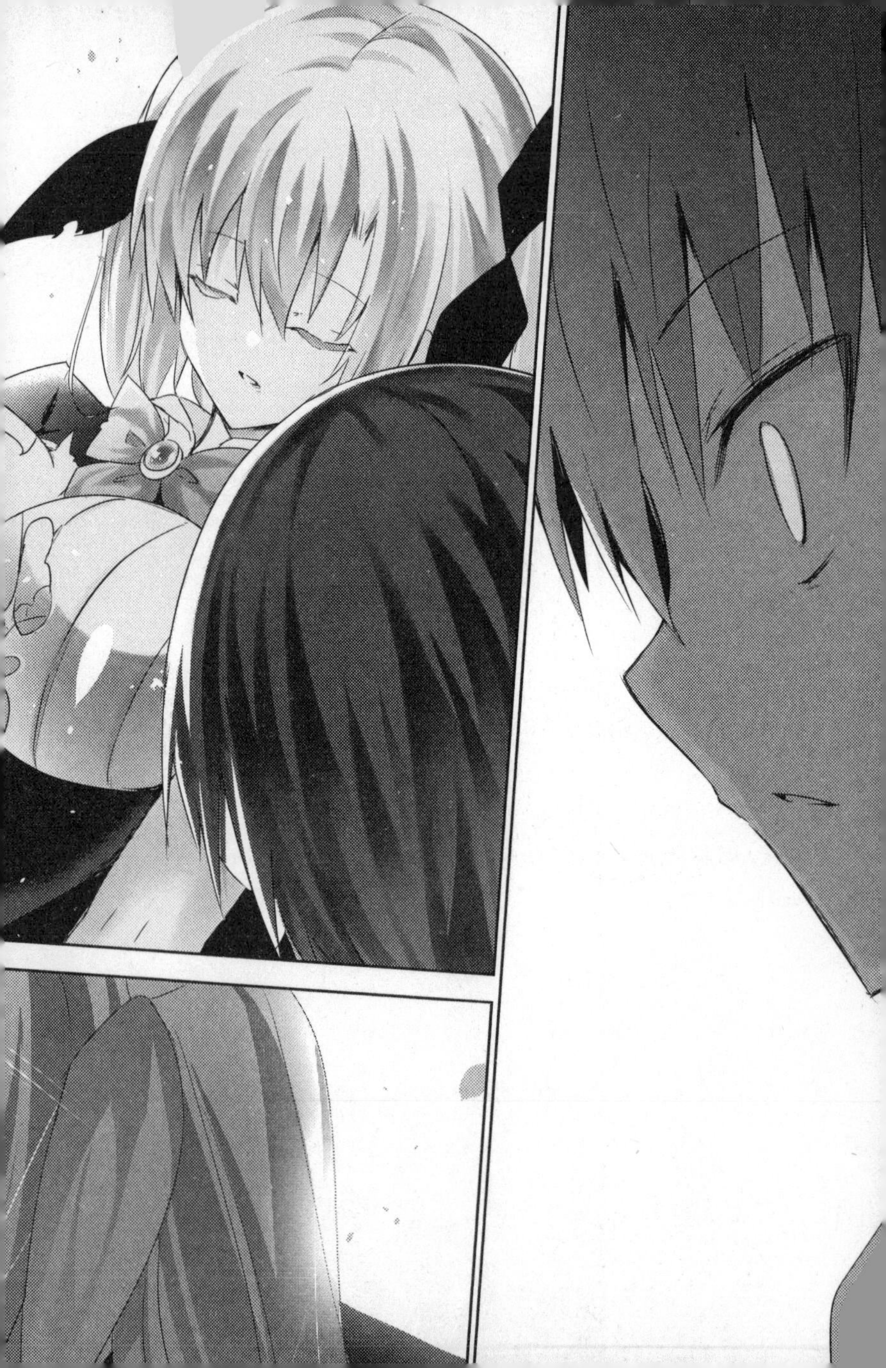

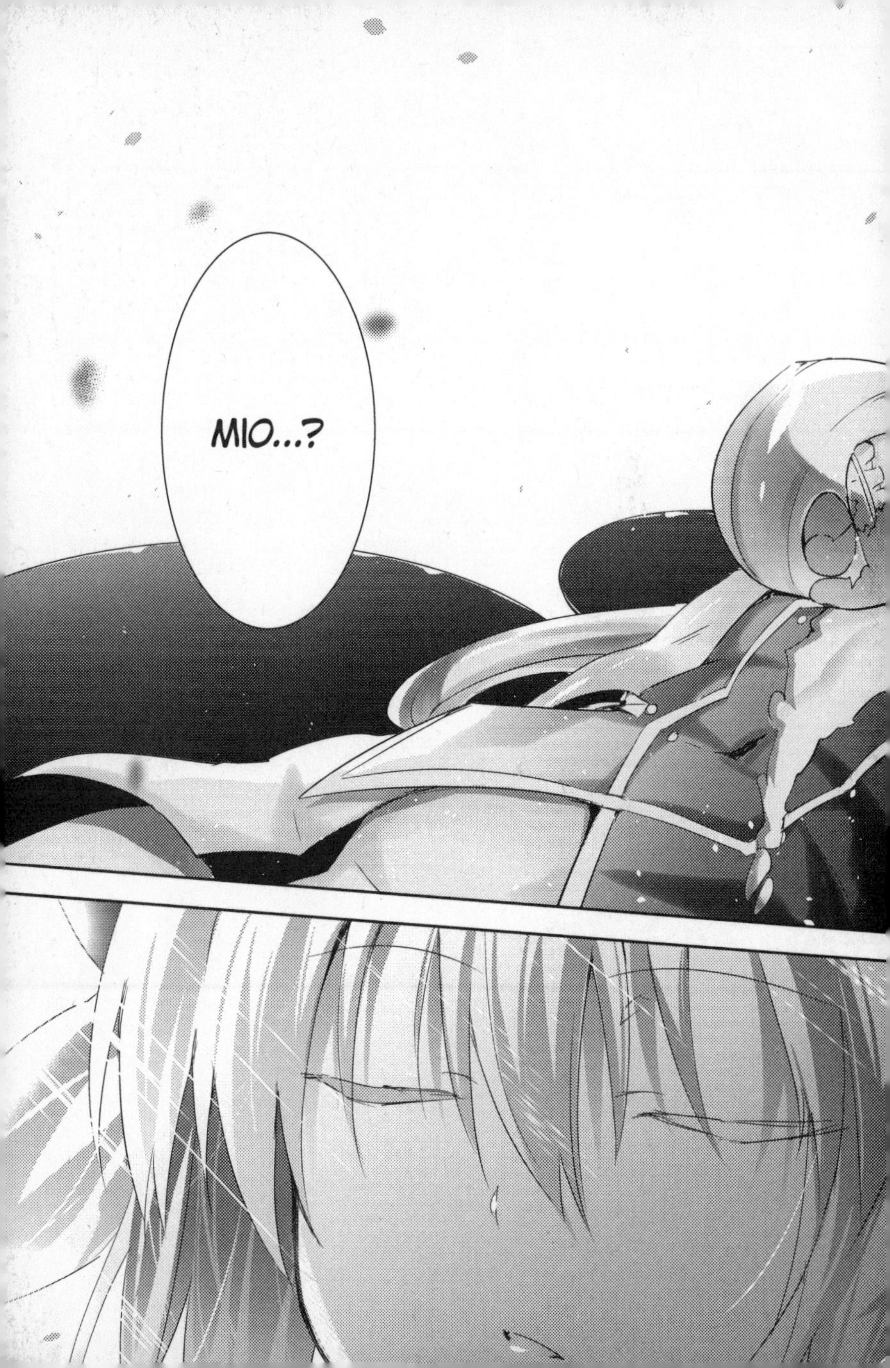
MIO...?

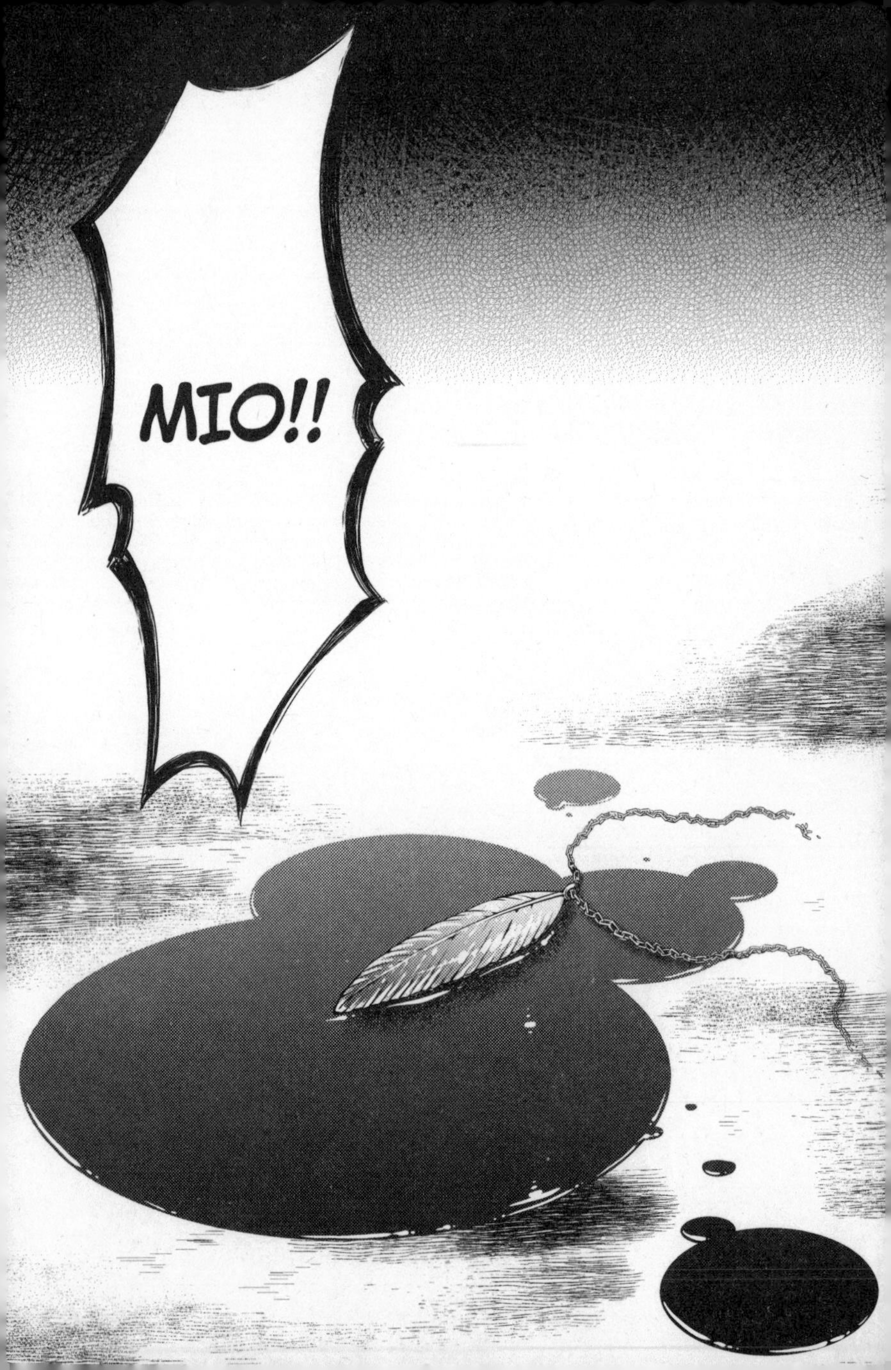
MIO!!

Magika
SWORDSMAN
AND SUMMONER

3

魔技科の剣士と召喚魔王

3

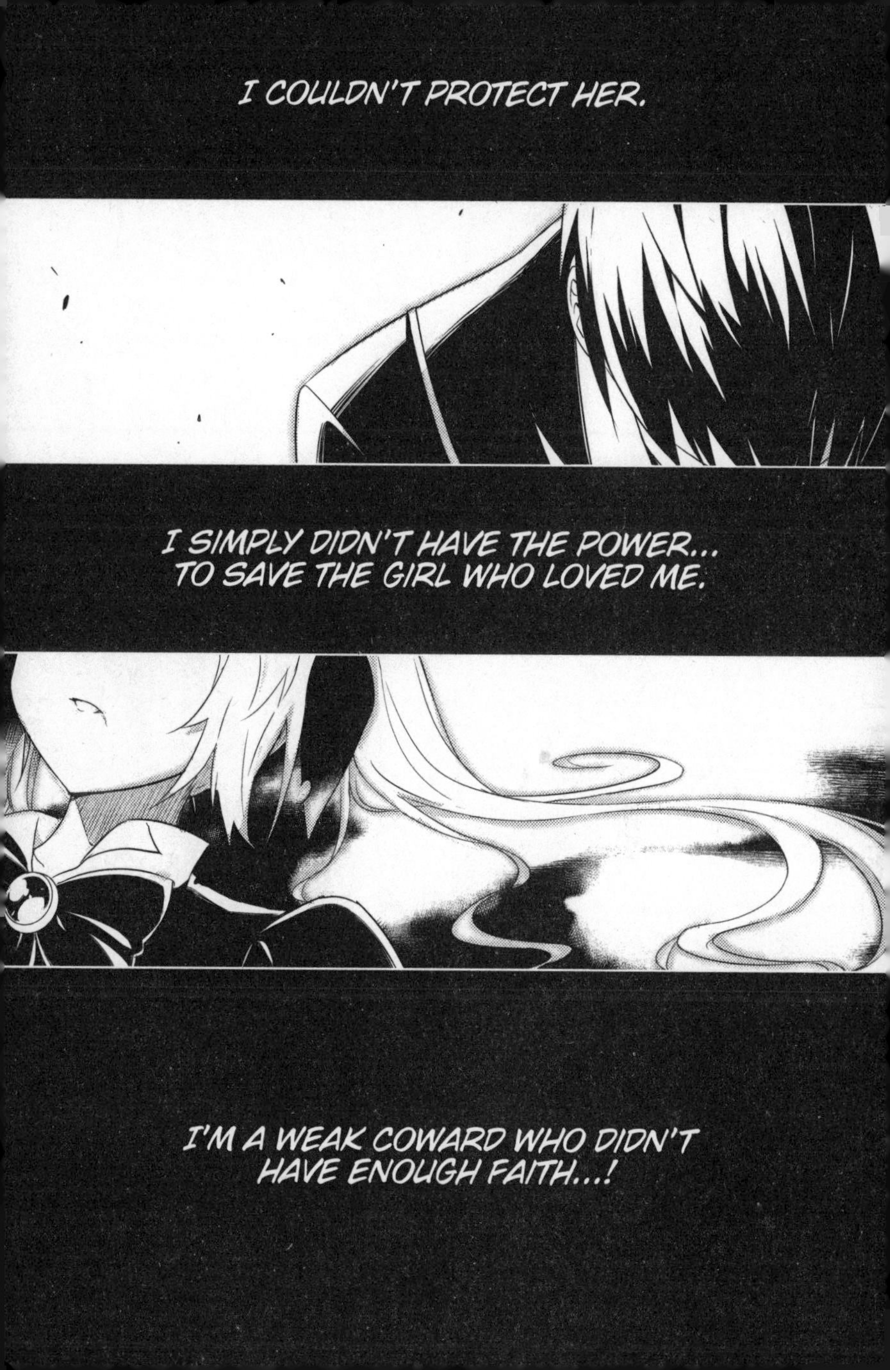
I COULDN'T PROTECT HER.
I SIMPLY DIDN'T HAVE THE POWER... TO SAVE THE GIRL WHO LOVED ME.
I'M A WEAK COWARD WHO DIDN'T HAVE ENOUGH FAITH...!

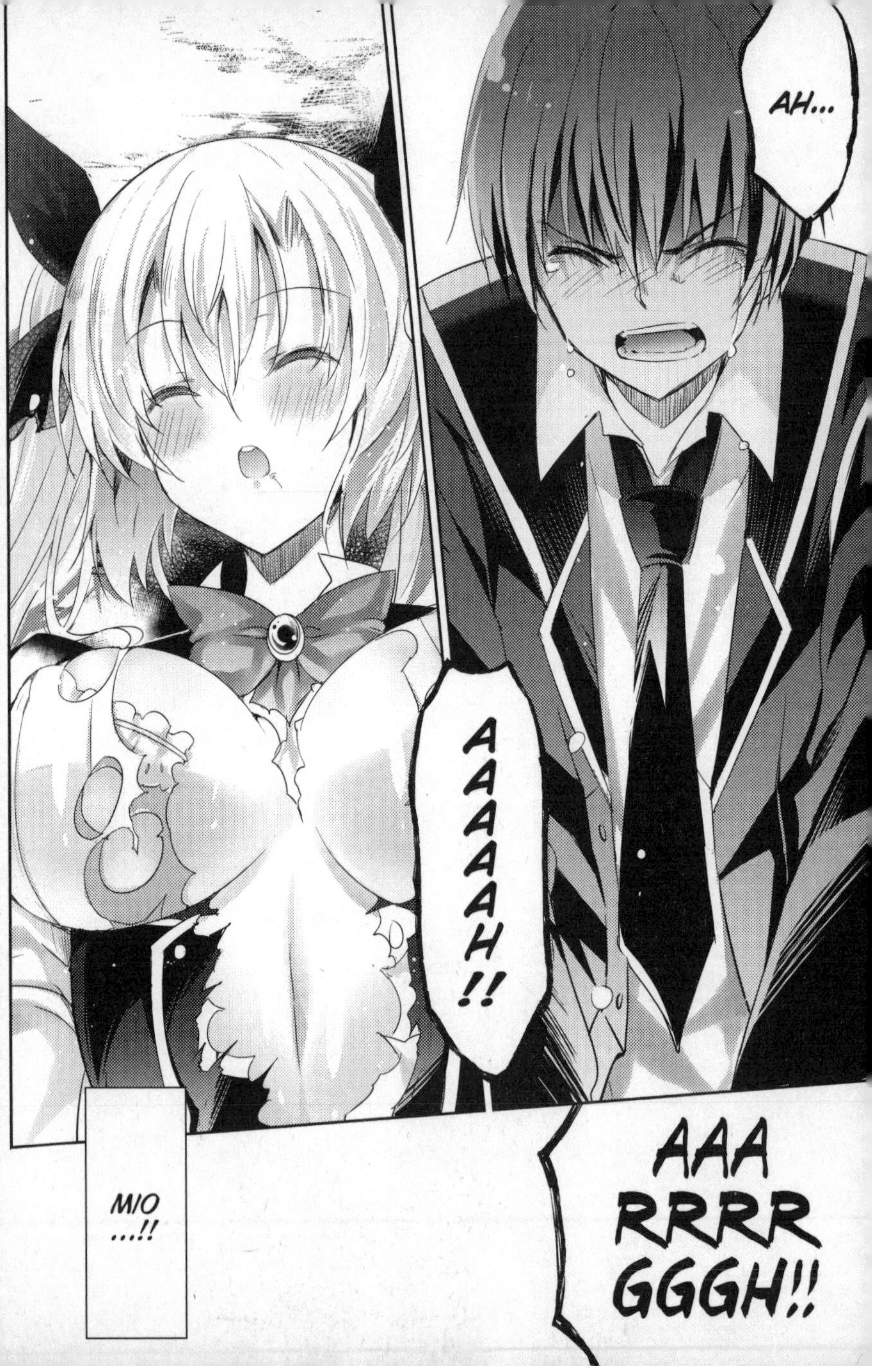
AH...
AAAAAAH!!
AAA RRRR GGGH!!
MIO ...!!

Chapter 15

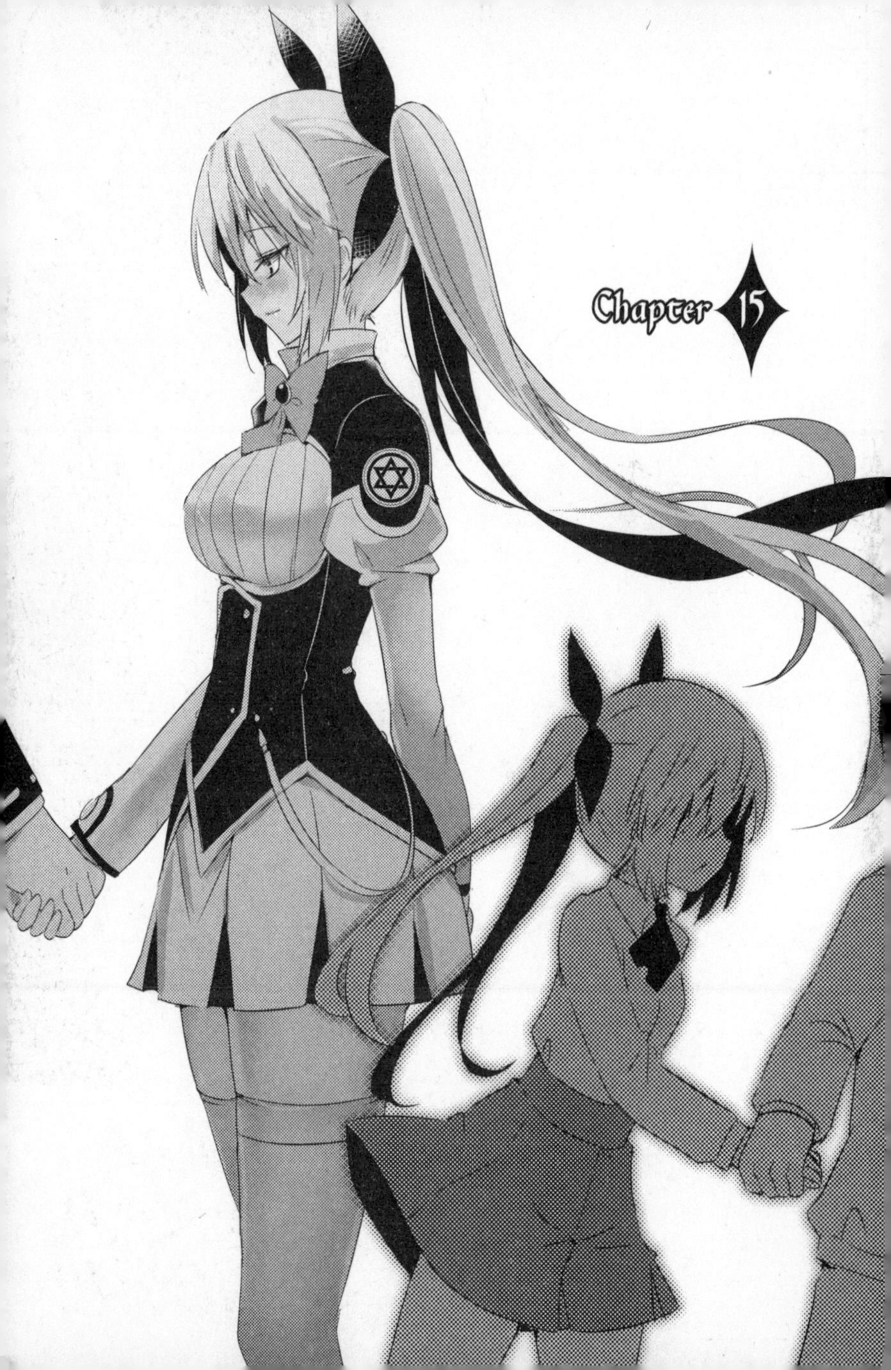

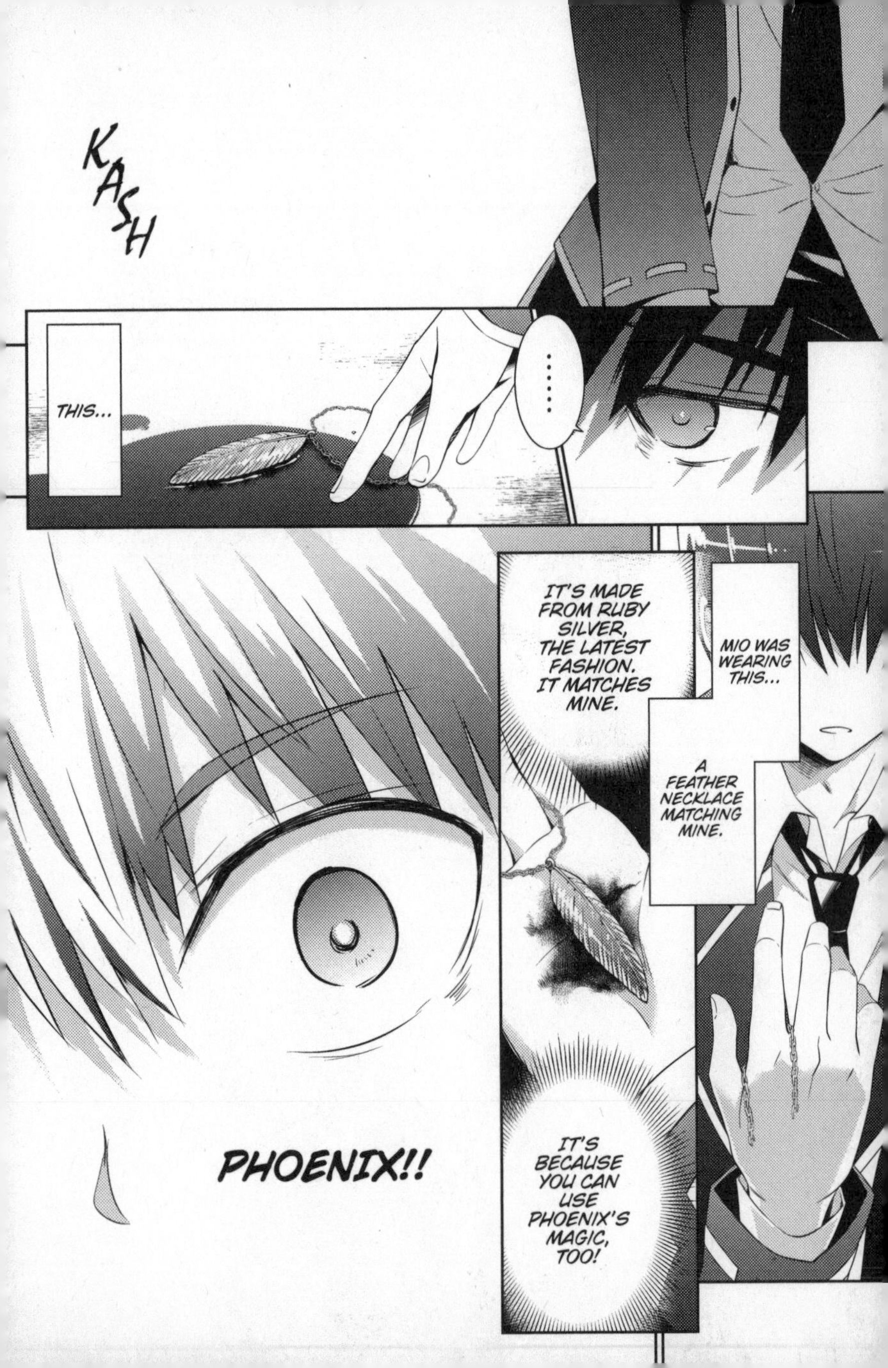
KASH
......
THIS...
MIO WAS WEARING THIS...
A FEATHER NECKLACE MATCHING MINE.
IT'S MADE FROM RUBY SILVER, THE LATEST FASHION. IT MATCHES MINE.
IT'S BECAUSE YOU CAN USE PHOENIX'S MAGIC, TOO!
PHOENIX!!

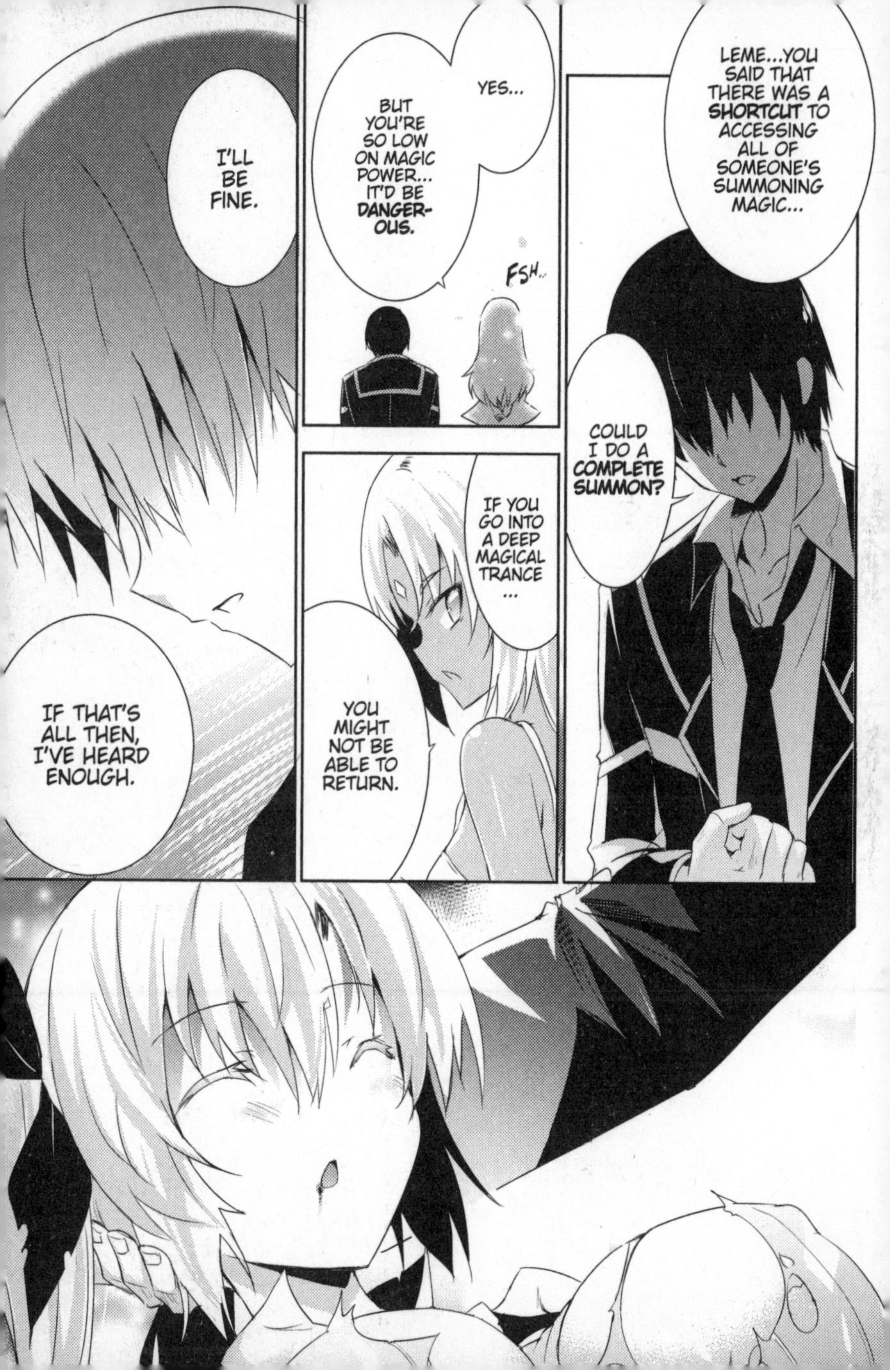
LEME...YOU SAID THAT THERE WAS A SHORTCUT TO ACCESSING ALL OF SOMEONE'S SUMMONING MAGIC...
COULD I DO A COMPLETE SUMMON?
YES...
BUT YOU'RE SO LOW ON MAGIC POWER... IT'D BE DANGER-OUS.
FSH..
IF YOU GO INTO A DEEP MAGICAL TRANCE ...
YOU MIGHT NOT BE ABLE TO RETURN.
I'LL BE FINE.
IF THAT'S ALL THEN, I'VE HEARD ENOUGH.

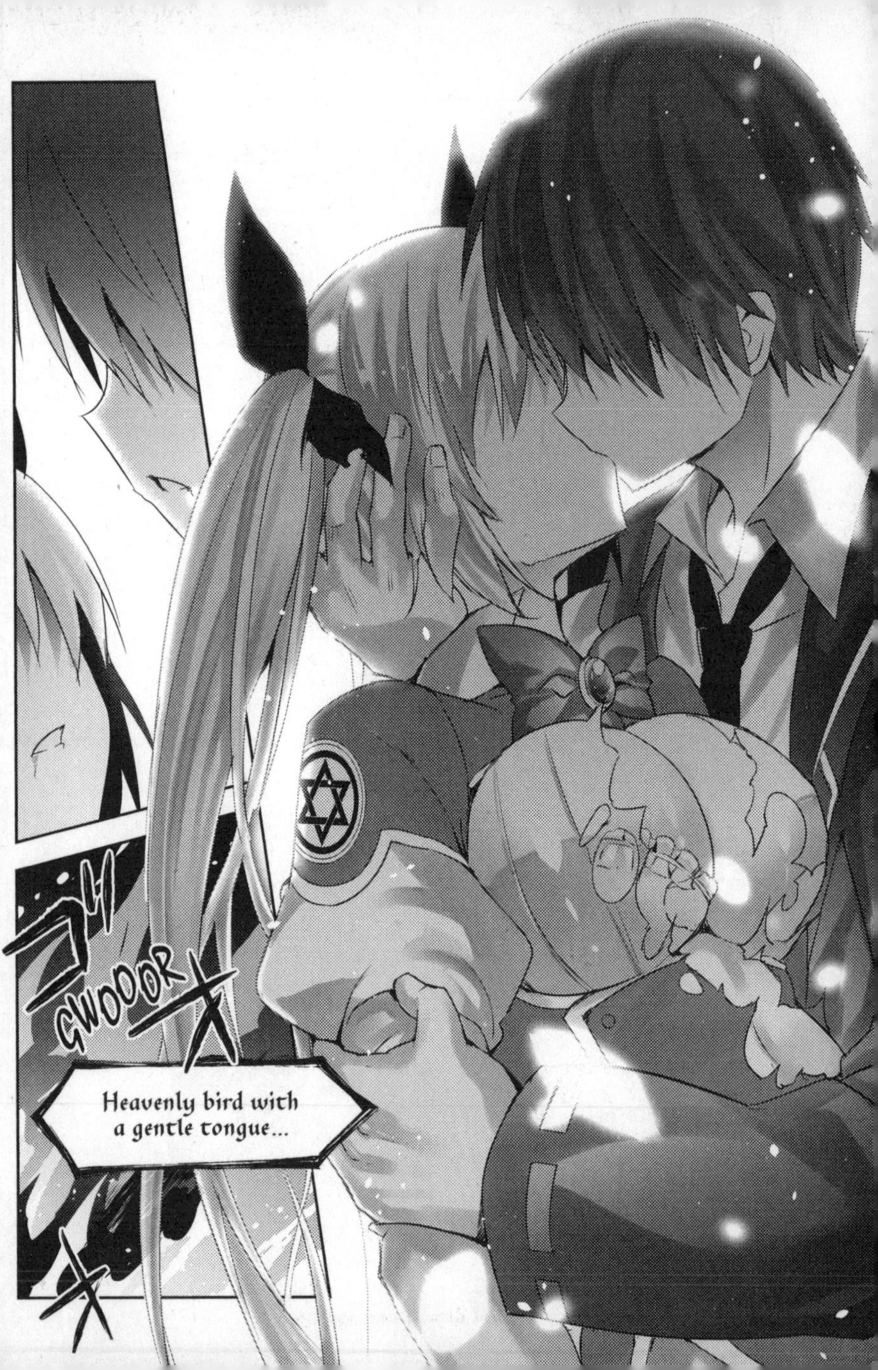
GWOOOR
Heavenly bird with a gentle tongue...

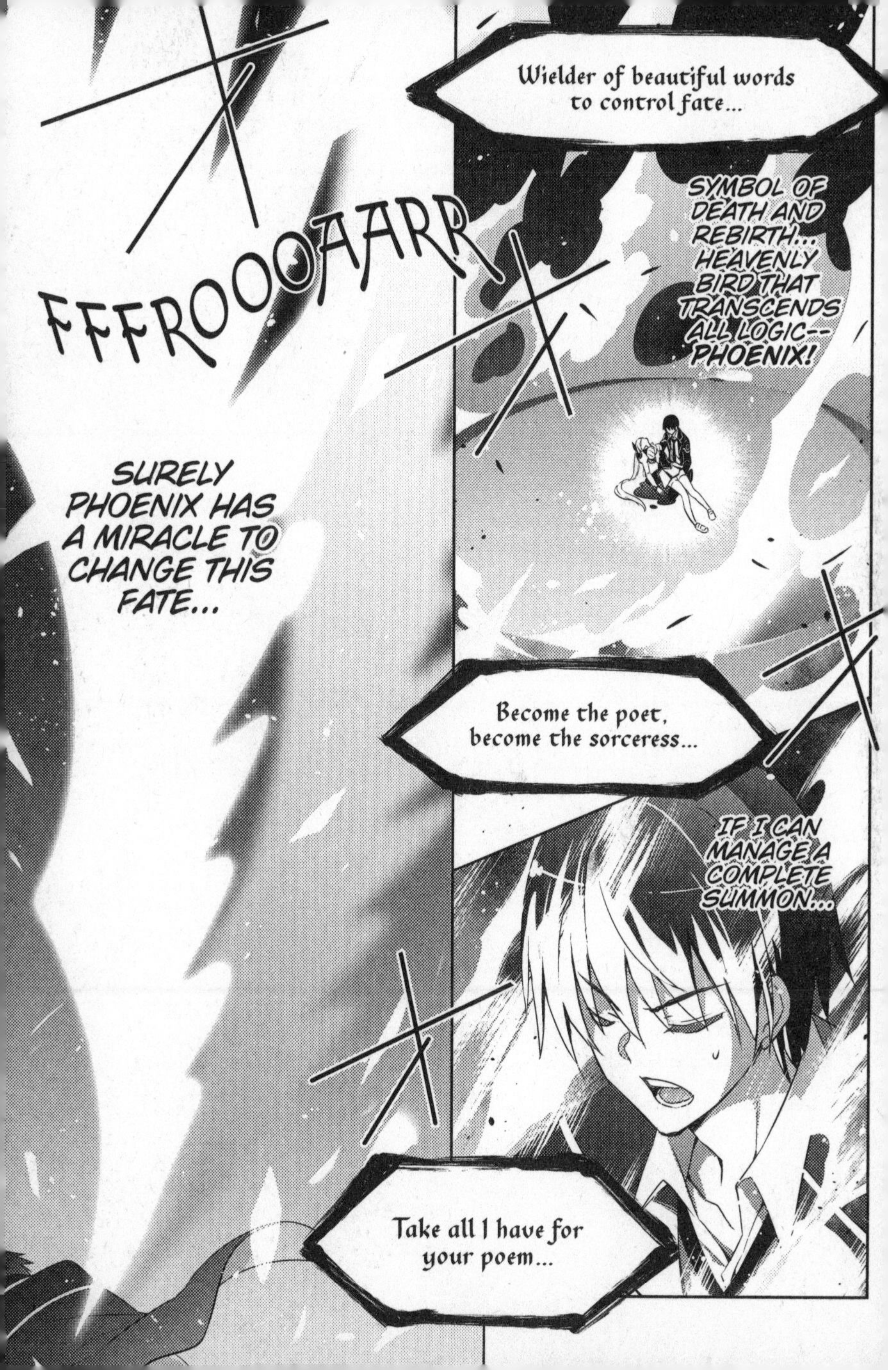
Wielder of beautiful words to control fate...
SYMBOL OF DEATH AND REBIRTH... HEAVENLY BIRD THAT TRANSCENDS ALL LOGIC-- PHOENIX!
Become the poet, become the sorceress...
IF I CAN MANAGE A COMPLETE SUMMON...
Take all I have for your poem...
FFFROOOAARR
SURELY PHOENIX HAS A MIRACLE TO CHANGE THIS FATE...

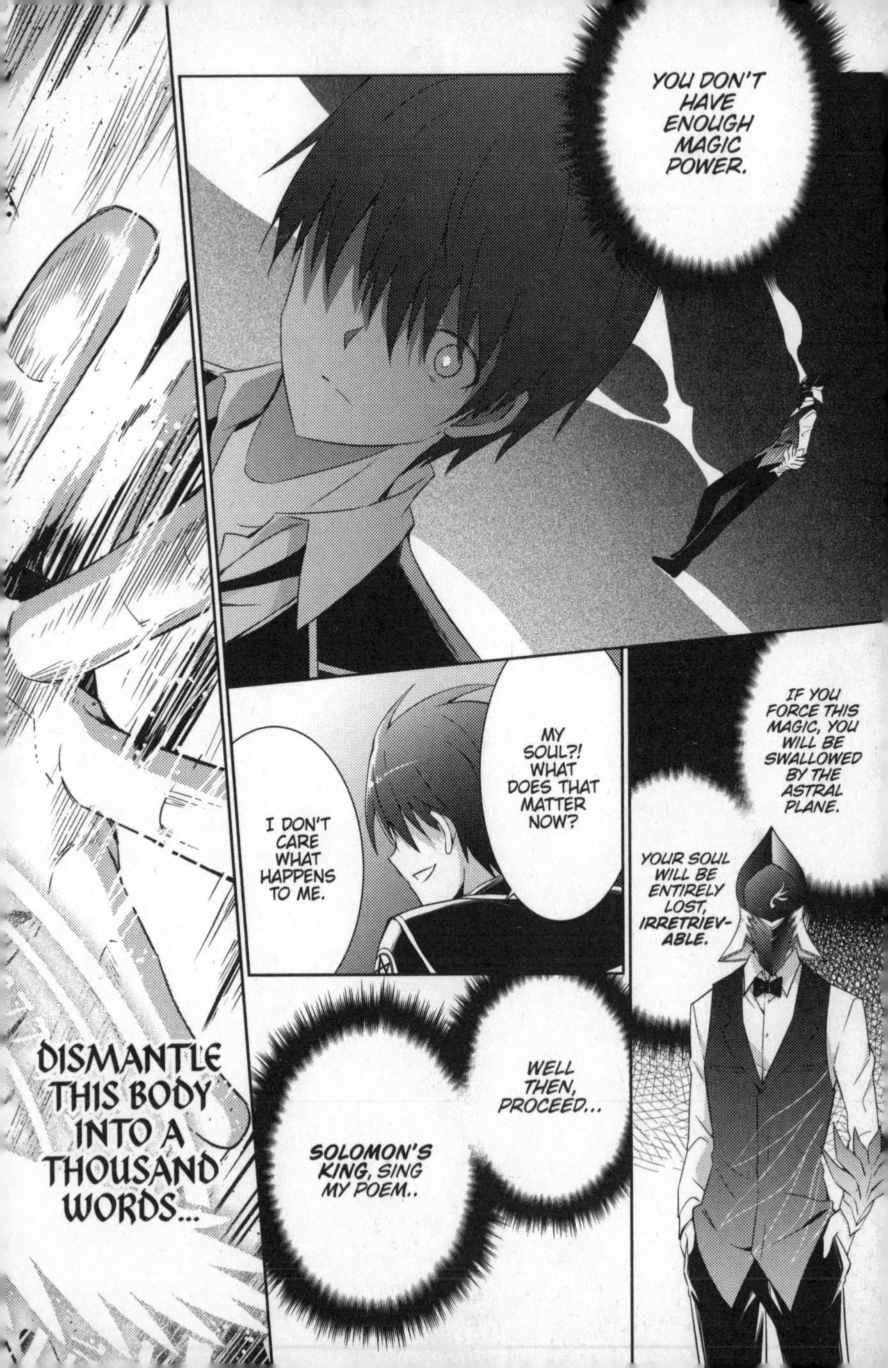
YOU DON'T HAVE ENOUGH MAGIC POWER.
IF YOU FORCE THIS MAGIC, YOU WILL BE SWALLOWED BY THE ASTRAL PLANE.
YOUR SOUL WILL BE ENTIRELY LOST, IRRETRIEV-ABLE.
MY SOUL?! WHAT DOES THAT MATTER NOW?
I DON'T CARE WHAT HAPPENS TO ME.
WELL THEN, PROCEED...
SOLOMON'S KING, SING MY POEM..
DISMANTLE THIS BODY INTO A THOUSAND WORDS...

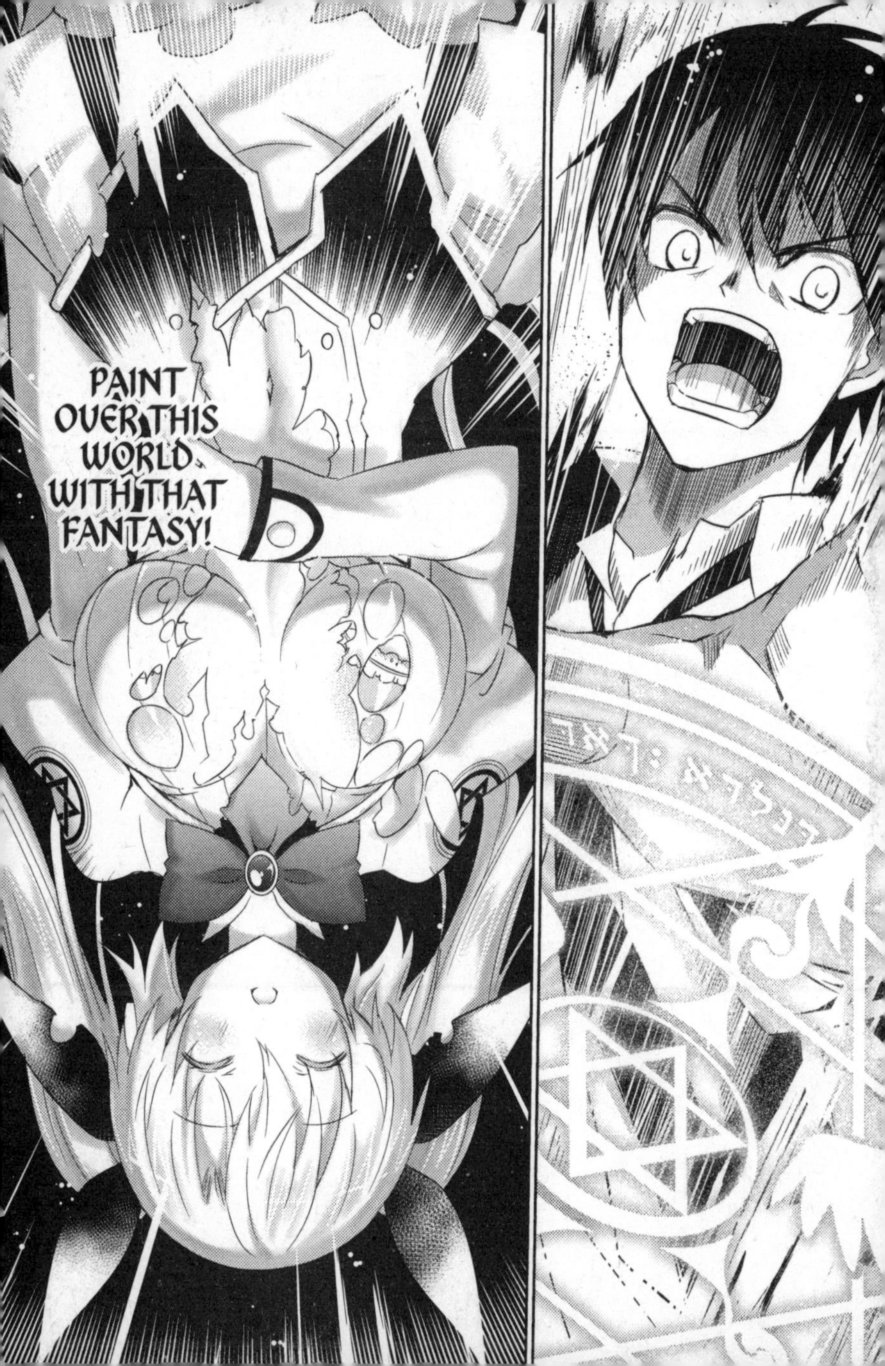
PAINT OVER THIS WORLD WITH THAT FANTASY!

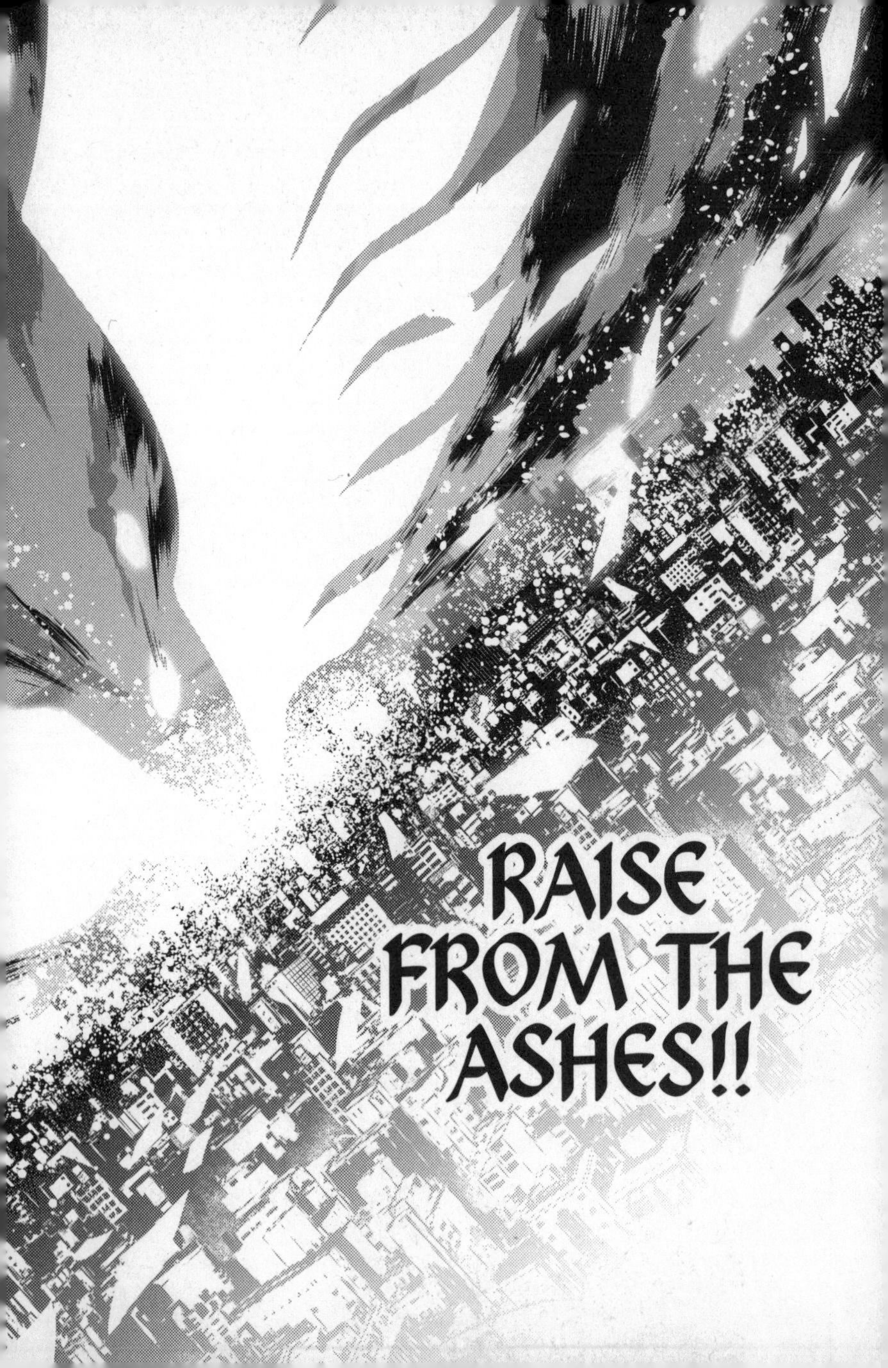
RAISE FROM THE ASHES!!

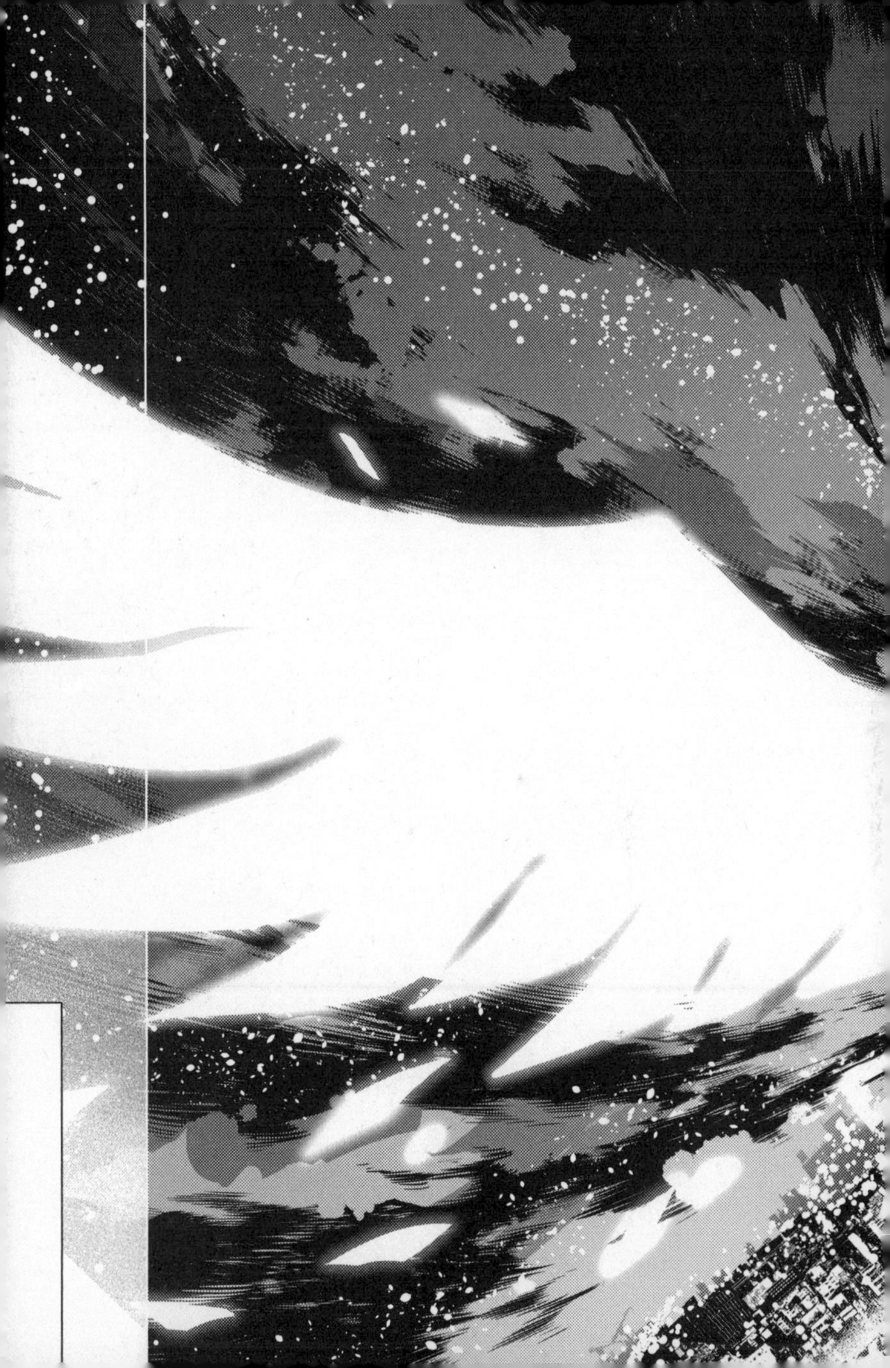

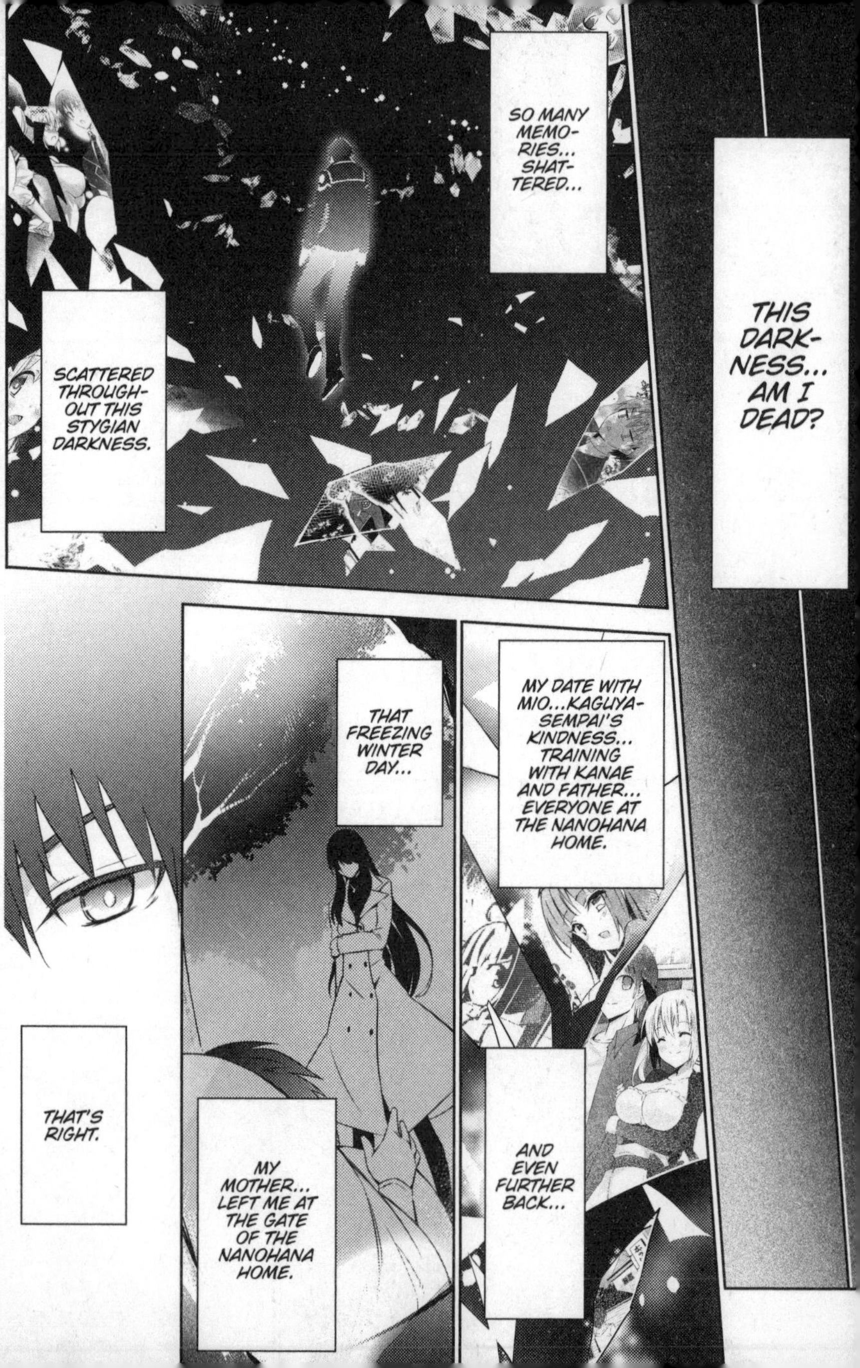
THIS DARK-NESS... AM I DEAD?
SO MANY MEMO-RIES... SHAT-TERED...
SCATTERED THROUGH-OUT THIS STYGIAN DARKNESS.
MY DATE WITH MIO...KAGUYA-SEMPAI'S KINDNESS... TRAINING WITH KANAE AND FATHER... EVERYONE AT THE NANOHANA HOME.
AND EVEN FURTHER BACK...
THAT FREEZING WINTER DAY...
MY MOTHER... LEFT ME AT THE GATE OF THE NANOHANA HOME.
THAT'S RIGHT.

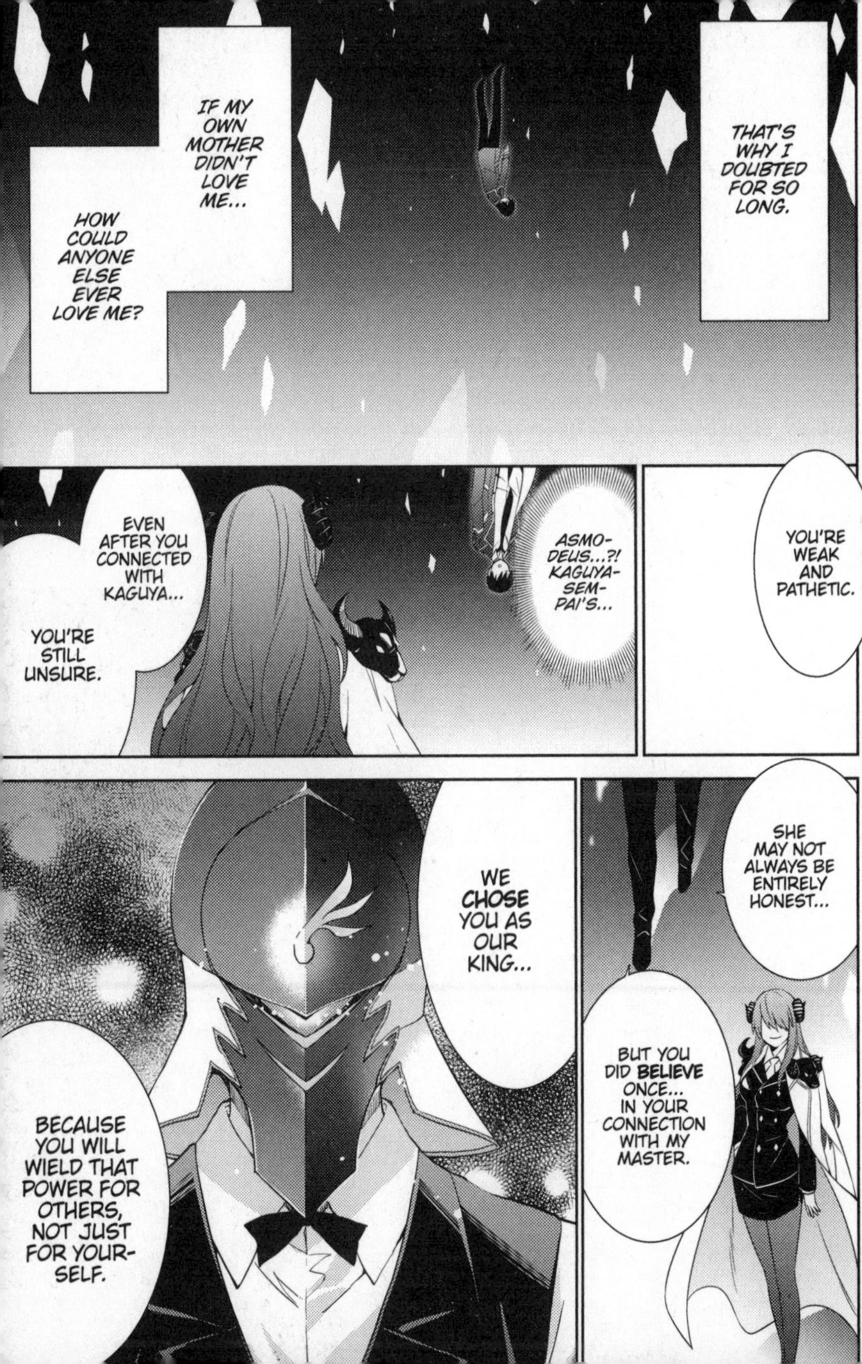
THAT'S WHY I DOUBTED FOR SO LONG.
IF MY OWN MOTHER DIDN'T LOVE ME...
HOW COULD ANYONE ELSE EVER LOVE ME?
YOU'RE WEAK AND PATHETIC.
ASMODEUS...?! KAGUYA-SEMPAI'S...
EVEN AFTER YOU CONNECTED WITH KAGUYA...
YOU'RE STILL UNSURE.
SHE MAY NOT ALWAYS BE ENTIRELY HONEST...
BUT YOU DID **BELIEVE** ONCE... IN YOUR CONNECTION WITH MY MASTER.
WE **CHOSE** YOU AS OUR KING...
BECAUSE YOU WILL WIELD THAT POWER FOR OTHERS, NOT JUST FOR YOURSELF.

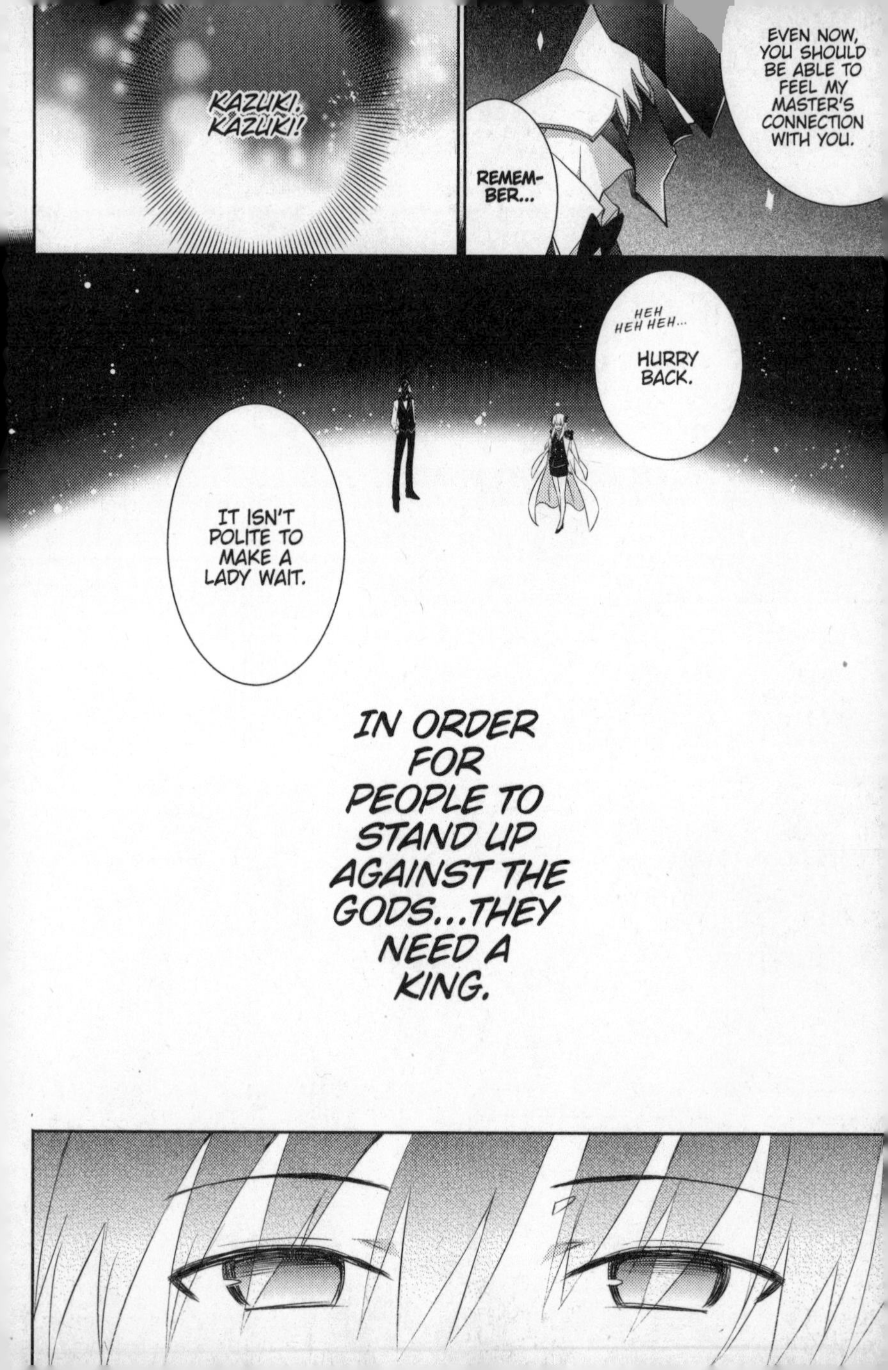
EVEN NOW, YOU SHOULD BE ABLE TO FEEL MY MASTER'S CONNECTION WITH YOU.
REMEM-BER...
KAZUKI, KAZUKI!
HEH HEH HEH...
HURRY BACK.
IT ISN'T POLITE TO MAKE A LADY WAIT.
IN ORDER FOR PEOPLE TO STAND UP AGAINST THE GODS...THEY NEED A KING.

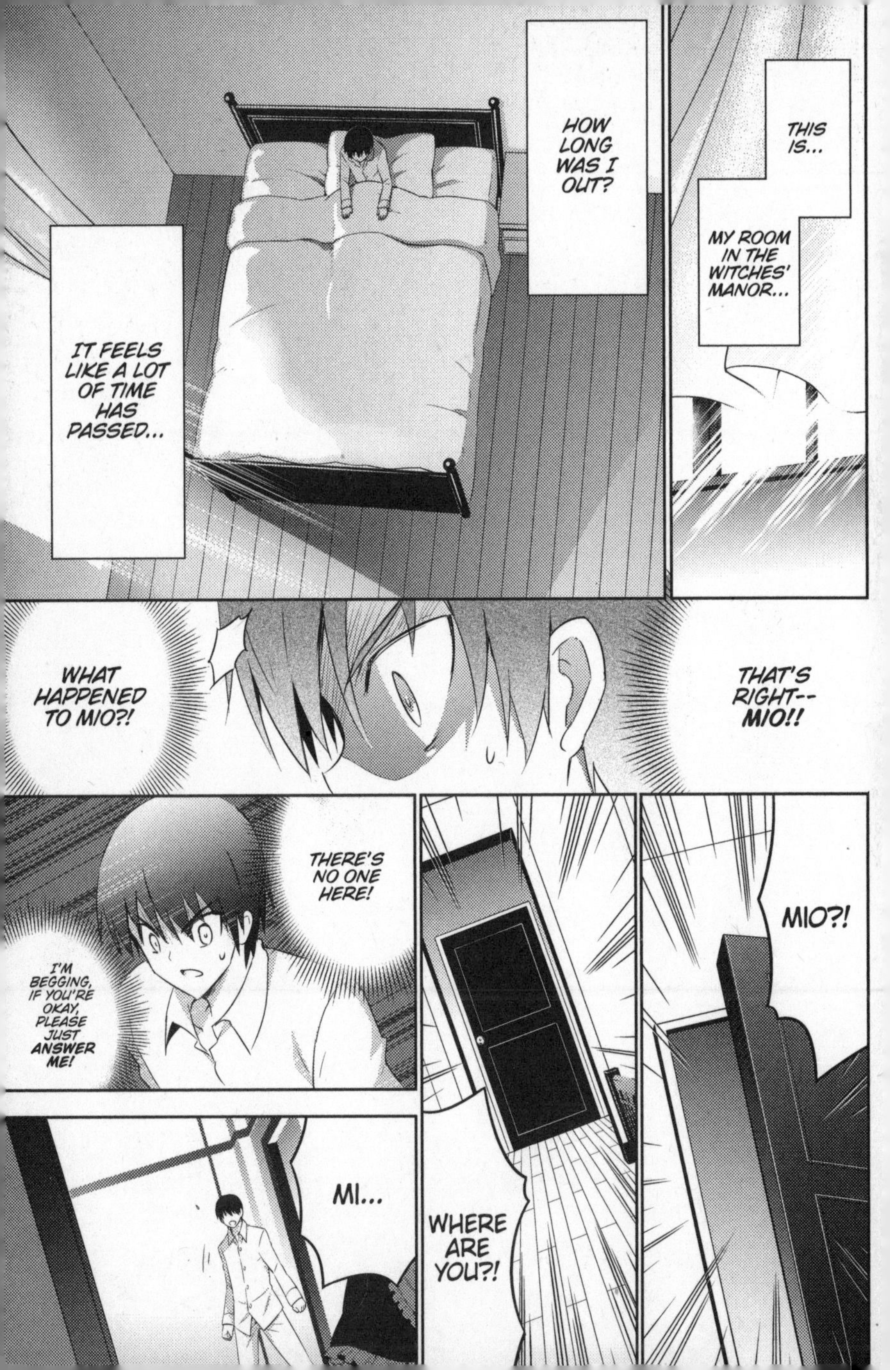
THIS IS...
MY ROOM IN THE WITCHES' MANOR...
HOW LONG WAS I OUT?
IT FEELS LIKE A LOT OF TIME HAS PASSED...
THAT'S RIGHT-- MIO!!
WHAT HAPPENED TO MIO?!
MIO?!
WHERE ARE YOU?!
THERE'S NO ONE HERE!
I'M BEGGING, IF YOU'RE OKAY, PLEASE JUST ANSWER ME!
MI...

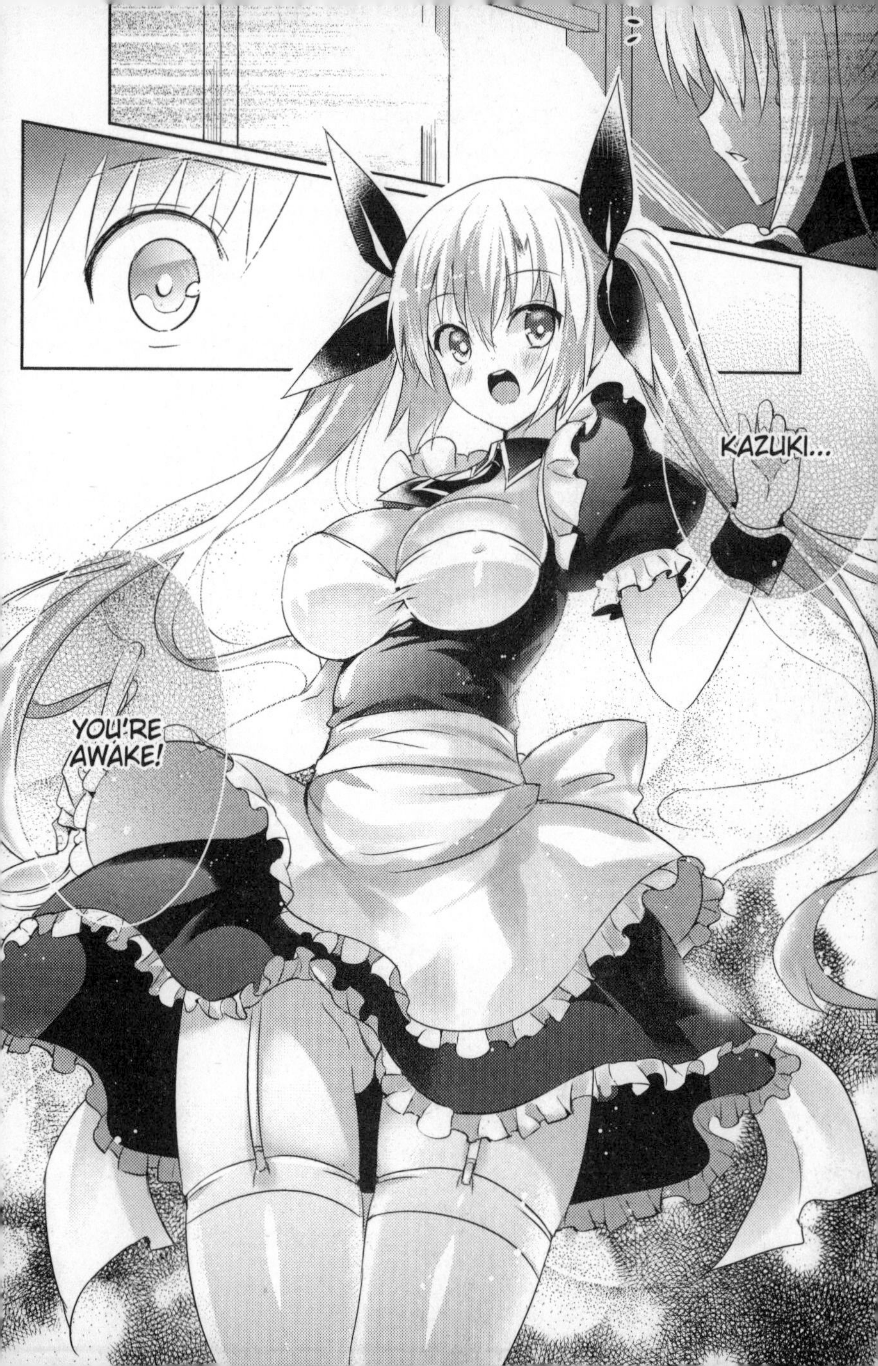
KAZUKI...
YOU'RE AWAKE!

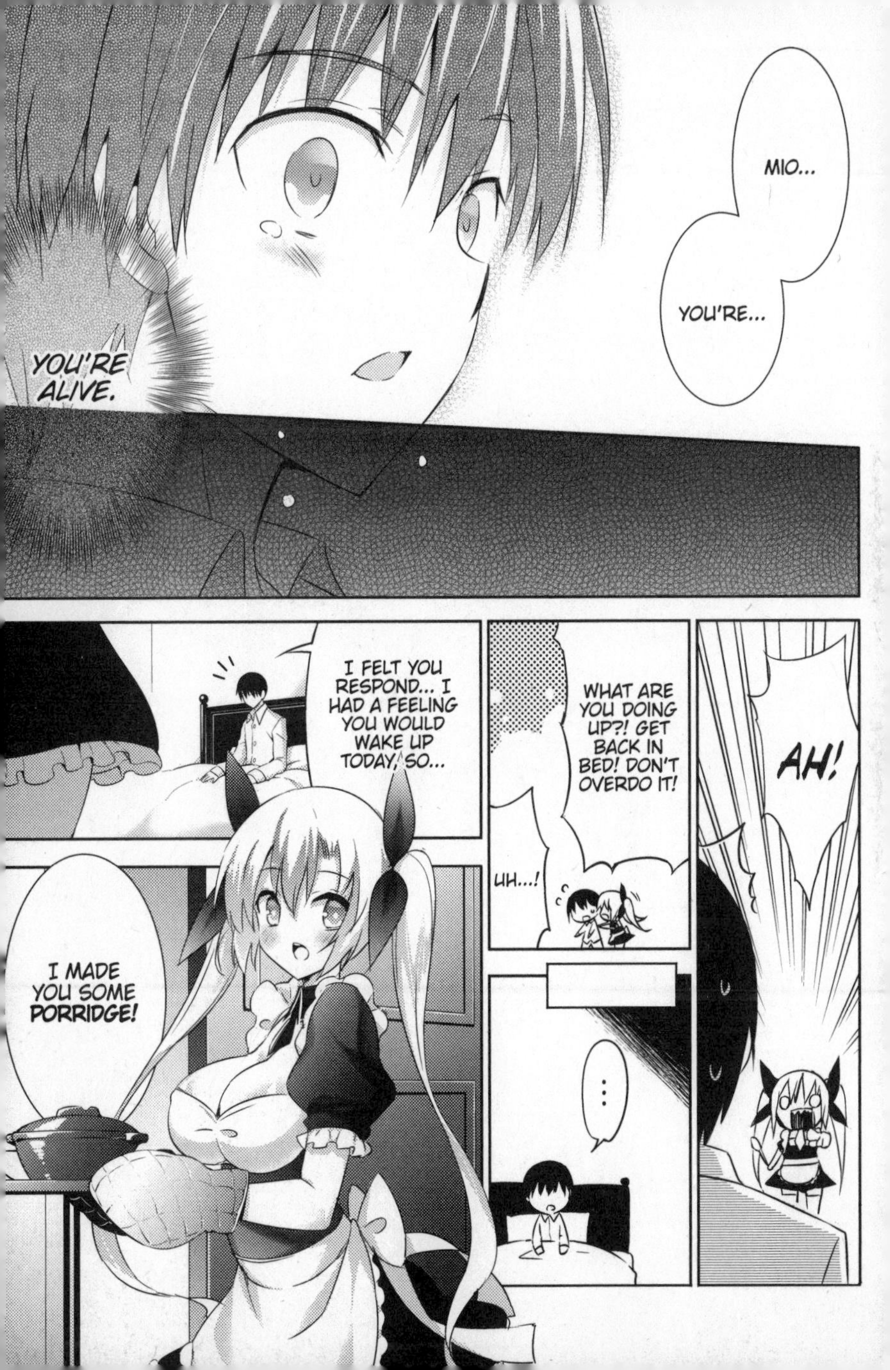

MIO...
YOU'RE...
YOU'RE ALIVE.
I FELT YOU RESPOND... I HAD A FEELING YOU WOULD WAKE UP TODAY, SO...
I MADE YOU SOME PORRIDGE!
...
AH!
WHAT ARE YOU DOING UP?! GET BACK IN BED! DON'T OVERDO IT!
UH...!

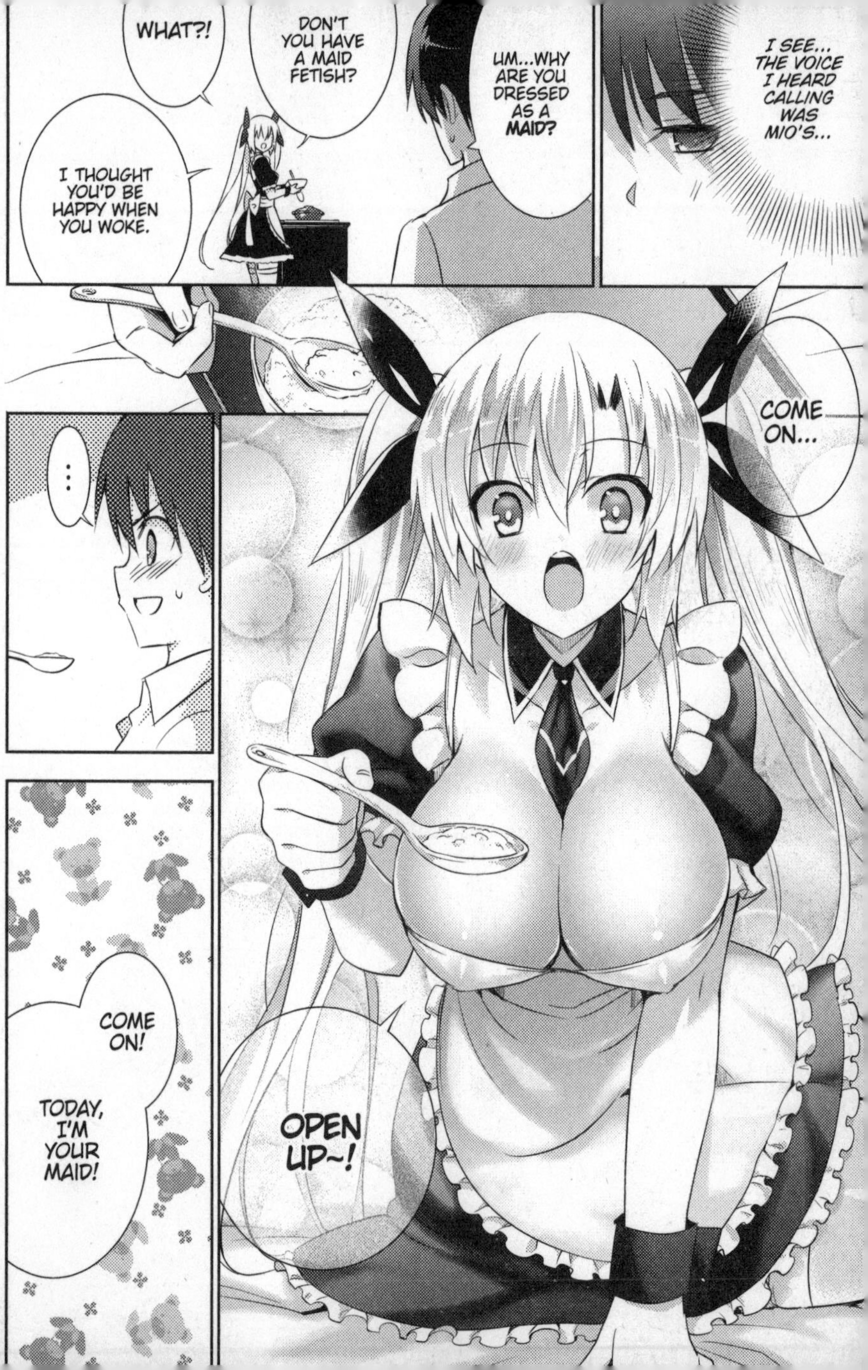
I SEE... THE VOICE I HEARD CALLING WAS MIO'S...
UM...WHY ARE YOU DRESSED AS A MAID?
DON'T YOU HAVE A MAID FETISH?
WHAT?!
I THOUGHT YOU'D BE HAPPY WHEN YOU WOKE.
COME ON...
...
COME ON!
TODAY, I'M YOUR MAID!
OPEN UP~!

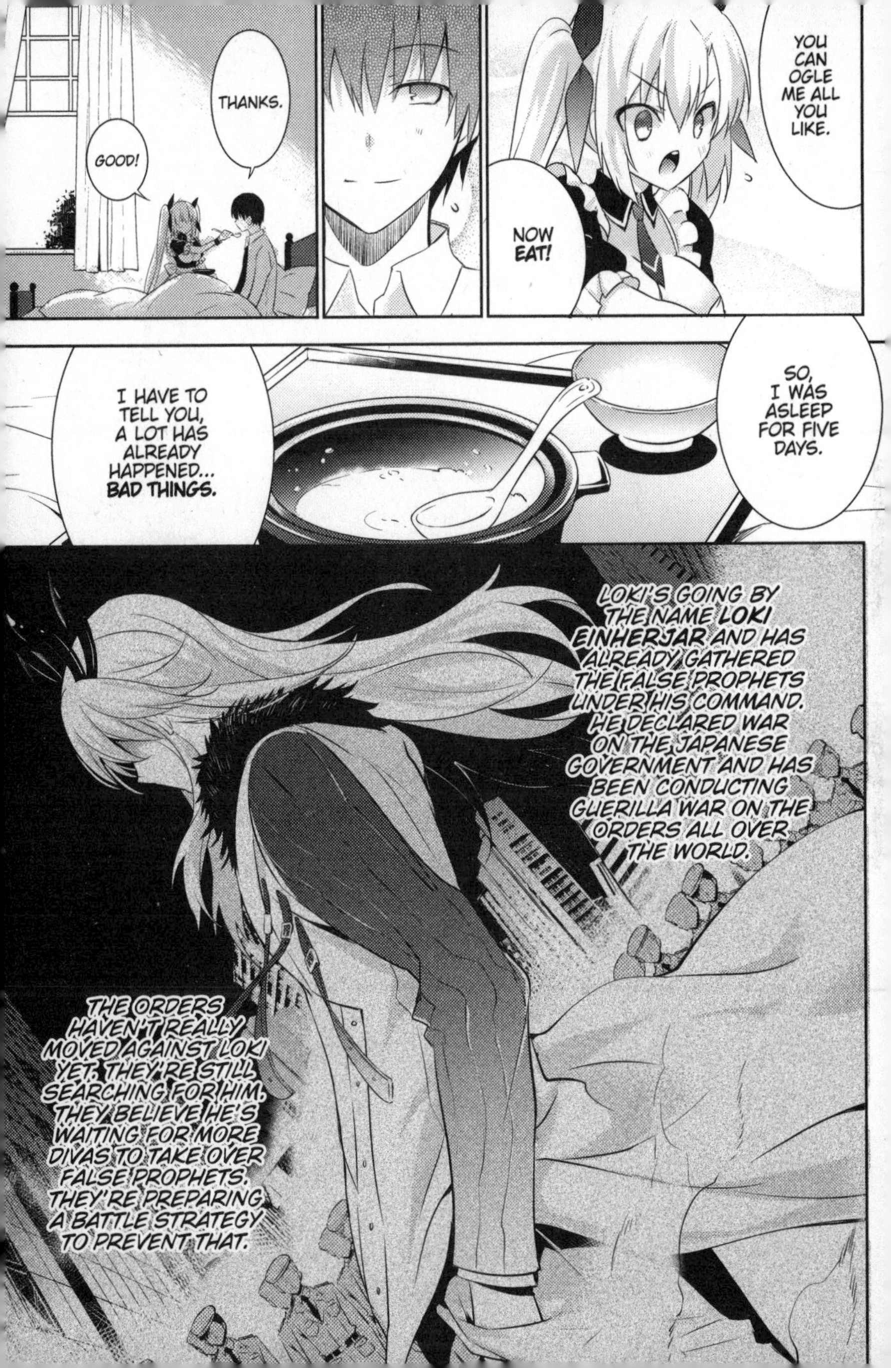
YOU CAN OGLE ME ALL YOU LIKE.
NOW EAT!
THANKS.
GOOD!
SO, I WAS ASLEEP FOR FIVE DAYS.
I HAVE TO TELL YOU, A LOT HAS ALREADY HAPPENED... BAD THINGS.
LOKI'S GOING BY THE NAME LOKI EINHERJAR AND HAS ALREADY GATHERED THE FALSE PROPHETS UNDER HIS COMMAND. HE DECLARED WAR ON THE JAPANESE GOVERNMENT AND HAS BEEN CONDUCTING GUERILLA WAR ON THE ORDERS ALL OVER THE WORLD.
THE ORDERS HAVEN'T REALLY MOVED AGAINST LOKI YET. THEY'RE STILL SEARCHING FOR HIM. THEY BELIEVE HE'S WAITING FOR MORE DIVAS TO TAKE OVER FALSE PROPHETS. THEY'RE PREPARING A BATTLE STRATEGY TO PREVENT THAT.

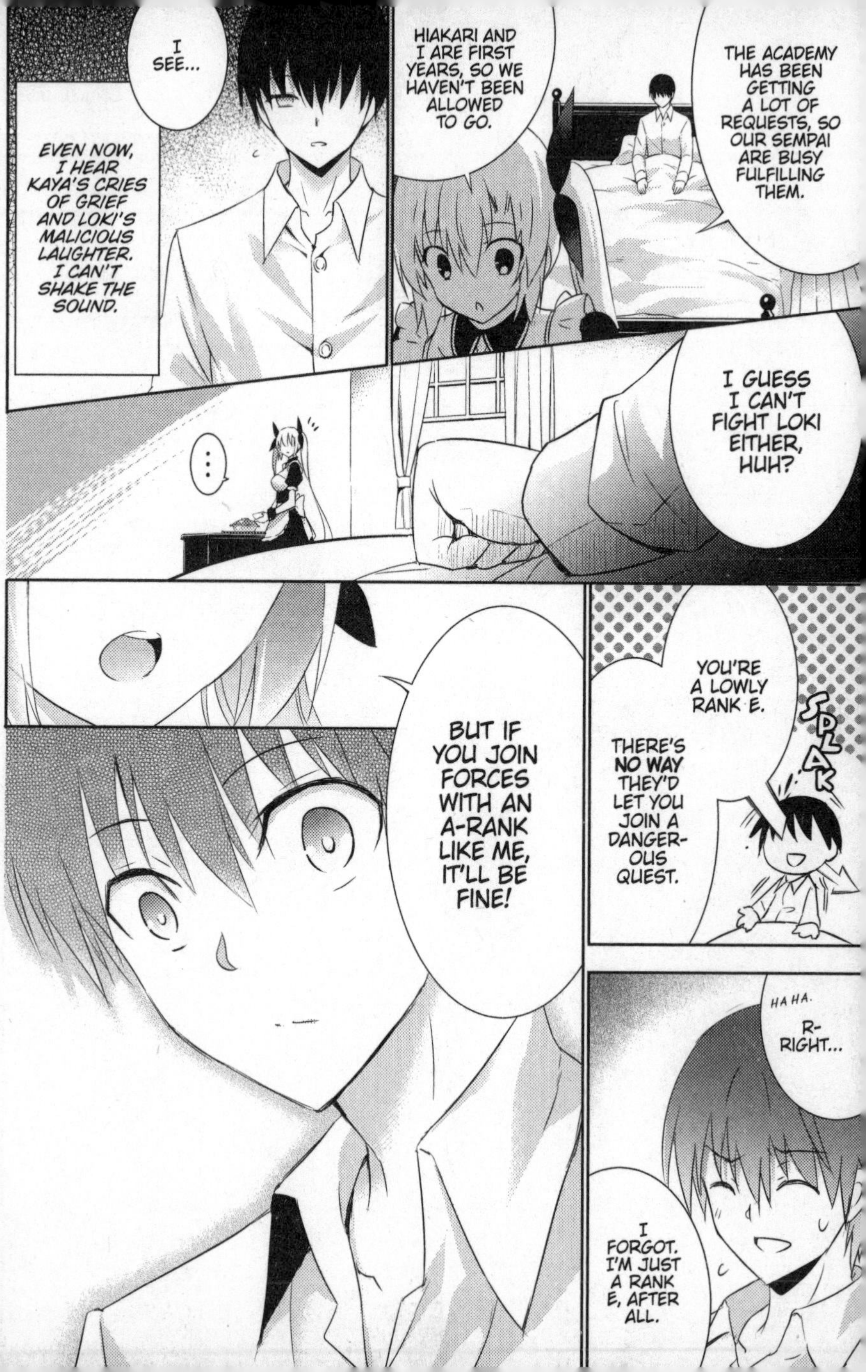
THE ACADEMY HAS BEEN GETTING A LOT OF REQUESTS, SO OUR SEMPAI ARE BUSY FULFILLING THEM.
HIAKARI AND I ARE FIRST YEARS, SO WE HAVEN'T BEEN ALLOWED TO GO.
I SEE...
EVEN NOW, I HEAR KAYA'S CRIES OF GRIEF AND LOKI'S MALICIOUS LAUGHTER. I CAN'T SHAKE THE SOUND.
I GUESS I CAN'T FIGHT LOKI EITHER, HUH?
...
YOU'RE A LOWLY RANK E.
SPLAK
THERE'S NO WAY THEY'D LET YOU JOIN A DANGER-OUS QUEST.
HA HA.
R-RIGHT...
I FORGOT. I'M JUST A RANK E, AFTER ALL.
BUT IF YOU JOIN FORCES WITH AN A-RANK LIKE ME, IT'LL BE FINE!

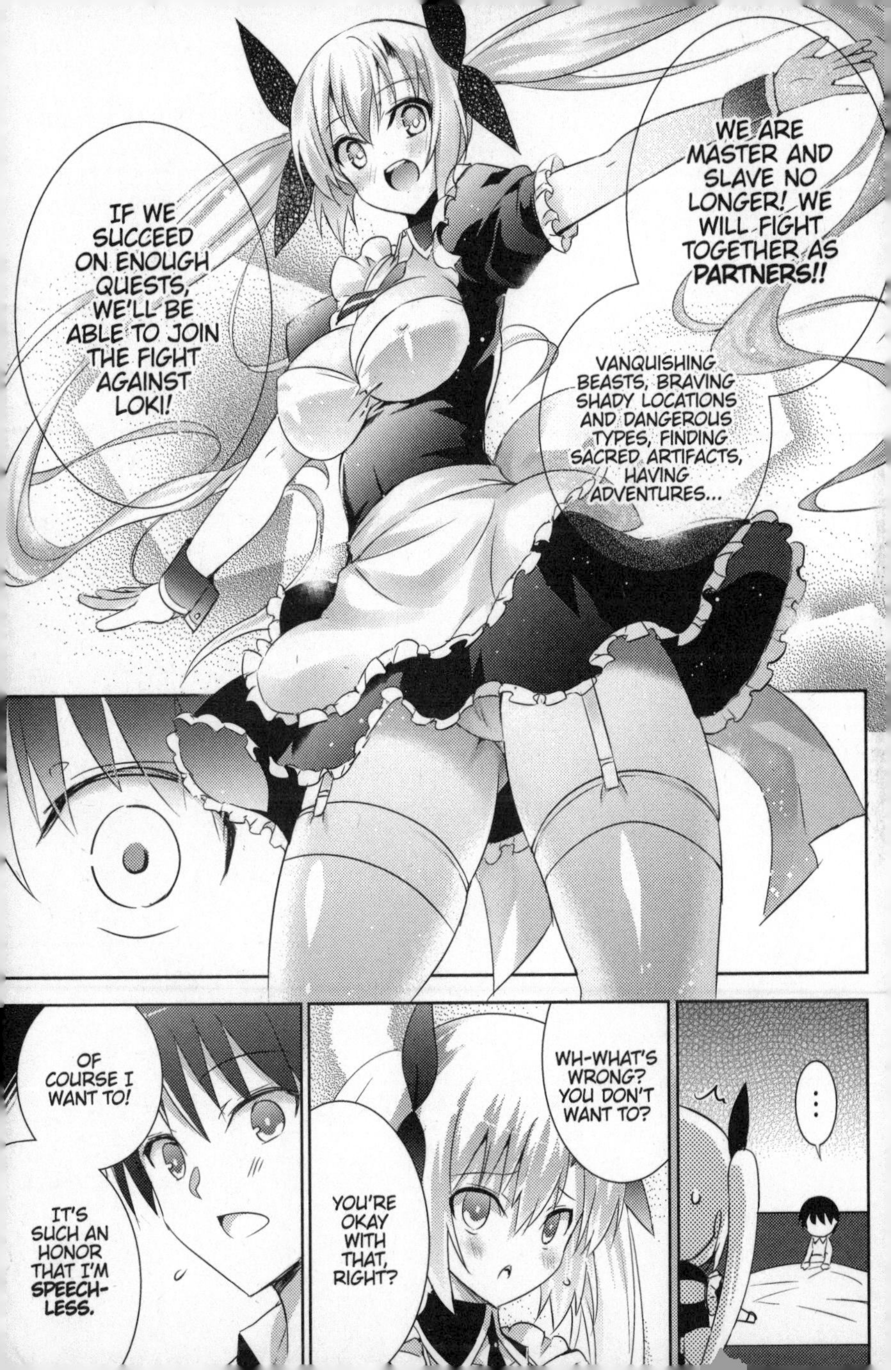
WE ARE MASTER AND SLAVE NO LONGER! WE WILL FIGHT TOGETHER AS **PARTNERS!!**
VANQUISHING BEASTS, BRAVING SHADY LOCATIONS AND DANGEROUS TYPES, FINDING SACRED ARTIFACTS, HAVING ADVENTURES...
IF WE SUCCEED ON ENOUGH QUESTS, WE'LL BE ABLE TO JOIN THE FIGHT AGAINST LOKI!
...
WH-WHAT'S WRONG? YOU DON'T WANT TO?
YOU'RE OKAY WITH THAT, RIGHT?
OF COURSE I WANT TO!
IT'S SUCH AN HONOR THAT I'M SPEECH-LESS.

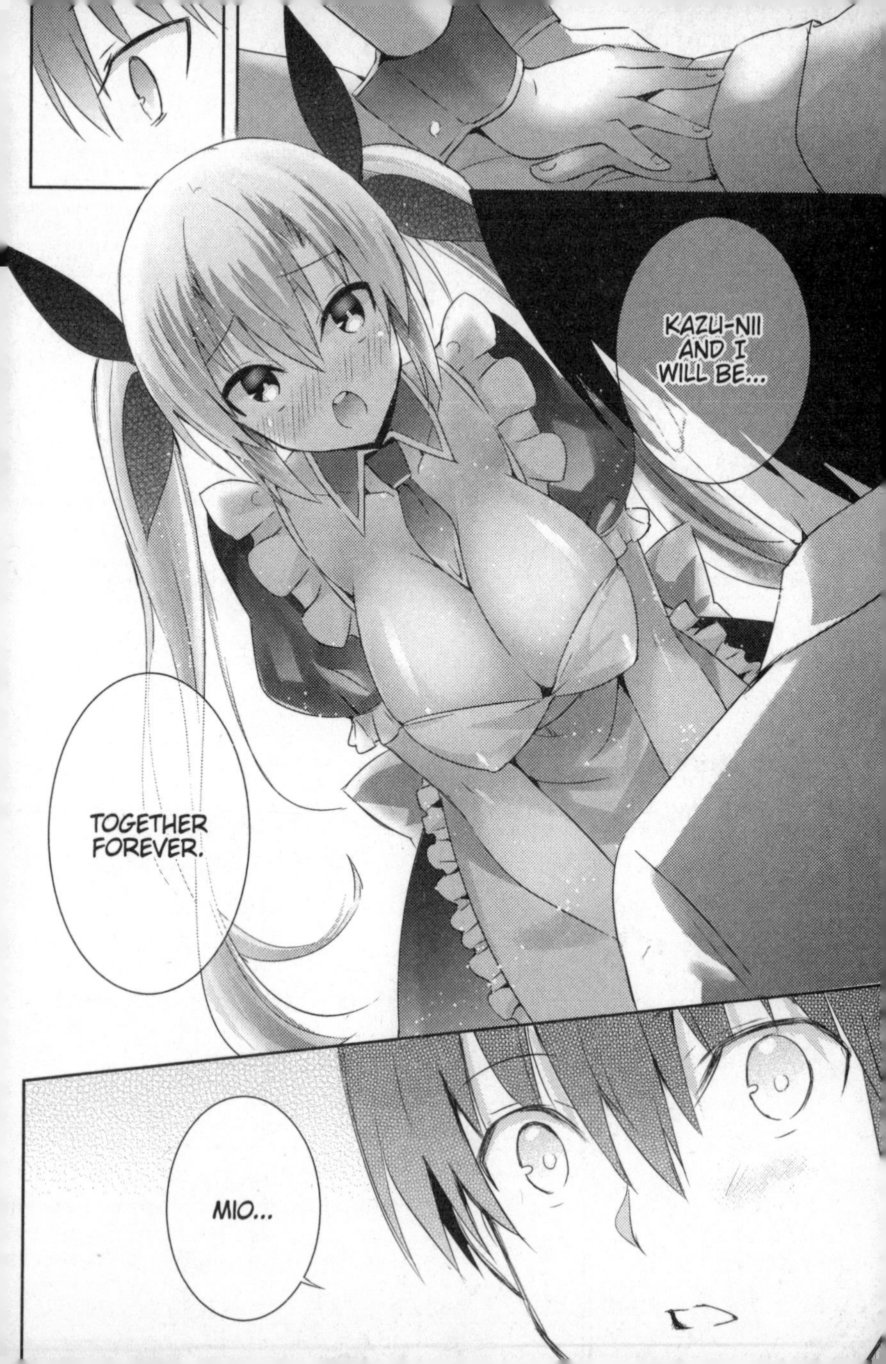
KAZU-NII AND I WILL BE...
TOGETHER FOREVER.
MIO...

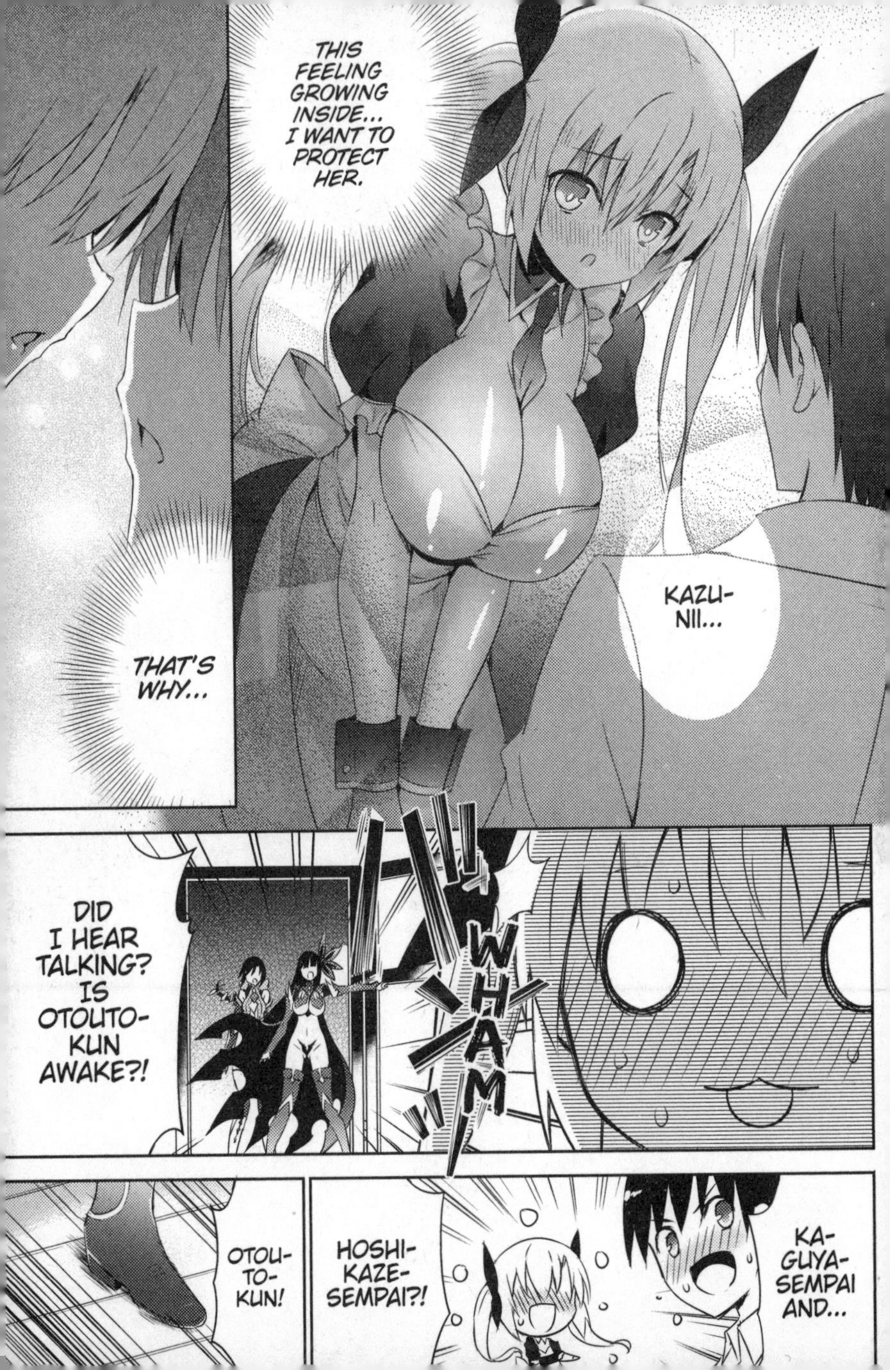
THIS FEELING GROWING INSIDE... I WANT TO PROTECT HER.
KAZU-NII...
THAT'S WHY...
WHAM
DID I HEAR TALKING? IS OTOUTO-KUN AWAKE?!
KA-GUYA-SEMPAI AND...
HOSHI-KAZE-SEMPAI?!
OTOU-TO-KUN!

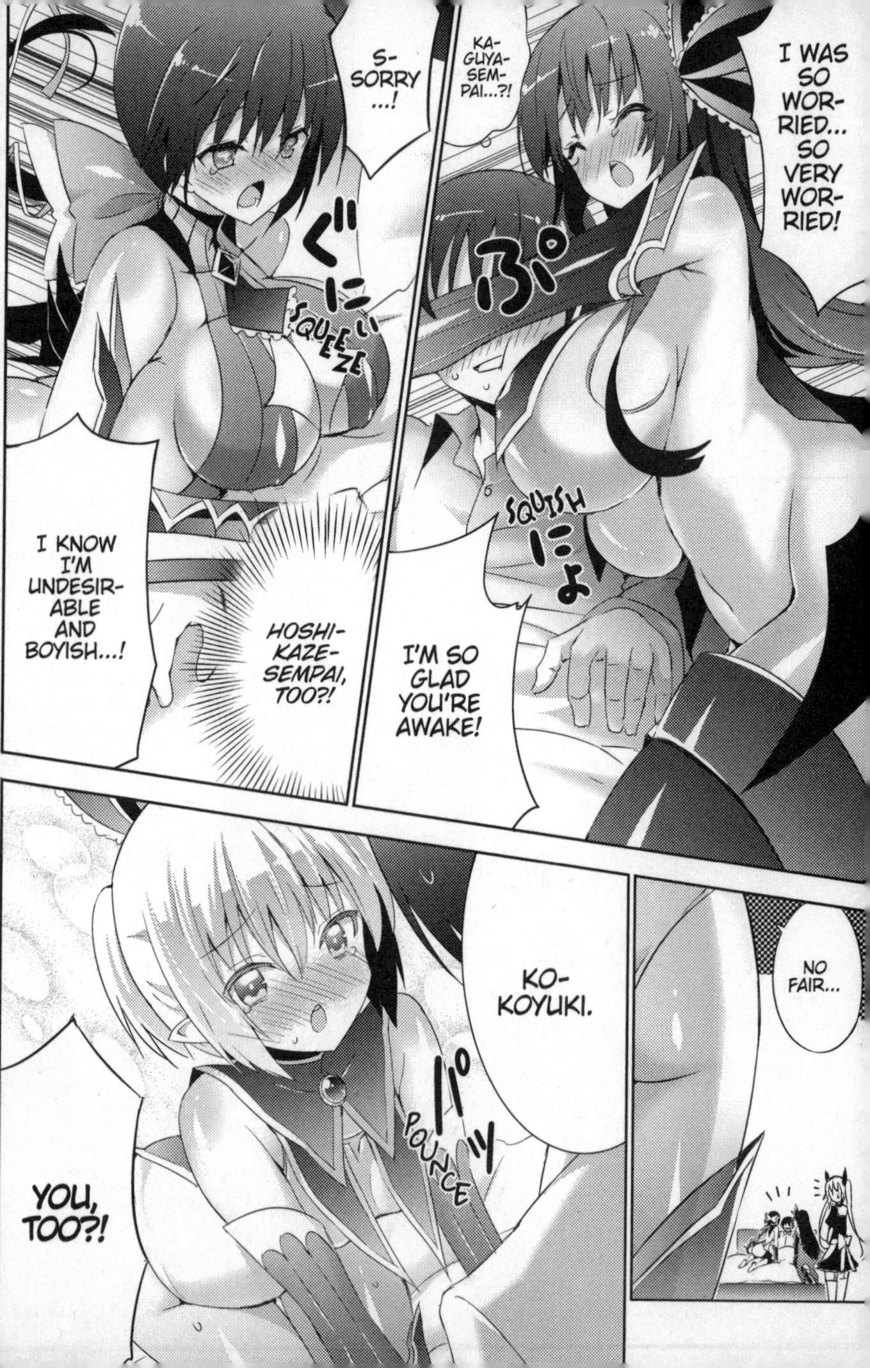

I WAS SO WORRIED... SO VERY WORRIED!
KAGUYA-SEMPAI...?!
ぷ
SQUISH
にょ
I'M SO GLAD YOU'RE AWAKE!
S-SORRY...!
ぐにぃ
SQUEEZE
HOSHIKAZE-SEMPAI, TOO?!
I KNOW I'M UNDESIRABLE AND BOYISH...!
NO FAIR...
KO-KOYUKI.
パッ
POUNCE
YOU, TOO?!

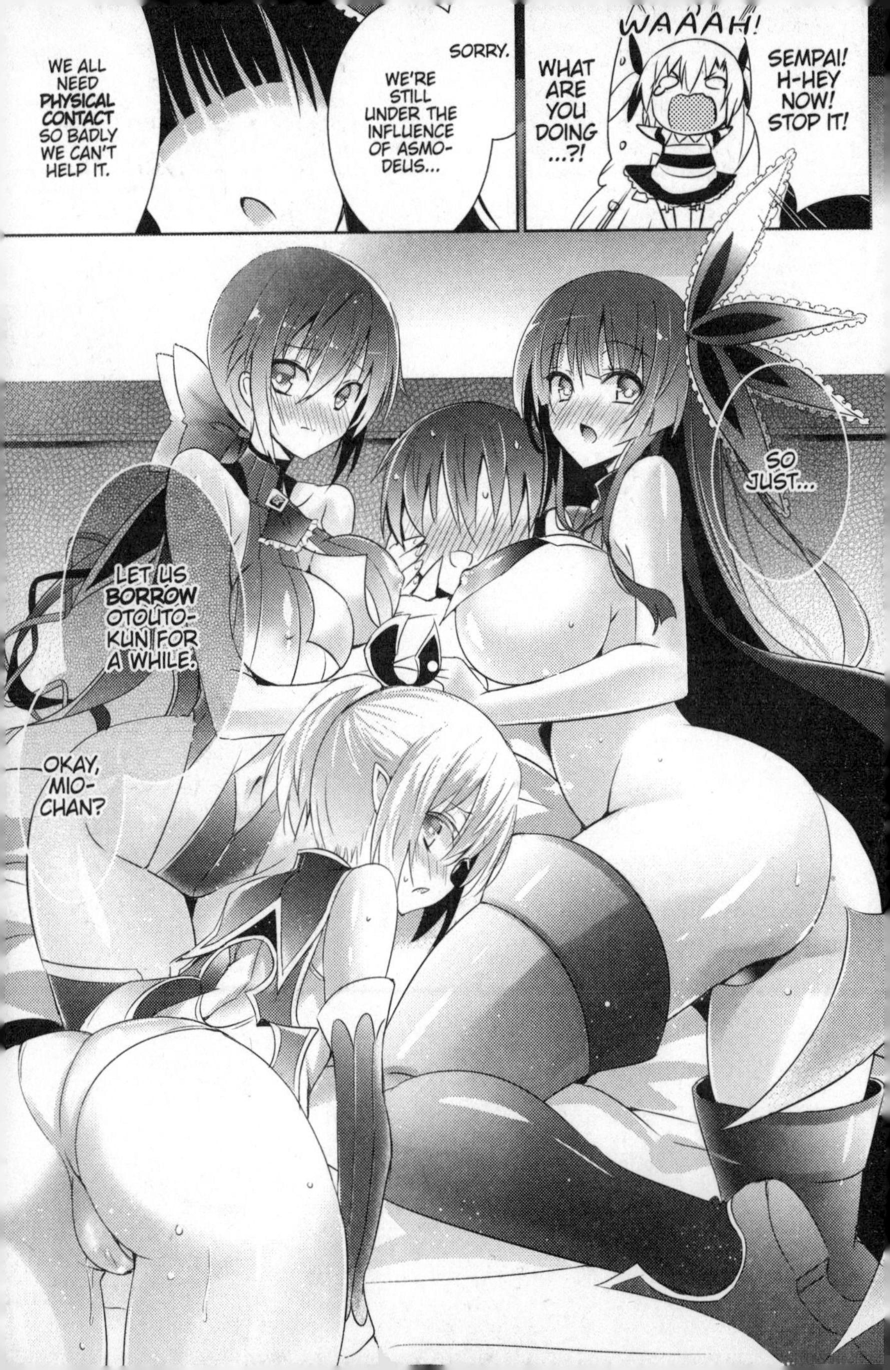
WAAAH!
SEMPAI! H-HEY NOW! STOP IT!
WHAT ARE YOU DOING ...?!
SORRY.
WE'RE STILL UNDER THE INFLUENCE OF ASMODEUS...
WE ALL NEED PHYSICAL CONTACT SO BADLY WE CAN'T HELP IT.
SO JUST...
LET US BORROW OTOUTO-KUN FOR A WHILE.
OKAY, MIO-CHAN?

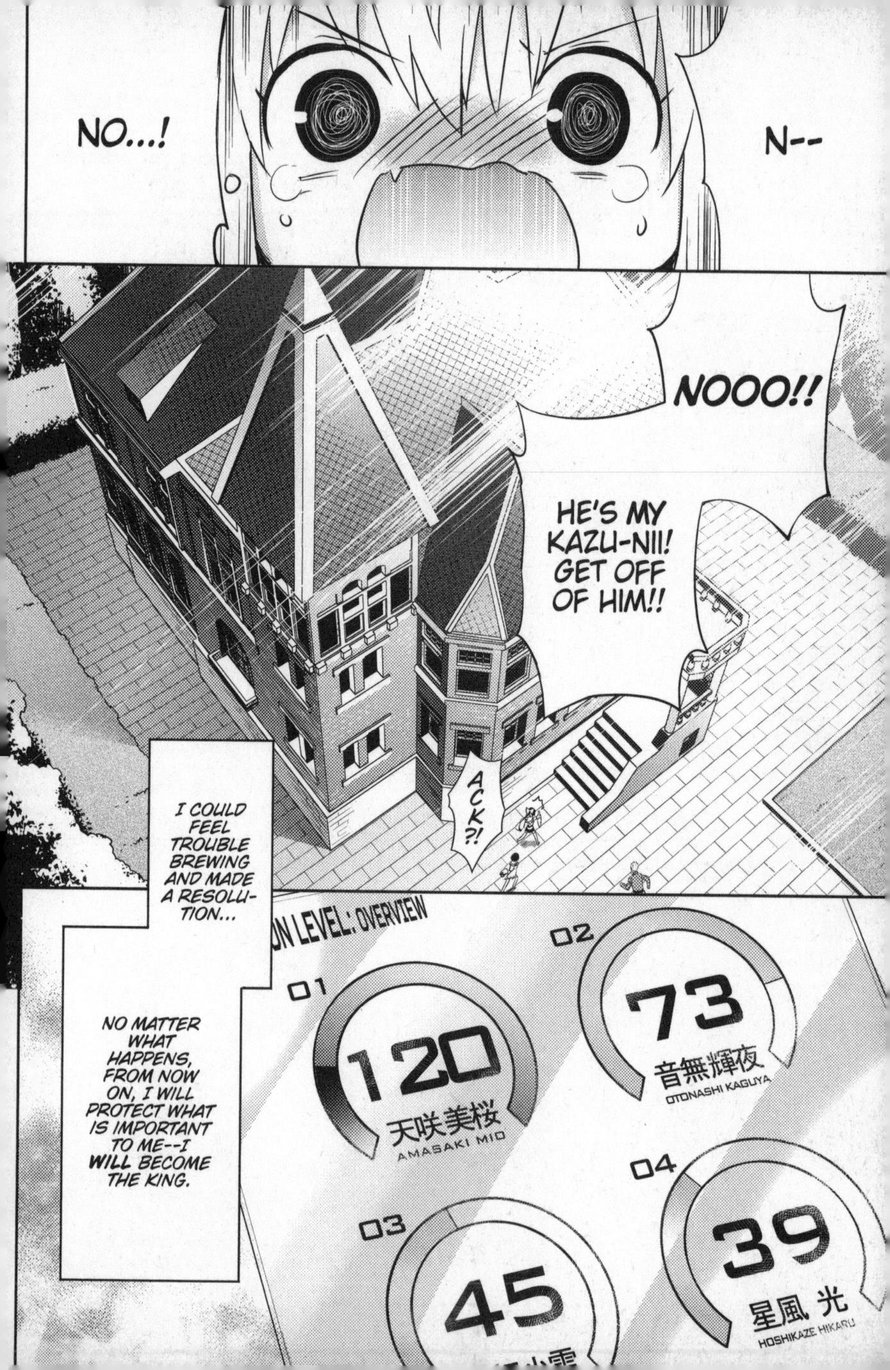
N--
NO...!
NOOO!!
HE'S MY KAZU-NII! GET OFF OF HIM!!
ACK?!
I COULD FEEL TROUBLE BREWING AND MADE A RESOLUTION...
ON LEVEL: OVERVIEW
02
73
音無輝夜
OTONASHI KAGUYA
01
120
天咲美桜
AMASAKI MIO
04
39
星風光
HOSHIKAZE HIKARU
03
45
NO MATTER WHAT HAPPENS, FROM NOW ON, I WILL PROTECT WHAT IS IMPORTANT TO ME--I WILL BECOME THE KING.

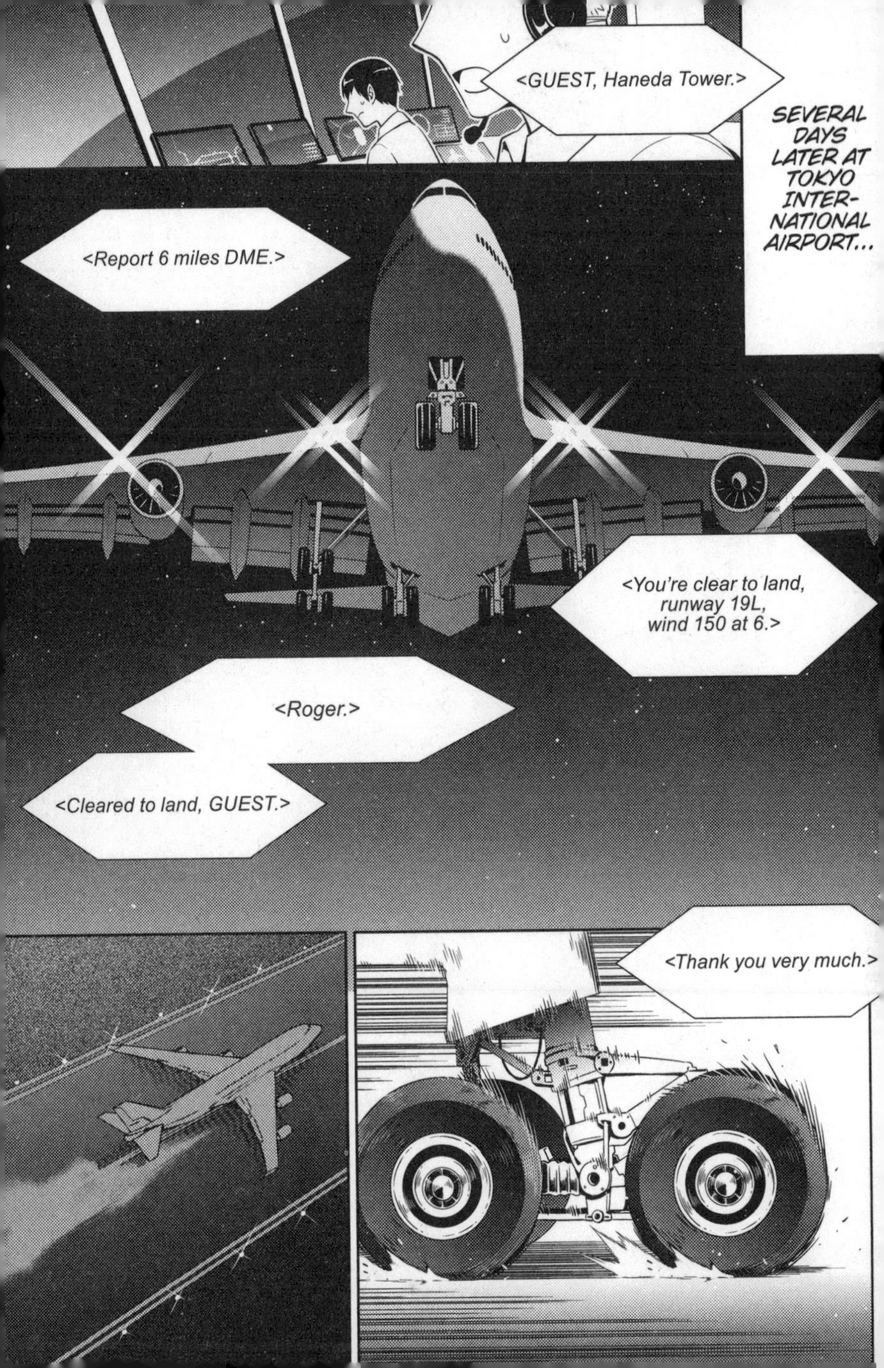
SEVERAL DAYS LATER AT TOKYO INTERNATIONAL AIRPORT...
<GUEST, Haneda Tower.>
<Report 6 miles DME.>
<You're clear to land, runway 19L, wind 150 at 6.>
<Roger.>
<Cleared to land, GUEST.>
<Thank you very much.>

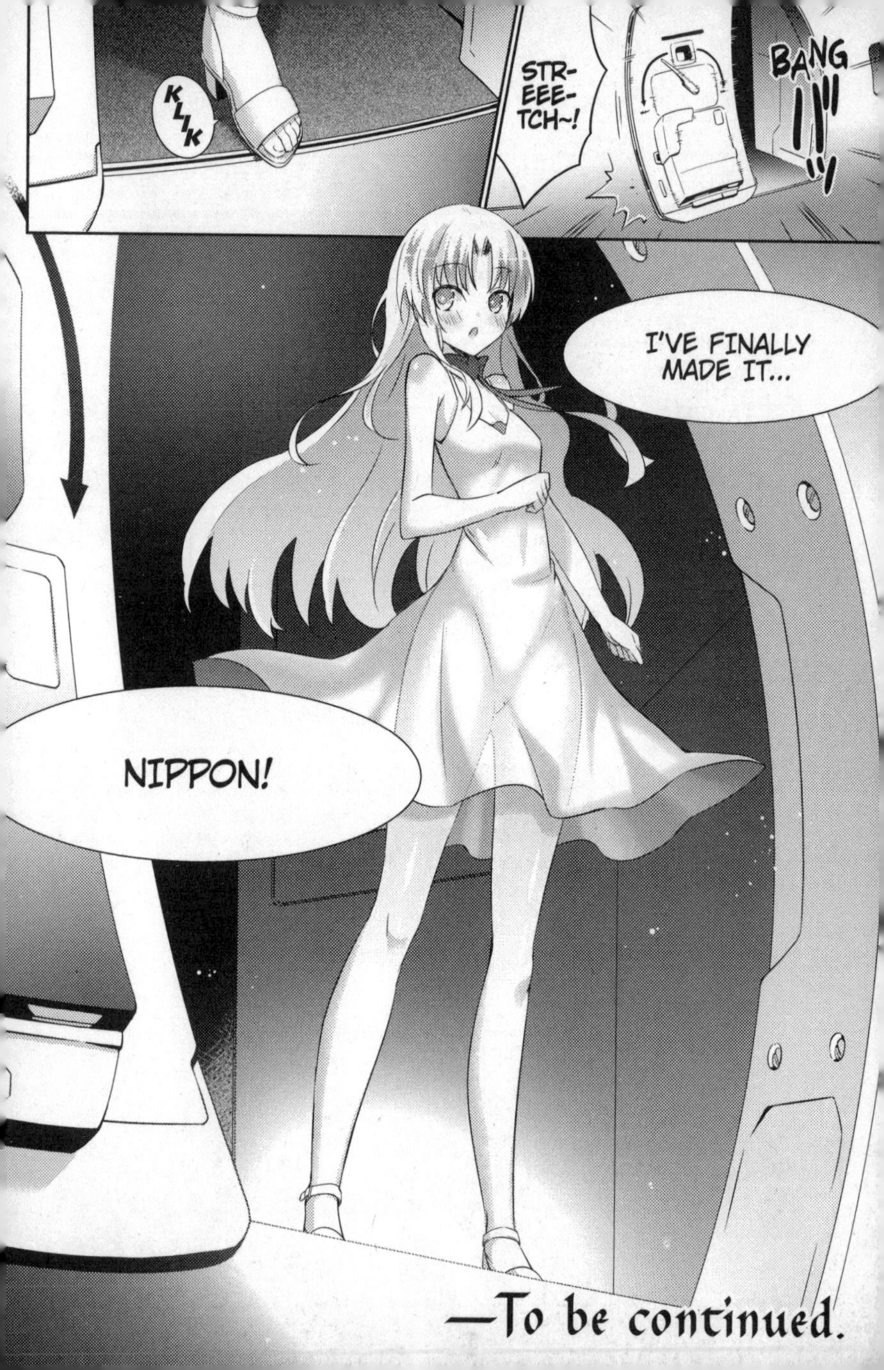
BANG
STR-EEE-TCH~!
KLIK
I'VE FINALLY MADE IT...
NIPPON!
—To be continued.

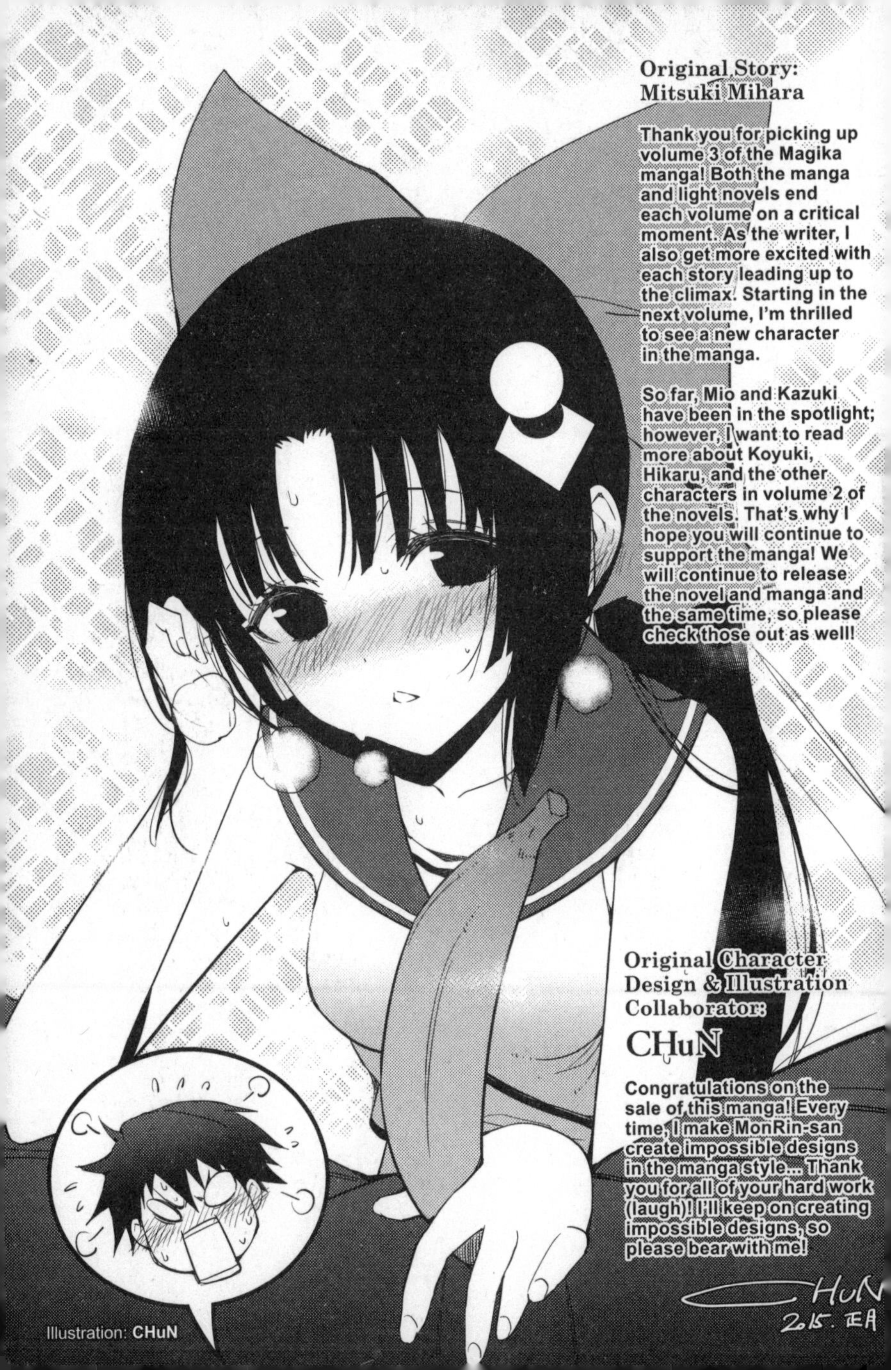
Illustration: CHuN

Original Story:
Mitsuki Mihara

Thank you for picking up volume 3 of the Magika manga! Both the manga and light novels end each volume on a critical moment. As the writer, I also get more excited with each story leading up to the climax. Starting in the next volume, I'm thrilled to see a new character in the manga.

So far, Mio and Kazuki have been in the spotlight; however, I want to read more about Koyuki, Hikaru, and the other characters in volume 2 of the novels. That's why I hope you will continue to support the manga! We will continue to release the novel and manga and the same time, so please check those out as well!

Original Character Design & Illustration Collaborator:

CHuN

Congratulations on the sale of this manga! Every time, I make MonRin-san create impossible designs in the manga style... Thank you for all of your hard work (laugh)! I'll keep on creating impossible designs, so please bear with me!

CHuN
2015. 正月

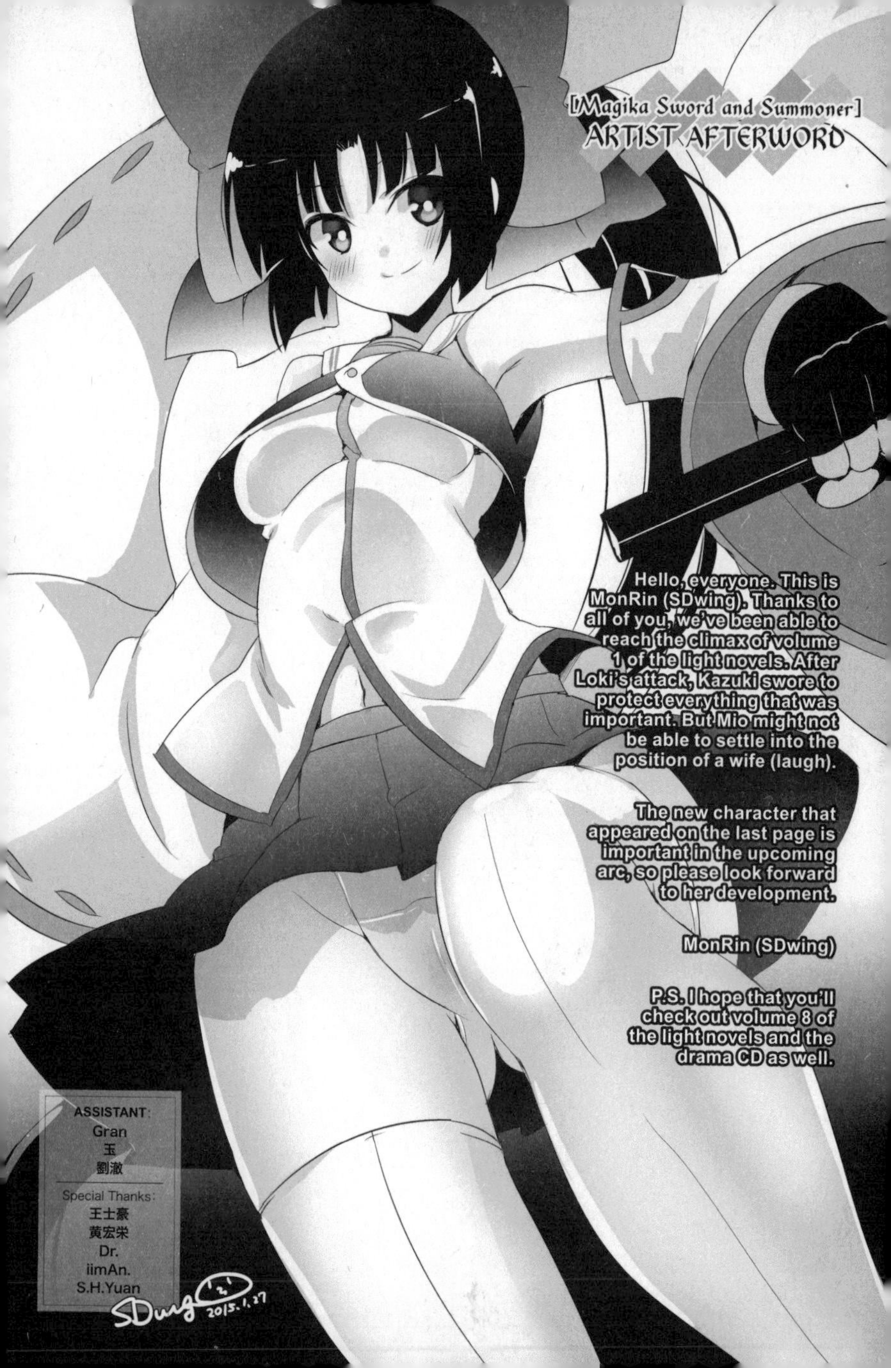
SDwing
2015.1.27

[Magika Sword and Summoner]

ARTIST AFTERWORD

Hello, everyone. This is MonRin (SDwing). Thanks to all of you, we've been able to reach the climax of volume 1 of the light novels. After Loki's attack, Kazuki swore to protect everything that was important. But Mio might not be able to settle into the position of a wife (laugh).

The new character that appeared on the last page is important in the upcoming arc, so please look forward to her development.

MonRin (SDwing)

P.S. I hope that you'll check out volume 8 of the light novels and the drama CD as well.

ASSISTANT:
Gran
玉
劉澈

Special Thanks:
王士豪
黄宏栄
Dr.
iimAn.
S.H.Yuan

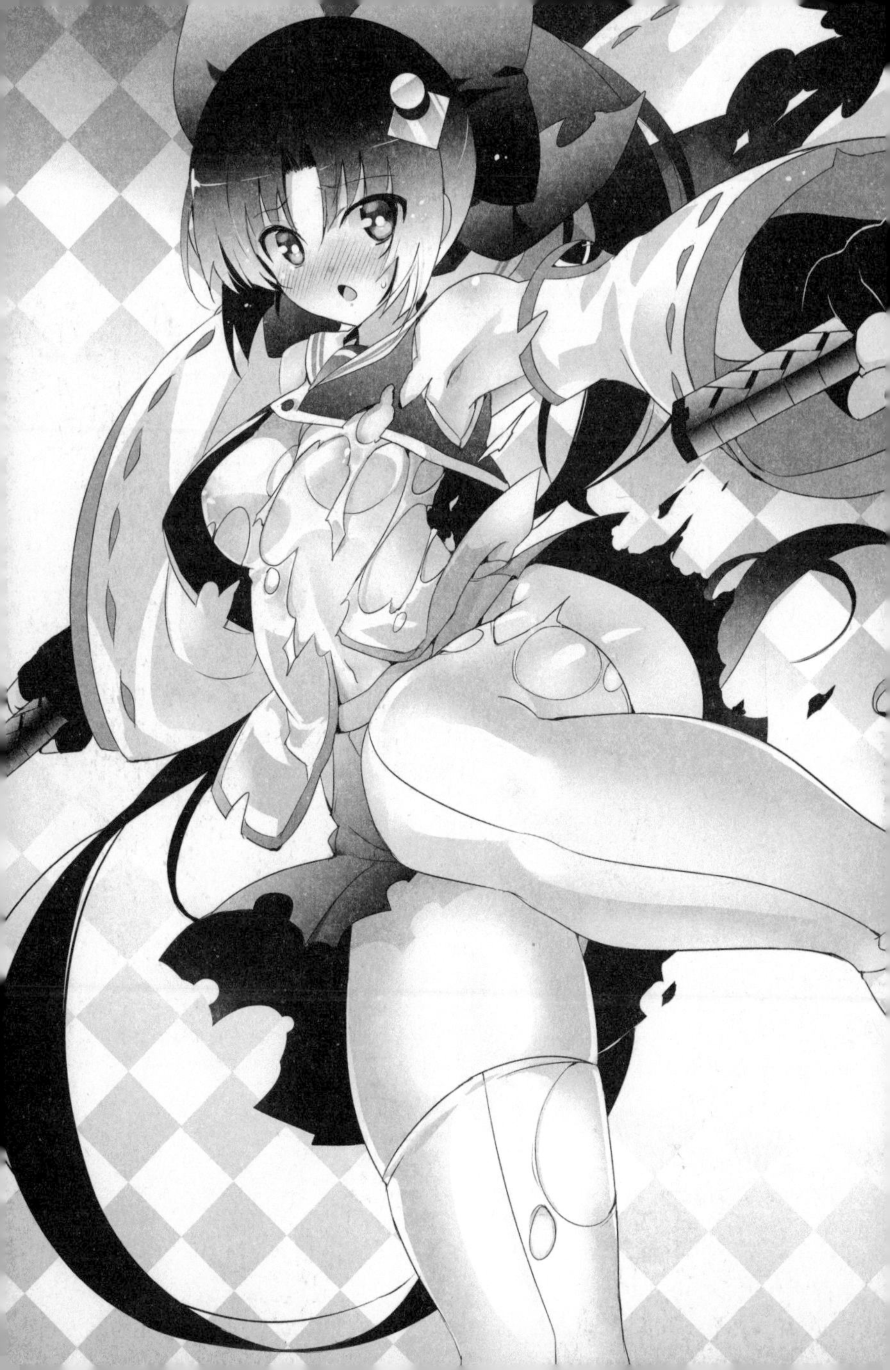

魔技科の剣士と召喚魔王

3

SEVEN SEAS ENTERTAINMENT PRESENTS

Magika SWORDSMAN AND SUMMONER VOL. 3

story by **MITSUKI MIHARA** / art by **MONRIN** / Original Character Designs by **CHuN**

TRANSLATION
Jill Morita

ADAPTATION
Lee Otter

LETTERING AND LAYOUT
Courtney Williams

COVER DESIGN
Nicky Lim

PROOFREADER
Janet Houck

PRODUCTION MANAGER
Lissa Pattillo

EDITOR-IN-CHIEF
Adam Arnold

PUBLISHER
Jason DeAngelis

ISBN: 978-1-626922-43-3
Printed in Canada
First Printing: February 2016
10 9 8 7 6 5 4 3 2 1

FOLLOW US ONLINE: ***www.gomanga.com***

READING DIRECTIONS

This book reads from ***right to left***, Japanese style. If this is your first time reading manga, you start reading from the top right panel on each page and take it from there. If you get lost, just follow the numbered diagram here. It may seem backwards at first, but you'll get the hang of it! Have fun!!

1
2
3
4
5
6
7
8
9

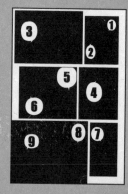